NURTURING RESILIENCE IN OUR CHILDREN

NURTURING RESILIENCE IN OUR CHILDREN

*Answers to the Most Important
Parenting Questions*

Robert Brooks, Ph.D., and
Sam Goldstein, Ph.D.

Contemporary Books

Chicago   New York   San Francisco   Lisbon   London   Madrid   Mexico City
Milan   New Delhi   San Juan   Seoul   Singapore   Sydney   Toronto

Library of Congress Cataloging-in-Publication Data

Brooks, Robert B.
    Nurturing resilience in our children : answers to the most important parenting
questions / Robert Brooks and Sam Goldstein.
        p.   cm.
    Includes bibliographical references and index.
    ISBN 0-658-02110-9
    1. Child psychology.   2. Resilience (Personality trait) in children.
3. Child rearing.   4. Parent and child.   I. Goldstein, Sam, 1952–   II. Title.

HQ772.B846   2002
155.4–dc21   2002071640

1 2 3 4 5 6 7 8 9 0   AGM/AGM   1 0 9 8 7 6 5 4 3 2

ISBN 0-658-02110-9

Cover photograph copyright © Julia Smith/Taxi/Getty Images

McGraw-Hill books are available at special quantity discounts to use as premiums and
sales promotions, or for use in corporate training programs. For more information, please
write to the Director of Special Sales, Professional Publishing, McGraw-Hill, Two Penn
Plaza, New York, NY 10121-2298. Or contact your local bookstore.

This book is printed on acid-free paper.

*For my wife, Janet. For my children, Allyson and Ryan,
whose resilient waters run deep and strong.*

S.G.

*In appreciation of my wife, Marilyn; my sons, Richard and Douglas; and
their lovely wives, Cybèle and Suzanne. Your optimism and resilience have
served as a wonderful source of strength for myself and for many others.*

R.B.

*Thanks again to Kathleen Gardner for her editorial assistance and guidance
in the preparation of this manuscript. Thanks also to our agent, James Levine,
and our editor, Matthew Carnicelli.*

S.G.

R.B.

Contents

Quick Solution Finder

Preface

In our first book, *Raising Resilient Children*, we set out to synthesize and present in a practical way a large volume of research about the qualities of resilience and the abilities of some children to face and overcome great adversity. We emphasized the importance of parents nurturing a resilient mindset in children from birth, a mindset that would help all youngsters deal more effectively with the many challenges that they might face. We characterized resilient children as being capable of dealing with stress and pressure and coping effectively with everyday challenges. They are optimistic and bounce back from disappointment, adversity, or trauma. They are capable of developing clear and realistic goals. They have learned to solve problems that are within their ability to solve and are confident that patience and persistence will lead to successful outcomes. Resilient children relate well to others, treat themselves and others with respect, and, very importantly, while they feel a sense of control of their lives, they do not possess a strong need to direct, control, or manipulate the lives of others.

Following the publication of *Raising Resilient Children*, we began to receive an increasing number of questions about resilience from parents, educators, and other professionals, particularly at our conferences and on our websites. We collected these questions and also reflected upon questions about resilience we had received in the past. We realized that although many of the topics and issues housed in these questions were discussed in our first book, in many cases the questions required more specific answers as to how the qualities of resilience, the mindset of parents capable of fostering resilience, and the attitudes and skills of resilient children impact on a variety of everyday life experiences within families, in the community, and at school. The many questions we received were the catalyst for writing this book.

We have written this book in a style that permits you to read and reread our words in different ways. In each chapter we have provided a set of questions that represent common themes in the inquiries parents have made concerning our work with families and the qualities of resilience. We have attempted to place the questions together in a logical framework so that by the close of each chapter the important guideposts, obstacles, and strategies for each resilient quality will have been presented and discussed.

Children come into this world with their own unique temperaments. Current research has suggested that qualities within children and qualities between children and their environments, as well as the characteristics of the general environment, all play a role in shaping a resilient mindset. Our focus is to examine primarily the middle set of factors, namely, those between child and parent, between child and teacher, between children and the world around them. Parents and other caregivers can strongly influence whether children develop the characteristics and mindset associated with resilience or whether they become burdened by low self-worth, self-doubt, and a diminished sense of hope. Developing a resilient mindset is not a luxury but an essential component of a successful future for our children, our culture, and our world. It is our hope that the ideas offered in this book will make a positive difference in your life and the lives of your children.

[R]ecent studies continue to corroborate the importance of a relatively small set of global factors associated with resilience. These include connections to competent, caring adults in the family and community, cognitive and self-regulation skills, positive views of self, and motivation to be effective in the environment.

ANN S. MASTEN

Raising children . . . is about identifying and nurturing their strongest qualities, what they own and are best at, and helping them find their niches in which they can best live out these strengths.

MARTIN SELIGMAN

We are linked by our resilience, that inbred, evolutionary ability to live and grow and love against all odds.

J. NOZIPO MARAIRE

1

The Dreams and Wishes of Parents

Weaving the Threads of Resilience

Question

People always seem to talk about the "good old days." When I watch old television programs like "Father Knows Best" or "Ozzie and Harriet," it seems that being a parent was so much easier then. I know that these are just television shows and that they probably exaggerate how simple things were, but I am wondering if being a parent is more difficult today than in my parents' or grandparents' time?

Answer

Although shows such as "Father Knows Best" and "Ozzie and Harriet" were just television programs, they do seem to capture a less complicated or complex time of parenting. While we believe the dreams and wishes of parents were likely the same in our parents' and grandparents' time as in ours, there is the sense that it is more difficult today to be an effective parent and to feel confident that our everyday acts of parenting will be successful in reaching the goals we desire for our children. Whether the vantage point is fifty years ago or today, all parents hope that their children will be happy, successful, and prepared to enter the world of adults possessing the inner strength to deal day after day with the challenges and demands they encounter. Though growing up has always presented its share of challenges and pressures for children, we believe there are many more challenges facing children today than fifty years ago. In our fast-paced, stress-filled world, the number of youngsters facing adversity and the number of adversities they face continue to increase dramatically. No child is immune. Even children fortunate to not encounter significant adversity in their lives or to be burdened by intense stress or anxiety experience the pressures around them and the expectations placed upon them.

> Though growing up has always presented its share of challenges and pressures for children, we believe there are many more challenges facing children today than fifty years ago.

We believe that as a culture becomes more technologically complex, an increased burden is placed upon children as well as parents to adapt to and cope with such systems. In a way it is a mixed blessing. Our children today have dramatically greater technology at their fingertips from information resources to medical support. In this regard, they are better off than their counterparts in past generations. Yet there is a price to pay. That price we believe is increased stress and pressure and the greater need for children at younger ages to develop coping strategies to master the stresses in their lives.

Some might argue that the solution lies in making the world a simpler place for our children. However, while making major changes in our children's environment may be an admirable goal, it has significant limitations, not the least of which are the many forces impinging on children beyond the control of parents. Instead, what seems to make the greatest sense is for parents to focus on what they do have some control over, namely, helping children develop the skills to deal with and, hopefully, change for the better the world we have created. The centerpiece of these skills is resilience. If we want to raise resilient children we must avoid expending all of our energy on attempting to change the world; rather we must begin by changing what we do with our children. We can no longer afford to assume that if our children don't face significant stress they will be unburdened as they transition into adult life.

Yes, we do believe today's children are growing up in a more complex, uncertain time than past generations. However, we are optimistic that these greater complexities will not lead parents to throw up their hands in frustration wondering what they can do. Rather, they will be prompted to search for guideposts to develop a resilient mindset in their children. Such a mindset will serve their children well in any environment.

Question

It seems that I am hearing the word resilient *more and more. Since the terrorist attacks on September 11, 2001, many people have used the word to describe the United States. A sportscaster once referred to a baseball team as resilient since they had many injuries but were still in first place. Then I heard a newscaster call a country resilient after an earthquake that destroyed many buildings and led to many casualties. Finally, I saw a news feature about a boy who was fighting cancer. The reporter said he was such a resilient kid. So what exactly does* resilient *mean?*

Answer

It does seem that the word *resilient* is heard more and more. Actually, the word was originally used to apply to physical properties and is defined in the dictionary as "springing back or rebounding." It is the act of returning to an original form or position after being bent, compressed, or stretched. In the last twenty to twenty-five years, the meaning of *resilience* has been broadened to include a psychological dimension, that is, to describe people who "bounced back" from stress, trauma, or adversity. All of the examples you mentioned capture adverse situations in which people have responded in a positive way despite stress, injury, or adversity.

> Resilience should be understood as a vital ingredient in the process of parenting all children, a process that directs our interactions as we strengthen our children's ability to meet life's challenges and pressures with confidence and perseverance.

Researchers studying resilience have typically focused on youngsters undergoing great risk such as the boy you mentioned with cancer. They have examined such risk factors as children being exposed to abuse, neglect, poverty, or mental illness in a parent. These are all worthy areas of study. However, we believe that the concept of resilience should be expanded to embrace not only children experiencing these and other hardships but to every youngster and that it should define a process of parenting that is essential if we are to prepare our children for success in all areas of their future lives. Resilience should be understood as a vital ingredient in the process of parenting all children, a process that directs our interactions as we strengthen our children's ability to meet life's challenges and pressures with confidence and perseverance. The principles involved in raising resilient children can serve as guideposts as we teach children about friendships, school, community, and dealing with challenges and mistakes, as well as meeting responsibilities.

Some may contend that our expanded application of the concept of resilience is so broad that it encompasses almost all aspects of raising children. We would not disagree, but we would see this more comprehensive definition as a positive phenomenon rather than as a watering down of an important concept. The development of resilience in our children is one of the most important tasks of parenting.

Question

In your lectures you talk about the importance of developing a resilient mindset in children. What does mindset really mean and what are the main characteristics of a resilient mindset? What impact does a mindset have in how a child actually behaves?

Answer

It seems that just as the word *resilience* is being increasingly used by many people, so too is the word *mindset*. When we write about a mindset, we are referring to a set of ideas, beliefs, attitudes, skills, and assumptions, all of which guide our behavior relative to a specific topic or issue. In this case we are referring to these qualities as they relate to resilience. Often we are not aware of or reflect upon the components of our mindset or how our mindset actually influences our behavior. Yet, as psychologists we believe strongly that our thoughts, feelings, and attitudes combine as powerful predictors in determining how we behave and ultimately deal with everyday life. In our experience it is not unusual to find that many parents have not thought about or challenged the assumptions they hold about parenting and their children's behavior.

As an example, one mother with whom we worked, had a temperamentally difficult-to-manage five-year-old daughter. The mother's mindset was that her daughter was acting difficult on purpose, and the mother told us that she was convinced that for some reason the girl was attempting to get her angry. Given this view, the mother reacted by becoming increasingly punitive, prompting the girl to feel unloved and resentful. Not surprisingly, the result was the establishment of a negative cycle between this mother and her daughter.

When we interviewed this girl, her mindset was that her mother was unfair and didn't love her. It wasn't until we helped change this mother's assumptions about her daughter by discussing the different temperaments in children and how her daughter was not placed on this earth to make her life miserable (a belief that mother had expressed in a moment of frustration), that the mother could accept our recommendations for working with a temperamentally difficult youngster. Without realizing it, this mother's assumption about her daughter's behavior was actually prompting her to respond in ways that worsened their relationship and lessened her daughter's ability to be resilient. Once this mother's mindset and subsequent behaviors changed, so did her daughter's in a positive way.

Another illustration that relates directly to the mindset of resilient individuals pertains to how children understand the reasons for the mistakes they make. Children who believe that a mistake is a sign of failure or inadequacy and something that is not easily corrected are likely to avoid mistakes at all costs or become increasingly helpless and unhappy in the face of failure. Such children may attempt to mask their feelings of failure by saying the task is stupid and quitting, or by becoming class clowns or class bullies. In contrast, another child dealing with the very same mistakes and issues may possess a decidedly different mindset, believing that mistakes are challenges to overcome rather than failures to avoid. This child's mindset will direct him or her to seek assistance from others and figure out ways of solving the problem.

> A resilient child is an emotionally healthy child equipped to successfully confront challenges and bounce back from setbacks.

Resilient children possess a mindset that is strikingly different from children who are not resilient and who have not been successful or able to overcome adversity. As parents understand the features of this mindset, they can help to nurture and reinforce it in their children. A resilient mindset is what we hope for all children. A resilient child is an emotionally healthy child equipped to successfully confront challenges and bounce back from setbacks. As we will discuss in our answers to questions in subsequent chapters, children possessing a resilient mindset feel special and appreciated. They have learned to set realistic goals and expectations. They develop the ability to solve problems and have confidence in their decisions. This leads them to view mistakes or obstacles as challenges rather than stresses. Children possessing a resilient mindset rely on productive coping strategies. Their self-concept is filled with images of strength and competence. They have developed effective interpersonal skills in their relationships with both children and adults. They are comfortable in seeking out assistance and believe that there are adults in their lives who care about and are available to them.

Our focus has been on how parents through day-in and day-out interaction with their children can develop and reinforce this "product" that we are calling a resilient mindset. The more parents are aware of the power of this mindset in their own lives and the lives of their children, the more they can make appropriate changes and become more effective parents.

Question

I heard you speak at a parenting workshop and was intrigued that as parents our mindset plays a large role in fostering resilience in our children. It's something I hadn't really thought about before, but I realize what an important concept it is. What are the characteristics of the mindset of parents who are more likely to nurture resilience in their children? And, as important, is it something that can be learned? One of the problems I see is that if I think too much about mindsets I might begin to analyze every assumption or every behavior of mine or of my children. I worry that if I do too much thinking about my parenting, I might become paralyzed in my interactions with my kids. Yet, I do want to increase my skills in understanding my mindset and that of my kids.

Answer

You raise some important questions. As we have noted, many caring, well-meaning parents have not thought about how our assumptions, including how we view ourselves, our parenting skills, and the behaviors of our children, really do determine the quality of a parent-child relationship. We believe that with awareness and practice, mindsets can be changed without having to analyze every behavior that appears in our household. We certainly don't want parents to become pseudo-psychologists poised to interpret every comment or gesture of their children, a stance that may create the appearance of a Woody Allen comedy (or tragedy). If parents understand the basic features of a resilient mindset, then we think that they will be better equipped to learn to interact with their children in a more natural and less artificial way as they reinforce this mindset in their children.

In essence, parents engaging in the process of raising resilient youngsters possess an understanding of what they can do to nurture a resilient mindset. We believe that it is a process that until now has not been actively attended to nor directly taught to parents. Some parents intuitively do it more effectively than others. However, it is our opinion that all parents are capable of learning about and appreciating the components of resilience. While the specifics of how we relate to each child will be different given their different temperaments, the process of nurturing resilience can be directed by an established set of guideposts and principles for every child. Keep in mind that children's lives are shaped by multiple factors, including their temperament, their family history and values, their educational experiences, and the culture in which they are raised. The guideposts for fostering resilience in children provide principles and ideas applicable for all children.

The mindset of a parent capable of fostering resilience in children is shaped and directed by ten important guideposts that we described in our book *Raising Resilient Children*. These form the foundation to help reinforce the mindset of resilient youth. Though some may seem obvious and commonsense activities or ideas that most reasonable parents would follow without difficulty, we have come to learn that what appears obvious requires continuous thought and reflection, so that we don't lose sight of what is truly important. The ten guideposts embedded in the minds of parents who foster resilience in their children, which we will address in greater detail in our answers to questions in subsequent chapters, include:

1. *Being empathic.* In the parenting relationship, empathy is the capacity of parents to put themselves inside the shoes of their youngsters and see the world through their eyes. Remember, empathy does not imply that you agree with everything your

children do but that you attempt to appreciate and validate their point of view. You learn to ask yourself such questions as: "Would I want anyone to say or do things to me that I am saying or doing to my children?" or "How do I say and do things in a way that my children will be most responsive to listening to me?"

2. *Communicating effectively and listening actively.* To influence their children, parents must develop the skills to listen actively to what their children are communicating. Parents must keep in mind that they must find time to give their children undivided attention and to validate what their children are attempting to say to them even if they do not agree with their children's views.

3. *Identifying and rewriting negative scripts.* Parents possessing a resilient mindset recognize that if something they have said or done for a reasonable time is not effective then they must change their script if their children are to change theirs. Many parents continue to believe that if they keep saying the same things to their children, it is the responsibility of their children to change. This often leads to the same negative behaviors occurring year after year after year. As one parent said, "My children are going to outlast me. I better think of different ways of responding to them!" We agree.

4. *Believing in their worth.* A basic guidepost for building resilience is the presence of at least one adult who believes in the worth of the child. They must love their children in ways to *help them to feel special and appreciated.* This implies finding time to be alone with each child so that each child has our undivided attention during the week.

5. *Being accepting.* One of the most difficult tasks for parents is to accept their children's unique temperament. This, of course, implies that parents are very aware of the impact of temperament on a child's development and behavior. By *accepting our children for who they are*, we can help to set realistic goals and expectations for ourselves and them, resulting in a more satisfying, less tense parent-child relationship.

6. *Focusing on strengths.* Resilient children do not deny the problems they face, but they recognize and focus on their strengths. Parents possessing a mindset to foster resilience help their children

experience success by identifying and reinforcing their islands of competence. Every child possesses these areas of strength. Parents must promote these rather than overemphasizing children's weaknesses.

7. *Viewing mistakes as learning opportunities.* Resilient children tend to view mistakes as opportunities for learning. When children make mistakes parents must use these opportunities to reinforce the message that *mistakes are experiences from which to learn.* It is important not to respond to our children's mistakes with comments that are demeaning or belittling. These only serve to erode the foundation for a resilient mindset.

8. *Fostering a sense of responsibility.* Resilient children possess a sense of responsibility. A major task of parents is to *help children develop responsibility, compassion, and a social conscience.* Although there are various ways to accomplish this, one of the most effective is by providing them with opportunities to make contributions to their home, school, and community.

9. *Building self-esteem.* Resilient children are those with high self-esteem who believe they are masters of their fate. They have a realistic sense of what they have control over and focus on those aspects of their lives. This implies that they also possess effective problem-solving and decision-making skills that are carefully nurtured by their parents.

10. *Using discipline to teach.* Finally, parents possessing a mindset to foster resilience understand that one of their most important roles is to be a disciplinarian in the true sense of the word. That is, they understand that discipline stems from the word *disciple* and is a teaching process, not a process of intimidation and humiliation. The ways in which we discipline our children either reinforce or weaken their self-esteem, self-control, and ultimately the capacity for resilience.

Question

I have a ten-year-old son. In observing him I would say he is resilient. If he loses a game he practices twice as hard the following week. If he doesn't do well on a quiz he will put in extra time studying for the next test. But I also notice he will sometimes put a teammate down if the teammate makes an error. He once talked about how stupid a girl in his class was since she never earned more than a C on a test. On the one hand he seems resilient, but I don't understand why he has to make fun of others.

Answer

You raise a very good point. We believe that if children are resilient they do not feel the need to put down their peers. Being resilient does not imply feeling superior to or better than others. Actually, in our view, resilience is associated with greater empathy, caring, and compassion. Resilience does not equate to insensitivity. Children who face and overcome adversity are not unaffected by their experiences. In fact, they are greatly affected. However, by possessing a resilient mindset and in particular by having certain supports available to them during times of adversity, they have been able to transform these negative experiences into a positive life outcome in which they are often more understanding and tolerant of their peers.

> Empathic individuals are able to "walk in the shoes of others."

Based on your description your son appears to possess many resilient qualities. He views mistakes as challenges. He accepts that if he doesn't do well it is his responsibility to work harder to succeed the next time. We suspect that your child has also developed reasonably good self-discipline and islands of competence. Given our relatively limited information, we are not certain if his self-expectations are too demanding, prompting him to place too much pressure on himself to succeed. However, what seems more apparent is that for whatever reason your son is not demonstrating one critical component of a resilient mindset, one that we would hope you would be able to help him develop, namely, empathy. Empathic individuals are able to "walk in the shoes of others." They can identify with the feelings, thoughts, and attitudes of others and would not say to their peers what they would not want said to them. Given the successes your child has experienced, we believe that your focus as a parent should be to nurture empathy in your son.

How best to do this? Begin by attempting to understand and reflect upon your child's perspective. Don't confuse empathy with giving in, spoiling, or being indecisive. It would appear that at this point your son is holding everyone to his standard. If he makes a mistake or doesn't do well he puts in extra time to perform better. This is fine unless you feel he is placing too much pressure on himself to succeed. If this is the case, you might help him to develop more realistic expectations and point out that everyone makes mistakes and the best way to learn from these mistakes is not to feel humiliated or intimidated by others. In a nonaccusatory way you can wonder how a teammate who makes an error or a classmate who earns a C on a test feels and what he might say to be more encouraging.

Sometimes when we engage in these conversations our children will respond that this is a particular classmate who has always done poorly and has been unable to improve. Once again empathy should be our guiding principle. Attempt to help your child understand that although he possesses the skills to learn from poor test performance and achieve higher scores some people may not. Remember that teaching empathy, similar to reinforcing any of the components of a resilient mindset, takes time. In the next chapter we will respond to a number of questions concerning empathy.

Question

I think my wife and I provide our children with a great deal of love, with a good education, and with enriching activities in the community. Our kids seem to enjoy school and these activities. Are these things enough to guarantee that our children will be resilient?

Answer

It seems that you and your wife are doing the right things to develop a resilient mindset in your children. However, there are no guarantees that even children from loving homes will easily develop resilience. Some children may be born with a greater capacity for resilience. In contrast, other youngsters, even when provided with love, a good education, and community activities, may struggle when faced with typical stress and adversity. For example, children confronted with such problems as depression, anxiety, Attention Deficit Hyperactivity Disorder, and learning disabilities, all of which have a strong biological basis, will face a greater uphill battle to become resilient. It is not that biology is destiny, but biology does play an influential role in a child's development.

> Parents focused on raising resilient children must appreciate how differ-ent each child is at birth and must develop realistic expectations for their children and for themselves.

Parents focused on raising resilient children must appreciate how differ-ent each child is at birth and must develop realistic expectations for their children and for themselves. This requires that the ways they communicate love, the kinds and number of community activities in which they involve their children, and their demands for school success be determined by their knowledge of the unique makeup of each child. In addition, when parents understand the differences in each child they will be better equipped to avoid the pitfall of assuming more responsibility for their children's success and more blame for their failure than is warranted, a situation that typically leads to greater frustration and anger.

We wish to emphasize that even given these strong innate influences, par-ents play a major role in their children's development. Adhering to the guide-posts we have described for nurturing a resilient mindset will ensure that you are doing the best you can in helping your child prepare to be a happy, suc-cessful adult. Just keep in mind that some children, particularly those with emotional, developmental, or behavioral problems, require more time and input than others in this process. Yet, the development of resilient qualities is even more important for these children as they face greater adversity in their current lives and, as researchers have demonstrated, in their teen and young adult lives as well.

Question

It seems from what I have read that resilient kids are kids who have overcome adversity. I have a five-year-old daughter and a seven-year-old son. When I look at them I want them to be resilient but it pains me to think of them facing adversity. I just feel like coming to their rescue or protection when they are upset by something so that they don't experience frustration or distress. Do my actions deprive them of an opportunity to become more resilient? How do I know when to step in to soothe them and when to let them handle things on their own?

Answer

Your question touches a very important point about when parents must let their children experience some frustration and failure and when it is time to move in. We have sometimes said at our workshops that being a parent is at times like walking a tightrope. It's a real balancing act in which you don't want to move sideways in either direction too far or you might fall off the tightrope. Some parents, picking up on this metaphor, have added, "And there doesn't seem to be a safety net underneath." Actually, we believe that typically there is a safety net from which parents can bounce back, be resilient, and attempt new approaches.

Addressing your question more specifically, the basic premise of our model is that children don't need to suffer in order to develop a resilient mindset or the qualities of resilience. They do, however, need to experience the typical successes and failures that are encountered by all youngsters, and when they do experience these situations, parents must respond in ways that reinforce a resilient mindset. Although the outcome of a specific issue or problem is important, even more vital are the lessons our children learn from the process of dealing with issues and problems. Regardless of success or failure, knowledge gained provides the experience from which the seeds of resiliency develop and flourish.

Thus, your role is to ensure as much as possible that your expectations are reasonable and your children are not exposed to undue hardship. When they succeed, you must help them to take realistic credit for their success in order to build up a reservoir of ownership and confidence. When they make mistakes or fail, you must avoid being judgmental or accusatory, but instead find ways of assisting them to see that they can learn from falling down. When they are feeling down, you must be empathic and acknowledge their feelings without rushing in to rescue them.

It is not always an easy call to know when to step in and when to let our children struggle a little. We advise parents to trust their instincts and judgment and to keep in mind how their past responses have impacted their children. If you find that in your attempts to keep your children from feeling frustrated, they are less apt to attempt new things or to persevere on difficult tasks, this is a strong cue you are overprotecting them and keeping them from opportunities to learn what they are capable of doing. In some situations it is helpful to communicate to our children that we are available should they need our help. If they call upon us, we can use our involvement as a learning experience to help them sort out what they can do by themselves and when they need our assistance. If they are having difficulty but don't call on us, we can also use that as a way of communicating we admire their perseverance but that it is sometimes helpful to enlist the input of others.

And don't worry. How to walk across the tightrope without falling off too often is a learning experience for all of us as parents. The more we do it, the better our balance will be.

Question

Sometimes I think we are in an "arms race" when it comes to raising children. We continue to create a more complicated world that is overwhelming to many children. Then we have to teach them to be more resilient. Wouldn't it be better if we could figure out how to make the world less complicated?

Answer

As we discussed in an earlier answer, it is a reality that our world is not going to become less complicated. But complexity does not necessarily have to equate with significant stress and adversity. We are distressed by the statistics reflecting the number of children who live below the poverty level, or who are abused or neglected in the United States and throughout the world. Technology and complexity are not to blame for these problems. We can have a complex yet humane child-focused culture. Even so we don't believe that changing the world around us offers a complete solution. We are not suggesting that we should not be involved in even small ways to change conditions in our community that will lead to a healthier emotional and physical environment for our children. However, we must be realistic of what we can change in the world and what we can change in our day-to-day interactions with our children. Even if we could do so, we are not in favor of freezing our culture in a time warp of years long past. A basic belief we espouse is that if we want to raise resilient children we must not concentrate all of our energy on changing the world around us, but we must begin by changing what we do with our children. Hopefully, the guideposts we have suggested to nurture resilience will provide direction as we interact and teach our children.

Always keep in mind the influence we have as parents to protect our children from undue stress and to instill in them a sense of hope and optimism even when the "outside" world is filled with painful events.

Question

I have twin brothers. They are fraternal twins. One of them is happily married, has a wonderful job, always has a smile on his face, and is upbeat. He was that way as a kid. My other brother is just the opposite. He never seems happy. He has been married three times, can't seem to hold a job for more than a few months, and just doesn't seem satisfied with anything in his life. How can they be so different having the same parents and growing up in the same environment? Is it all genetic? If they were identical twins would they be exactly the same? The reason I have even more of an interest than ever before is that I have two-year-old fraternal twin boys and I am already seeing differences in them even though I think my husband and I treat them the same. Is there anything else I should be doing?

Answer

Your question touches on several important issues related to factors that help children develop a resilient mindset, which as you indicate take on greater personal relevance since you have fraternal twin boys of your own. First, you ask, "Is it all genetic?" We know that temperamental characteristics are present at birth, and as one parent said at a workshop, "It's in the genes." While that statement is true to some extent, it only captures part of the story. The full picture is more complex.

Obviously, identical twins are the siblings most likely to have the same temperamental features given that they emerge from the same egg and sperm, but even with identical twins there may be differences at birth. Fraternal twins genetically are similar to different age brothers or sisters; they will have more of a probability of sharing similar temperamental characteristics than those who are not blood relations but not to the same degree as identical twins. Thus, in the case of your fraternal twin brothers whom you describe as very different even as kids, we would not be surprised to find that they were already quite different from birth.

> Many parents find it easier to relate to and be affectionate with one of their children than another.

However, as we constantly emphasize, a child's temperament alone does not determine all facets of his or her thoughts, emotions, and behavior. This is where the influence of parents enters and a complicated picture emerges (is there anything that is not complicated in parenting?). Although parents may say that they treat all their children the same or that they love all of their children the same amount (however one measures love), this is rarely the case. Many parents find it easier to relate to and be affectionate with one of their children than another. This phenomenon may be based on several factors including a child's temperament. Some children love to be held, while others don't. Some loved to be kissed, while others back away. Some are cheery and always smiling—as is the case with one of your brothers—while others are more difficult to interact with since they are needy and perpetually unhappy, which seems to be the situation with your other brother.

Subtly or not so subtly most parents enjoy interacting with a child who makes them feel good as a parent. Children are rather perceptive in knowing if a parent likes to be with them. However, children are often unaware of how their own actions play a role in influencing their parents' behavior. Thus, a child with an unhappy, difficult-to-please temperament is likely to evoke negative feelings from his or her parents, negative feelings that lead the child to conclude, "My parents don't love me," "My parents aren't fair," "My parents love my brother more than they love me," or "My brother always gets much more than I do." When children feel this way, they are prone to respond in a negative, less cooperative manner with their parents, which invites further parental anger and frustration. A negative script is set in motion.

Also, even if your brothers' temperaments were similar, your parents might have had different feelings about them based on such factors as their physical appearance or birth order. We once worked with parents who had fraternal twin girls. In the course of therapy, the mother became more aware of the fact that the older twin reminded her of herself while the younger one was more similar in looks to mother's younger sister, whom mother described as "selfish" and "always opinionated." Without realizing it, these perceptions of her sister colored this mother's view of her twin daughters.

Thus, even if children are raised in the same home, their images of themselves and of others may be markedly different based on their temperament, their parents' response to their temperament, and their perception of their parents' actions. As is evident, many factors contribute to the emergence of a child's personality.

In terms of your own twins, try to appreciate each one's unique temperament and respond accordingly. Being fair does not mean you should do the same thing with each of your sons but rather that you should respond to each based on what each needs. Examine whether the perceptions you have about your twin brothers impact on how you see and respond to each of your sons, always keeping in mind that although your sons are fraternal twins just as your brothers are, your sons are different from your brothers. Also, find time to be alone with each of your sons, and your husband should do the same. This is important for all siblings but sometimes of greater urgency when you have children who are often lumped together under the label "the twins." Use all of your interactions to foster a resilient mindset in each of your sons.

Question
This may seem like a silly question but I have been thinking a lot about it. Is resilience inherited, at least in part?

Answer
Your question is not silly and is raised in different ways by many parents. We doubt there are "resilience genes." However, as we have alluded to in a number of our other answers, we believe strongly that there are qualities of human temperament and behavior that protect and insulate children, increasing the likelihood that one child will be resilient while another will be at-risk. Some children are very easy to comfort from birth while others are much more difficult to calm and comfort. This latter group often expe-

riences a very low emotional threshold and a high intensity of reaction. That is, small amounts of negative stimulation in the environment, amounts that usually don't result in much distress for other children, distress these children a great deal.

It might be helpful to imagine that you are one of these easily stressed children. Consider what life is like if multiple times during the day the minor stresses that have little, if any, impact, on most children are very upsetting to you. Imagine that when you are upset, you respond primarily through tantrums. How would these reactions influence your self-image and the manner in which you perceive others treat you? Because of your low emotional threshold the often innocent actions of others are experienced by you as very distressing and thereby "intended" to upset you. Certainly this type of temperament would work against the development of a resilient mindset. We are not suggesting that children with this temperamental style are incapable of developing resilience but rather that parents need to understand that the development of resilient qualities may require more effort, consistency, tolerance, and support on their part.

Although resilience genes may not exist, what do exist are inborn characteristics that will predispose children toward becoming more or less resilient. Although children may begin at a different point along a "resilience continuum," where they end up along this continuum will be greatly determined by their daily interactions with their parents and other adults.

2

Teaching and Conveying Empathy

Through the Eyes of Others

Question
I have heard the word empathy *used a great deal in terms of being a more effective parent. But I'm not exactly certain what empathy means or in what ways it is so important. Also, is empathy the same as sympathy? If not, how are they different?*

Answer
We believe that the ability to be empathic is one of the most important skills in any relationship, husband-wife, friend to friend, parent-child, teacher-child. Basically, we define *empathy* as the capacity to put yourself inside the shoes of another person and to see the world through that person's eyes. In the parent-child relationship, empathy implies that when parents interact with their children, they have "trained" themselves to ask how their children would describe them at that moment, or how their children are experiencing what they have to say, or how their children are viewing a particular situation.

> It is much more challenging to be empathic when we are upset or annoyed or disappointed with our children.

The importance of empathy impacts on all aspects of our parenting and yet is much more difficult to develop than we realize. We have found that most parents consider themselves to be empathic. It is not unusual to hear parents say, "We always try to understand our child's perspective" or "We do try to see the world through their eyes." However, we have discovered that it is much easier to be empathic with those people whose ideas totally agree with ours or with our children when they do what we ask them to do. It is much more challenging to be empathic when we are upset or annoyed or disappointed with our children. For instance, think of the last time you were upset with your child. Perhaps you even raised your voice (as most parents do) and yelled. As you were yelling did you ask yourself, "I wonder how my child would describe me at this moment?" Most of us do not ask this question when we are upset since our main goal is for our child to listen to us. Unfortunately, as many of us know from firsthand experience, our children are less likely to listen to us when we yell but we continue to do so since it is difficult to remain calm when we are angry.

If we want our children to listen to and learn from us, if we want them to develop a resilient mindset, then we must think about how we come across to them and how our words and actions are received. For example, many parents tell us at our workshops that their children are unmotivated. A typical response to this apparent lack of motivation is for parents to exhort their children to "try harder and put in more of an effort." The problem with this kind of statement is that most, if not all, youngsters experience this as accusatory and judgmental. As one young man told us, "How do they know I'm not trying? Does anyone have a test for trying?" Thus, when parents tell their children to try harder, their goal is to motivate their children to do more work. But if their children perceive this statement as judgmental they are likely to do less work.

How might empathy help in this situation? Empathic parents might ask themselves, "How did I feel when someone told me to work harder and put in more of an effort?" Interestingly, when we ask parents this, most recall instances where they became angry. We even say at our parenting workshops, "Imagine if you had a tough day as a parent, that nothing seemed to go well, but we happened to be consulting with you that day and said that we had diagnosed the problem. You eagerly asked us what we found, and we answered, 'You're just not trying hard enough.' How many of you would say, 'What a helpful remark!'?"

In essence, empathy allows us to understand more clearly the view of our children and to respond in ways that create a climate in which they will learn from us rather than resent us. It is a vital interpersonal skill. Some people confuse empathy with sympathy. While at times they may appear to overlap, sympathy is to feel sorry for someone else. Empathy is to understand that other person's perspective, to put ourselves in that person's shoes.

One final comment about empathy. You might wish to do the following exercise, one that many parents have found quite revealing and helpful. Divide a sheet of paper in two. On one-half of the sheet write down all of the words you hope your children would use to describe you and reflect upon (a) why you hope they would use those words and (b) how you are behaving toward them so that they are likely to use those words. Then on the other side of the page, write down the words you think they would actually use. Compare the words on both sides of the page. Some parents discover that the two lists are similar. However, many parents with whom we work quickly recognize that the words they believe their children would actually use to describe them are far apart from the words they would hope they would use. The larger the discrepancy between the words on the two lists, the more we must strive to practice empathy.

Question

Can a parent learn to be more empathic? In calmer moments when my kids are not there, I tell myself to be more empathic, to put myself inside their shoes. But then when they don't listen to what I have to say and when I have to keep reminding them to do certain things, I find myself saying things to them that I wouldn't want anyone to say to me. I actually said to my son the other day when he hadn't cleaned his room, "Do you have a brain to remember things?" You can imagine that this made the situation tenser, and I immediately regretted saying it. What might help me not to say these things?

Answer

Most parents can certainly relate to your situation, having said or done things that they wish they could take back. We believe that all of us can strengthen our capacity for empathy, but it is not always an easy task. If it were, then one brief exercise would lead to immediate change. As we often highlight in our parenting workshops and as we mentioned in the previous answer, it is easier to be empathic toward our children when they are doing what we want them to do. It is also easier to be empathic when we are calm and not stressed. However, as your question indicates, when you become angry it is much more of a challenge to practice empathy. In many respects the true test for being empathic is when we are feeling stressed, angry, or annoyed. Practicing empathy is even more important when we are stressed or angry since it is at these times when we are most prone to say or do things likely to be hurtful toward our children.

> Practicing empathy is even more important when we are stressed or angry since it is at these times when we are most prone to say or do things likely to be hurtful toward our children.

There are things we can do as parents to help maintain empathy even during very exasperating times. A first step is to accept that as parents we are human and that even the most loving parents will at times wonder why they ever decided to have children. Frustration and anger are normal emotions that surface in our role as parents. Once we have accepted that such feelings will arise, we can become more aware of what triggers these feelings as an important step toward learning to deal more constructively with them. We can begin to notice what it is that leads us to be angry and less empathic. We can ask ourselves certain questions such as: Are these situations we can predict? Are they situations that we can avoid? Are they situations in which we can find more effective ways of responding so that our frustration is kept to a minimum and we can help to develop a resilient mindset in our children?

You mentioned that one of the things that frustrates you is when you constantly have to remind your kids to do certain things such as to clean their rooms. From what you wrote it appears as if their failure to meet responsibilities occurs with great frequency, almost something that you can predict will happen. In our clinical work we have learned that many frustrating experiences occur with some regularity, an observation we will discuss in greater detail in Chapter 4. What might be helpful is for you to sit down with your kids and discuss why fulfilling responsibilities is important and then ask them what might help them to remember to meet these responsibilities. By doing this, they become part of the solution to the problem, increasing the likelihood of their being cooperative, thereby lessening your frustration and anger.

Humor might also help as long as it is not experienced as sarcasm. How do you think they would respond if you were to ask them, "Do you think I nag you a lot and say some things that you wish I didn't say?" More than likely, they will answer in the affirmative. Some children might even say, "You finally realized that you're a nag!" Remain calm regardless of what they say. You can even ask them how would they like you to remind them in those rare instances when they forget to do certain things such as put their toys away.

Even with preparation, however, parents will face situations that prove frustrating and exhausting. Accept that these situations will occur and have a plan in place with how to handle your anger without compromising your ability to be empathic and caring. One mother found herself becoming very angry with her eleven-year-old daughter. This led her to tell her daughter to go to her room, which was typically met with, "No I won't!" You can imagine how quickly empathy disappeared from the scene. However, the futility of trying to send her daughter to her room prompted this mother to say, "I need a time-out. I'm going to my room." Interestingly, after the mother exited the room, the girl knocked on her mother's door and asked if she could come in. The mother reported that much to her surprise they had a calmer discussion and she was able to remain more empathic. The important message is for you to develop a number of strategies to use when you feel you are getting angry, strategies that will help you maintain a calmer demeanor.

And finally, when you do "lose it" and say or do things that you wouldn't want said or done to you, it's okay to apologize as long as you don't find yourself repeating the same behavior and apologizing every day. When you lose your composure, ask yourself what prompted your anger, and then consider different ways you can deal with the situation in the future.

Question

I think I am an empathic parent with my two daughters. They are eleven and fourteen years old. Yet I think they take advantage of my empathy. For example, the other night my eleven-year-old wanted to stay up past her bedtime to watch television. I told her I knew how she felt, that it was past her bedtime and she couldn't watch TV. She said if I really knew how she felt, I would let her watch. She also said that all of her friends were watching the show. I ended up feeling sorry for her and let her watch the program. So much for empathy! What else could I have done?

Answer

Your question has been raised by many other parents. The concept of empathy is sometimes confused with giving in to children or letting them get away with things or not holding them responsible for their actions. Part of the problem is that some parents mistakenly believe that if they are empathic, their children will always do what they are asked and not get angry with them. However, when their children do not respond in a cooperative way, parents blame empathy, feeling that they are not holding their children accountable. In addition, some parents have difficulty tolerating their child's anger and will in fact "give in" to ensure their child's love. As one mother told us, "I want my child to love me and not be angry with me." The wish to avoid our children becoming upset with us may prompt parents to acquiesce to their children's demands and then cast aspersions on empathy as the culprit. One mother equated empathy with "being wishy-washy."

> Empathy does not necessarily imply that you agree with another person but rather that you attempt to understand that person's point of view.

Let's examine once again what empathy means so that hopefully we can clear up the misconception that empathy leads children to take advantage of us. As we have emphasized earlier, empathy involves the ability to put yourself in the shoes of another person and to see the world through that person's eyes. Empathy does not necessarily imply that you agree with another person but rather that you attempt to understand that person's point of view. Actually, as parents, the more we can assume the perspective of our children, the easier it will be to establish limits and expectations in ways that our children are most likely to hear and respond positively to us. An empathic parent not only asks, "In anything I say or do with my children what do I hope to accomplish?" but also, "Am I saying or doing things in a way in which my children are most likely to hear me rather than tune me out?"

This second question can guide us to validate what our children are communicating, but we must remember that validation doesn't mean we agree with them or give in to their demands. When your daughter said that if you really knew how she felt you would let her watch the show, one response might have been, "I think I know how you feel and how much you want to watch the show, but you know that there is a time for you to go to bed and the show is after your bedtime." Don't be surprised if your daughter fails to say, "Thank you for validating what I am feeling" since most kids don't thank us for setting limits. However, by being empathic and validating your daughter's feelings, she should be better able to accept the limits you have set.

In Chapter 11 we will discuss the obvious drawbacks of giving in to our children when they make us feel that we are being unfair or that we are not doing a good job as parents. Suffice it to say that in the future, don't allow your daughter's protests that "all of her friends were watching the show" keep you from setting established bedtime limits. If you felt the show was appropriate for your daughter to watch, you might even offer to tape it for viewing the next day.

The more we can be empathic and the more we can validate our children's feelings, the better relationship we can have with them and the more effective disciplinarians we can be.

Question

My four-year-old son Billy doesn't like to be left with a babysitter when my wife and I go out. Actually I was the same way when I was his age so I can understand how he feels. When the babysitter came over I thought it would help if I let Billy know that we could be reached if he became upset. So I told the babysitter in front of Billy that if he cried I would give her the number where she could reach us. When I said that, Billy reacted by beginning to cry. Wasn't I being empathic? Where did I go wrong?

Answer

Without wishing to sound too technical—but we suspect as psychologists we do fall prey to using jargon at times—your question helps us to distinguish between empathy and what some therapists call "overidentification." While the two concepts may appear to have some common characteristics, in fact they are different. As we have noted, empathizing with our children means attempting to see the world from their perspective. Obviously, in doing so, our assumptions about how they are feeling and thinking will be somewhat biased since they are based, in part, on our own life experiences. However, empathic parents can basically separate what they are feeling from what their children are feeling.

In contrast, when we overidentify with our children, we often "read into" their feelings and thoughts. Frequently, when we overidentify we assume that they are feeling what we felt when we were children or feel even today. In the example you cited, you assumed that Billy would be very upset when you and your wife went out and that he would experience separation anxiety and cry. Certainly what you told the babysitter was based on your love for Billy and your desire to help him feel as comfortable as possible when you left him for the evening. Billy's past problems with separation most likely added to your motivation to warn the babysitter of what might occur when you left.

What was very revealing in your question was your very honest statement that when you were Billy's age you felt the same way he did. Although Billy also seems worried about separation, in this instance your memories of how you felt as a child may be contributing unintentionally to Billy becoming increasingly anxious. In assuming that he would be upset when you left and telling the babysitter how she could get in touch with you if he began to cry, the message Billy heard was that it was very probable that he would become upset and require you either to return home or at least comfort him on the phone. In essence, seeds of anxiety were planted.

If Billy tends to have separation problems a better approach that should help him to deal more effectively with these problems and become resilient is to find strategies for dealing with his anxiety. He should get to know a new babysitter at a time when you are home. You can talk with the babysitter—with Billy present—about the activities that Billy enjoys. If Billy is comfortable with a night-light, the babysitter should be told this. Also, some parents make it a "special" evening with the babysitter by allowing their child to stay up an additional fifteen minutes. The more experience

Billy gains with having you leave and return, the better equipped he will be to handle separations from you.

> As parents we must be careful not to make assumptions about how our children are feeling and thinking based solely on our own experiences as children.

Another example of a well-meaning parent intensifying a child's distress is captured by a shy mother who constantly exhorted her shy daughter to speak with other children. The first questions she asked her daughter after school were, "Did you speak to many kids today? Did you invite anyone over to play?" This mother constantly lived with the pain of her own shyness and thus, from an early age attempted to help her daughter be more outgoing, believing her daughter was lonely. Her pressure to change the situation actually increased her daughter's anxiety.

As parents we must be careful not to make assumptions about how our children are feeling and thinking based solely on our own experiences as children. When we confuse our feelings with theirs, we are not being empathic; rather we may be distorting the perspective of our children. Since all of us make assumptions about the behaviors of others, the difference between empathy and overidentification can be a thin line at times but it is important to maintain this line as much as possible.

Question
Can parents help their children learn to be more empathic? Sometimes I'm surprised by the mean things that my ten-year-old son and my thirteen-year-old daughter say to other kids or even to each other. I don't know why they would say these things since my husband and I don't speak that way to them or to each other or to other people. What can we do to help them be more considerate and empathic?

Answer
Many parents have reported their surprise at how mean their children can be at times. Even children who grow up in loving homes and by and large

are caring and compassionate individuals can fall into the trap of saying and doing hurtful things. The reasons are varied. Certainly in the early adolescent years, insecurities reign supreme. It is a time when children are increasingly separating themselves from their parents and seeking acceptance from their peers. It is not unusual that acceptance by one group often brings with it the need to set oneself aside from or reject another child or group. To have an "out" group serves to define an "in" group, to which most children yearn to belong. It is for this reason that some kids will communicate hurtful things only when in the presence of their group but not when they are with only one other peer.

Also, when we are feeling insecure, we are less likely to be empathic and compassionate. Many parents have told us that when they are more anxious and stressed, it is difficult to practice empathy. Thus, it is little surprise that youngsters would respond in the same way when they are feeling pressured. Many adults when thinking back to their childhood and adolescence recall times when they did things toward peers of which they are now ashamed. One caring father at our workshop reported how he and some of his friends teased another boy who had pimples on his face and was not very athletic or popular. He said, "If I saw someone doing that to another child today, I would be furious."

Even though some teasing may be a natural part of growing up, it does not mean that parents should accept it. When they observe their children engaging in behavior that lacks empathy and compassion, they can discuss this behavior with them. In doing so, it is important for parents to maintain empathy and not come across as accusatory, lest their children tune them out. In your situation, when you observe or hear about either of your children saying hurtful things to each other or to others, you might say to them, "I know many kids put each other down but I wonder how the person being put down feels." You might wonder how they have felt when they have been on the receiving end of cruel comments. If you can do so without lecturing, you can share a time when as a child or adolescent you were teased and how that made you feel. Concerning how your two children treat each other, you can set limits on how they speak with each other, explaining, "I know that sibs fight and get angry with each other at times, but you will have to figure out a way to show your anger without hitting or putting each other down."

We know that one discussion with our children is not going to immediately change a situation that has been in existence for a while. We know that many children will offer numerous reasons or excuses for why they do what they do. However, it is important for our children to know how we feel about unkind behaviors and to remind them to place themselves inside the other person's shoes. Our messages become the foundation for the emergence of more empathic, less bullying behaviors. Remember, because your children may engage in these less than desirable behaviors does not mean that they lack empathy or will grow up to be uncaring adults. They may be very caring, but once in a while they need reminders of what is and what is not acceptable in terms of their interactions with others.

Question

I heard you say at one of your workshops that it's easy to be empathic with our children when they do what we want and make us feel good as parents. But my kids are just like most kids and don't always do what we want. When mine don't, I go on autopilot and say and do things without thinking. Most of the things I say and do were things my parents said and did to me when I was a kid that I didn't like. Last night after they failed to put their dishes in the dishwasher, I told them that they were never considerate or helpful. I hated when my parents used words like never *or* inconsiderate. *It just made me more angry when I was a kid and less likely to cooperate. What can I do to break this chain?*

Answer

Your question is a very important one and similar to that raised by many parents such as the parent we discussed earlier who found herself asking her son, "Do you have a brain to remember things?" when he failed to clean his room. We hope we're not being unfair when we say that based on what you wrote, you see negative comments as programmed in you by your own parents, ready to be released without much thought at times of frustration. In essence, the script of your parents has become your script, much to your disappointment. Although you did not like your parents' script toward you, it was the script you learned and the one you are most likely to use with your own children.

We will discuss changing negative scripts in greater detail in Chapter 4, but let's look at how to begin to change what you are doing. Your use of the word *autopilot* aptly describes what is occurring in your response to your children. It is as if your response is pre-set and automatic, not permitting any other response to surface. As you struggle to change, keep in mind that one of the main goals of parenting is to develop a resilient mindset in children and that to accomplish this we must turn off autopilot and begin to consider other possible maneuvers. When we have been on autopilot for a long time, it is a struggle to assume control of our lives but it can be done.

> Don't permit your childhood memories to control your life, but instead use them to increase your empathy by placing yourself inside your own shoes when you were a child.

In a calmer moment, sit down and ask yourself, "How else can I respond when my kids are not meeting their responsibilities?" Remind yourself that words like *never* or *inconsiderate* serve to increase resentment, as they did to you during your childhood. As you described your situation, it is obvious that you are currently feeling trapped by your childhood experiences. Instead, ask yourself how you might use these experiences as a motivation to change. Don't permit your childhood memories to control your life, but instead use them to increase your empathy by placing yourself inside your own shoes when you were a child.

As a possible aid, make a list of several things that your parents said to you that were not helpful and then consider what might have been a better response. To assist you with this task, you might recall things your parents said or did that either boosted or lessened your self-worth. The more you can reflect upon your own childhood memories and feelings, the more likely you will be able to consider alternative responses with your children.

We know one father who remembered the many hurtful reprimands he received from his parents as a young boy and how he was saying the same things to his children. Following our suggestion he made a list of things he could say and do differently when his children did not fulfill their responsibilities, including not losing his temper, sitting down with them to discuss what made it difficult for them to remember to help out, and asking them if they felt it would be useful if he reminded them of what was expected. His calmer, less accusatory approach permitted his children to come up with some excellent suggestions including that the responsibilities of all members of the family be posted in the kitchen and when each responsibility was completed it would be checked off. They also agreed that if a responsibility had not been completed, any family member could place a cutout red circle on the poster that had the word *reminder* written on it. The idea worked very well but would not have been possible had this father not reflected upon his own memories of childhood as a catalyst to turn off the autopilot.

Creating a list of things our parents said to us that are now part of our inner "program" can help us to become more aware of this program. Awareness and insight set the foundation for changes to take place. In addition, if we free ourselves from a negative autopilot mode, we can examine more closely our expectations for our children and our response to their behavior, setting the stage for us to consider more effective ways of reinforcing a resilient mindset in our children.

And one final word, which we constantly emphasize. If you have been on autopilot for many years, don't get discouraged if you and/or your children fail to disengage immediately from that mode. As much as we all want to be our own pilots and masters of our fate, it often takes time to free ourselves from flying by autopilot. When we are able to do so, however, the rewards are great.

Question

I've begun to notice something in my interactions with my two sons that is bothering me. Whenever we begin to argue, especially when they haven't met their responsibilities, such as cleaning their rooms or finishing their homework, I start to feel that they are primarily acting in this way to get me angry. This leads me to become even angrier with them and a vicious cycle gets going. I hate to admit this but the other day when I came home from work and one of my sons had left his baseball bat on the floor near the door and I almost tripped on it, I had this feeling that he did it to get my goat. I was so angry that I told him he could not play with the bat for the next month. What can I do in situations like that instead of assuming the worst and getting very angry?

Answer

As you point out, one of the common assumptions of parenting is that when our children are unable to gain or obtain their immediate goal they will retaliate by acting in obstructive, negative ways that appear designed to make us angry. We suspect that almost every parent has on at least one occasion perceived that their children's behavior was designed to fuel parental anger.

As we have noted in our responses to other questions about empathy, once we are angry it is difficult to be empathic. Empathy is challenged when we experience negativity from our children. Anger and disappointment quickly reduce empathy and tend to blind parents to the negative power of their words and actions.

When anger dominates our emotions we are less likely to be reflective. In such situations we tend to believe that our children can control the majority of their negative behaviors if they wanted to. As long as we adhere to the opinion that our children's negative behavior is within their control and that they are engaging in this behavior on purpose, then our words, the tone of our voices, and our actions will be driven by this belief. If we are to be empathic we must learn to be in greater control of our own feelings and actions. Being in control reduces the likelihood that an argument will begin. When your children don't meet their responsibilities, the reasons, though important to understand, should not provoke an argument. Even if you perceive that your child's goal is to make you angry, by becoming angry in return, you simply throw fuel on the fire. Remaining calm and in control, not always an easy task, is more likely to set the stage for your children ceasing their negative behavior.

Let's look at other ways you could have responded. If this was the first time a bat was left out, you might pick it up and return it to your son with a comment that in case he was looking for it you found it. If this type of problem has occurred before we suggest you deal with the problem, rather than becoming distracted by the motive for the problem. It will be important for you to sit down with your sons and arrive on an agreed upon plan as to what will happen if their possessions are left around the house. Finally, if responsibilities involving chores and homework haven't been met, a similar approach should be taken, helping your sons develop a set of strategies to meet their responsibilities.

> When your children don't meet their responsibilities, the reasons, though important to understand, should not provoke an argument.

Question

I am really concerned my children will take advantage of me if I am empathic. I know that when I was a kid, all I had to do was shed some tears or say to my parents that what they were doing was unfair and they would let me do whatever I wanted. I remember that when I was fifteen years old and wanted to go to a party my parents asked if there would be an adult present. I said yes, and they said they were going to check. I started to cry and said if they really trusted me they wouldn't have to check. They said they did trust me and didn't check. In fact, there was no adult at my friend's house and several of us got drunk. Looking back, it could have been a dangerous situation and I'm not sure why my parents didn't call. I would have been angry if they had checked, but it would have been the right thing to do. Now, I see my fourteen-year-old daughter trying the same things so I'm not sure it helps to be empathic and give in.

Answer

As we have noted on several occasions, empathy should not be equated with giving in, backing down, spoiling, or allowing children to do whatever they want. In fact, empathy has everything to do with helping children learn to accept limits as we make an effort to understand their point of view.

> Empathy fosters the skills to communicate to our children in ways in which they are most likely to listen not only to our words but to the intent of our message.

Many parents fail to understand that we can be empathic yet disapprove of our children's actions. To be empathic means to communicate that your child has been heard. In the situation described, empathy allows you to respond to your daughter that making a phone call or attending a party is not going to be used as a "test of trust." You can certainly point out the many situations in which your trust of your child is unquestioned and in fact trust is not the issue in the current situation. If you feel comfortable you can say, "I trust you but sometimes a situation can get out of hand even for a responsible child."

Don't expect your children to thank you for your actions. Instead recognize that they will respect you if you consistently do what you say and promise. Keep in mind also that even when you're empathic, there will be situations in which your children will continue to respond with difficult behavior. We believe, however, that empathy is the best place to begin changing children's behavior and building strong parent-child relationships. It is the place we begin in helping children foster a resilient mindset. Empathy fosters the skills to communicate to our children in ways in which they are most likely to listen not only to our words but to the intent of our message.

Question

When I'm calm it seems so easy to be empathic. But the other day I was really feeling hassled and my nine-year-old son came home from school, threw his book bag on the floor, and started to shout that school stinks. He then said that the teacher had yelled at him. Even though I was angry with him, I tried to be empathic and said, "That must have made you upset." He yelled back, "Why do you think you always know how I feel?" His answer made me even angrier, but I told myself to remain calm and I said, "If a teacher yelled at me when I was your age, I would have been upset." He yelled at me again, "That's how you felt! I'm not you." He then stormed out of the room. What happened? What could I have done differently?

Answer

Your first statement is absolutely correct. It is easy to be empathic when our children behave well and meet our expectations. It is harder to put empathy into place during trying times. Yet, it is exactly during those times that empathy may be most important. Remember that to be empathic requires you to be thoughtful as well as to believe that if you want to be heard and understood you have to begin by first listening and seeking understanding.

In the situation you reported it was evident that you wanted to assist your child. Unfortunately, he did not experience your comments as very helpful. If anything, it seems as if he felt you were being intrusive. In the future you might begin by asking yourself why did my son come home and tell me how he was feeling about school? Despite his shouting and complaining, he was willing to communicate about his day. We suggest you begin by saying in a low-keyed way that you are glad he could tell you what happened. You can even ask him how he felt before you offer your thoughts. If he's not certain how he felt, you might say that you have some ideas based on your own experiences and ask him if it's okay to share these with him. If he says no, then simply say, "If at any point you would like to hear them, please let me know." You might also say that if there is anything you can do to help he should also let you know.

Let's assume he is interested in how you felt and you answer that it would make you upset and he still responds with, "Why do you think you always know how I feel?" You might say, "I'm sorry if that's what it sounded like. I guess I'm really not sure how you felt. Maybe you can tell me." Given his negative feelings, it seems he experienced your comments as not hearing him and instead, telling him how he should feel. His response, "That's how you felt! I'm not you" bears this out.

To review and expand upon our answer, we suggest you begin with empathy. Instead of telling your son how he feels, we suggest you ask him how he felt or simply reflect that he appears upset. Ask him to tell you a little more about what happened in school. Show an interest without coming across as intrusive. Depending upon his response you can ask him what he would like to do about this problem. Based on your past interactions he may seek your help to develop some strategies. He may tell you that he is so upset that he doesn't want to think about it right now, a request that should be respected. If he has had ongoing problems with his teacher and expresses a sense of hopelessness that nothing will help, you must begin by honoring that feeling. In response, we suggest you offer your availability and assistance if your child would like some help dealing with this problem. The key word in this situation is *acceptance*. It is not most important to tell your children how they feel, what they've done, or what they should do but to let them know that you accept them and are available to help.

Question

My wife and I are really concerned about our twelve-year-old son. He often says that he is "dumb" and "stupid." We try to be encouraging and say, "No, you're not." This seems to get him angry and he says, "Yes, I am." We thought we were being empathic but when we tell him he's not dumb or stupid, he gets into an argument with us insisting that he is. We're not sure what to do. It hurts us so much to hear him say he's dumb and stupid.

Answer

It is painful for anyone to hear people whom they love and care about speak negatively about themselves. When people believe they are dumb or stupid, every activity, task, or assignment is colored by this negative feeling. Such feelings can quickly become self-fulfilling prophecies. No one finds it very helpful when they express how they feel, think, or believe, regardless of how negative those thoughts or actions are, to have someone respond by telling them they are wrong to feel this way. This is particularly true when we deal with issues that don't have right or wrong answers. When people feel dumb or stupid they filter daily experiences through this belief. They tend to magnify the negative and minimize the positive.

Though it is one of the most painful experiences of parenting to hear our children speak negatively of themselves, it is important in this situation not to attempt to talk your child out of his thoughts, feelings, or beliefs. It is also important for you not to become so angry or distressed that you are unable to be of assistance to him. Children may have negative self-feelings for a variety of reasons. Some children seem to come to the world with a temperament to view things negatively. For others, feeling dumb and stupid is the result of failure in the classroom or on the playground. In these situations we suggest you begin by validating and reflecting what you have just heard. "Sounds like things have happened to you that make you feel you're dumb or stupid." We then suggest you continue by conveying empathy. "Most people who have had this problem feel this way. We are glad you could tell us how you feel. We also know that most people, with some help, can learn strategies to successfully deal with their problems. We're here to be of help." By saying these things, you are empathizing with and validating your child; once you do this, he or she will be more receptive to hearing your message of help and hope. In our experience your children will also be more willing to take steps to change these negative feelings.

Question

My husband and I heard you speak, and we've been doing a lot of talking about the concept of empathy. You mentioned that we serve as models for our kids and that they notice what we do more than what we say. You also mentioned that you often ask kids to describe how their mothers and fathers treat each other.

What are some of the most important things that kids notice about how parents treat each other that affects their own ability to be empathic?

Answer

We are not aware of any research studies that have made an effort to count, measure, or rank the most important things kids notice about their parents when it comes to developing empathy. In our experience, however, the strength of the parents' relationship is closely tied to children developing empathy. We focus on four main qualities in parent relationships: Trust, respect, availability, and communication. We summarize these as TRAC. When parents get on the "express TRAC" they begin setting the stage to help their children develop empathy. A strong parental relationship is established when parents respect and trust each other, communicate effectively, and are available to each other and to their children. In research studies, availability between parents and children has been found to be one of the best predictors of success during the teenage years. When parents respect, communicate effectively, and are available to each other they build the foundation of a trusting relationship, a relationship capable of bearing the strains that often come with adversity. When children observe this kind of relationship in their parents and when parents behave in the same way toward their children it serves as a model for their children. A resilient mindset thrives in such an atmosphere. To help you keep these thoughts in mind, as you interact with each other ask, "How would our children describe how we are treating each other?" Seeing your relationship from their perspective can serve to correct any aspects of the relationship that is not "on TRAC."

Question

I have a nine-year-old son and twelve-year-old twin daughters. I hate to admit this but I feel my three children are really lazy and I'm not sure why. My wife and I meet our responsibilities. We will go out of our way to help our kids such as driving them places even when it's not convenient for us. Yet, they constantly have to be reminded to do their chores. Earlier this week one of my daughters asked me to drive her to pick up a book that she had forgotten at her friend's house. I said, "I will but I'm not sure I should since you didn't make your bed or put your clean clothes away." She said, "Why do you always throw in my face what you do for me? If you don't want to do it, then don't do it but don't throw it in my face." All, I'm trying to do is motivate her to meet her responsibilities. Can empathy help this situation in any way?

Answer

Yes, empathy can certainly help this situation. One of the myths of irresponsibility is to equate doing chores with being a responsible, caring person. Many parents even refer to the first responsibilities they expect their children to meet as *chores*. Believe it or not a label such as chores may make a difference in a child's perception of our request. Not surprisingly, we have found that children do not like to do chores. Yet, when these same children are asked to help out, they often respond in a positive way. When we become preoccupied with day-to-day chores we often lose sight of the many ways our children are responsible.

> When we become preoccupied with day-to-day chores we often lose sight of the many ways our children are responsible.

Although telling your daughter that you don't want to drive her to her friend's house since she hasn't met her responsibilities might seem like an appropriate strategy for motivating her to help out, what we have found is that such an intervention frequently prompts children to respond in the same angry fashion as your daughter. In many cases a power struggle is set in motion. We believe a more effective approach is for you to adopt a more empathic stance. Talk with your daughter at a calm moment about how her contribution to the family means a great deal to you. You might discuss what responsibilities are especially important. Also, there may be some responsibilities that are truly not very important that can be dropped. For instance, if you felt that making the bed was not essential, you could even say to your daughter, "I've been thinking about what would be really helpful to me. I need help setting and clearing the table and having you put your clean clothes away. If you can help in that way, I'm not really concerned about the bed being made." While some parents might wonder if they are giving in by doing this, it has been our experience that a parent's flexibility and willingness to modify some "nonessential" task requirements will actually result in children being more cooperative.

Finally, we should keep in mind that by serving as a model of empathy and responsibility we can help our children become empathic and responsible. Certainly we are not suggesting that all privileges should be provided "free of charge" but rather that when we take the time to help our children develop responsibility in many areas of their lives, when we avoid overfocusing on chores as the only means of demonstrating responsibility, and when we are willing to demonstrate kindness and love to our children in noncontingent ways, we set the stage for helping them to develop into responsible and caring individuals. Our task is facilitated when we can place ourselves in their shoes and be empathic.

3

Communicating Effectively

To Listen, to Learn, to Influence

Question

I am really confused about something. When things seem to be calm in our home, our ten-year-old son finds a way to say or do something that upsets everyone. When we try to talk to him about it, he responds that we are always on his back and he doesn't want to listen to us. What should we do so that he will listen? The way things are going now I feel like screaming back at him, which I must admit I have done at times. This doesn't seem to be the road to building a resilient mindset.

Answer

The proverbial generation gap is often reflected not only by differences in musical taste or clothing preference or even diverse opinions, but also by an inability to communicate. We have found that most parents struggle with how to speak with their children in ways that their children will at least listen to what they have to say and not immediately react with anger or tune them out. It is for this very reason that we have emphasized the importance of establishing effective lines of communication with our children if we are to nurture their resilience.

Many parents have asked us, "What exactly is effective communication?" At our workshops some have expressed the belief that it involves children complying with our requests while others perceive it as pertaining primarily to the solution of problems. One father, perhaps only half-kidding, offered another definition when he said, "To me effective communication is when my children answer questions with more than one word."

> Effective communication allows us to model and reinforce empathy, hope, optimism, and problem solving, as well as enhance self-worth and a sense of control or ownership over one's life.

We believe effective communication goes far beyond our children doing what they are told or addressing only problematic areas. It encompasses the quality of communication that occurs minute-to-minute, hour-to-hour, day-after-day in all types of situations. Effective communication allows us to model and reinforce empathy, hope, optimism, and problem solving, as well as enhance self-worth and a sense of control or ownership over one's life. The ways in which we communicate our feelings and thoughts is a foundation for developing and strengthening all of these qualities as well as reinforcing resilience in our children.

Effective communication is rooted in empathy, in listening to our children and learning what they are attempting to express before offering our opinions and thoughts. As any parent can attest, this is easier said than done. Think how often you may have interrupted your children when they communicate ideas and opinions that are different from those that you hold. Our communication must be nonjudgmental and nonaccusatory. We must serve as a model of honesty and dignity.

Yet, even in the best of circumstances, some children are more prone to respond adversely to our messages. To answer your question about how best to speak with your son so he will listen to you, we would obviously need more information, such as whether your son's provocative, negative style has existed from an early age. As you describe him he seems to display the characteristics of a temperamentally difficult child. Such children appear to come into the world "informing" their parents immediately that "parenting me will not be easy." Genetic or biological factors contribute to this pattern of behavior. These children are more prone to oppositional and defiant behavior. They may respond adversely to even low levels of stress, often expressing very negative thoughts and attitudes, many of which are seemingly unfounded in the face of the problem being encountered. Much to the confusion and frustration of parents, these children are frequently disobedient, defiant, and hostile, often for no apparent reason.

Even parents with a long fuse when faced with these behaviors are vulnerable to losing their temper. In such situations effective communication gives way to shouting matches and a loss of empathy. In the heat of the moment, most loving parents have said things to their children that afterwards they are upset they said. A mother at one of our workshops smiled and said, "I hope that if my daughter ever writes her autobiography, she will be kind enough to leave out certain things I've said to her or to use a fictitious name."

Whether or not your son is biologically predisposed toward negative behaviors and/or other factors are operating, it's important for you to ask this question: "How can I discuss my son's behavior with him without him immediately feeling I'm always on his back and becoming very angry with me?" This is where empathy plays such an important role. One approach is to find a quiet moment to talk with your son about the problem in as clear and nonaccusatory a way as possible. We realize that this will not be easy since your son is prone to hear almost any remark as judgmental. You can say that you have something you want to discuss with him that has to do with the family getting along better. You can add that if at any point he feels you are criticizing him he should let you know. We have found that when parents bring up the issue of possible criticism, their child is better able to listen to them.

Next describe the problem as a family problem and engage him in a discussion of ways he believes the family can relate more harmoniously. Discuss times he has handled a situation well and times he has not. Share with him that when he screams or shouts it is difficult for you to listen to him and raise the question of other ways in which he might communicate his feelings. Also, say that you do not want him to feel that you are always on his back and ask, "What's the best way of speaking with you so you don't feel we're on your back?" If he responds, "I don't know," you can say, "That's okay, it will take time to think about. We can talk more about it in the next few days." Many children feel put on the spot when we ask them for input or solutions; thus, it is important to build in some time to think.

If he answers that he wouldn't shout if he were treated better, you can ask him to be more specific about how he feels you can treat him better. The important thing is to listen closely to what he has to say, to validate his perspective (validation doesn't mean you agree but that you hear his point of view), and to offer your own view if it differs from his. If you can engage him in this way, it will be easier to work out a plan of action for what he can do when he gets upset. You can also discuss with him consequences for his screaming and yelling.

An alternative but similar approach would be to have a "family meeting" where all members of the family discuss both the positive things that are occurring in the family as well as things that each would like to see changed. It is important to set guidelines that establish such a meeting as a time for the family to solve problems and not attack one another. The presence of all siblings can help the child who is having the most problems not feel that he or she is being singled out.

Whether your discussions with your son take place with him alone or in the context of a family meeting, or a combination of both, changing his behavior will be an ongoing process, not one solved in one interaction. However, by establishing a more positive, empathic communication style and not overreacting to his behavior, you will set the stage for him being less volatile and more cooperative. You might wish to read the book *From Chaos to Calm* by Janet E. Heininger and Sharon K. Weiss, which has been especially written for parents of children whose behavioral challenges are similar to yours.

Question

My wife and I heard you speak. You emphasized that it is important for parents to become "active listeners." We think we listen very actively to our children and try to understand what they are saying to us. Yet they often tell us we don't understand them and then they become angry. A good example occurred the other night. Our eleven-year-old daughter was frustrated because her homework was difficult. In response she told us she hated homework. She said homework was stupid and that it didn't help kids learn. If anything it turned them off to school. We listened closely, trying to understand what she was telling us. We knew how frustrated she was. I responded, "Homework can be a pain but it has to be done." This only made her more upset. Is there something else I could have said that would have worked more effectively?

Answer

It is obvious how much you are attempting to understand and respond to your daughter. The first part of your response to her, "Homework can be a pain" was empathic. You were communicating that you recognize that homework is a burden for her. However, when you quickly added that "it has to be done" (which is true) you were not giving her the opportunity to share with you why it is such a pain. It appears that the way she experienced your comment, even though it was not intended that way, was that you knew it was a pain but that didn't matter, she still had to do it. Thus, from your daughter's perspective, she may have thought you did not understand or care about her distress.

What else could have been said so that your daughter would feel you really heard her and, thus, she would be more receptive to listening to what you had to say? Once you observed, "Homework can be a pain," it might have been helpful to ask her what it is that she doesn't like about homework. You could have wondered if there was any homework that was not a pain. Although your daughter might respond that all homework is a pain, there is a chance she might recall a homework assignment that was less stressful. If this were the case, it would provide an opportunity to gain a clearer picture of what is most challenging to your daughter and perhaps open a problem-solving dialogue.

We should note that your daughter is actually correct in suggesting that there is very little scientific support for the benefits of homework, in particular during the elementary school age years. However, homework helps young children develop responsibility and self-discipline toward school. These are skills that will become critically important as they progress into the later school years. It is during junior and senior high school that homework becomes a vehicle by which children teach themselves. Your daughter is incorrect in suggesting that homework is the cause of turning all kids off to school. Research suggests that students succeeding in school usually complete homework without much difficulty. Those struggling at school often do not. Thus, homework may simply mirror these students' classroom-based problems.

All of us become frustrated when we are assigned a task that we don't understand or can't complete. If your daughter resists, dawdles, or leaves homework unfinished, first make certain she understands what to do. Of course, this will be easier to accomplish if you are able to establish an empathic dialogue with her. A lack of understanding is the most common reason children don't complete homework. Some don't understand the material and/or the homework instructions. Make certain you investigate whether your daughter's problem with homework is the result of confusion over what to do or how to do it. Once you have gained a better understanding of the problem, it is important for you to use your communication skills, in this case to communicate with your child's teacher about what is occurring.

> A vital component of effective communication is to be an active listener, which implies that we begin without preconceived notions or assumptions.

A vital component of effective communication is to be an active listener, which implies that we begin without preconceived notions or assumptions. We must understand the feelings, thoughts, and beliefs our children are communicating. We must be careful not to allow our own agendas or need to get our point across to interfere with our ability to appreciate what our children are attempting to tell us. Features of a resilient mindset, including empathy, problem solving, and learning to feel more in control of a situation, are reinforced when parents are active listeners. Thus, as we noted earlier, rather than telling your child that homework is a pain but needs to be done (something she probably already knows), we suggest you empathize with her, elicit her observations, and explore whether in fact she understands and is capable of completing the homework. If you can do this, then together you can develop strategies for her to complete her homework.

Question

When I was growing up, I always felt my parents nagged me. They constantly reminded me to do things, even before they were supposed to be done. I remember one time when I was about eleven years old I became so angry with my father. He told us it was time to sit down to eat dinner. Then he said, "Don't forget to clear the dishes after you finish." I remember screaming back, "Why do you always have to remind me? I'll do it." He sent me away from the table. I told myself I wouldn't do the same thing with my kids. Yet I find I am constantly nagging. My kids are clearly angry with me, just as I became angry with my parents. I tell them that I have to remind them to do things since they often don't remember. I just don't like the tension in our home. How can I say things differently?

Answer

Your question addresses an obstacle that often prevents well-meaning parents from communicating effectively with their children and is tied to the concept of negative scripts that we will discuss in Chapter 4. If a parent grew up in a home in which the family communication style lacked empathy, it is typically more difficult but not impossible for that parent to communicate spontaneously in ways that foster a more positive home atmosphere. Whether we realize it or not, nagging tends to become a self-fulfilling prophecy. That is, parents nag and then children complete tasks. However, the task is completed not because the child has developed an internal sense of responsibility and self-discipline but rather to escape from under the "parent's thumb." This pattern increases rather than decreases the likelihood that when the situation arises in the future the child will not follow through unless the aversive consequence—in this case the parent's thumb—is provided. In addition, nagging is seductive. When parents do it, it frequently appears to work. Yet it is ineffective in the long run in fostering self-discipline and responsible behavior. Even more so, as you point out, nagging is often a powerful fuel to fire anger and resentful feelings between parents and children.

> Many parents have been pleasantly surprised that their seemingly irresponsible children become more responsible when nagging is reduced.

You may not realize it but you have already taken the first step toward a more positive solution by recognizing that history is being repeated. You have also acknowledged that nagging has become an automatic response for you. You do it without even thinking or meaning to do so. Many parents are not as aware as you are of these patterns and continue to engage in them, constantly blaming their children when things do not change.

In Chapter 4 we will describe a number of strategies that you can use to modify your existing script. However, we would like to suggest a couple of things for you to try now. One is the time-honored but often effective method of counting to five (or ten) before reminding your children to do something. During that time ask yourself what will be accomplished if you remind them and would it be best to say nothing and see if they will act responsibly. Many parents have been pleasantly surprised that their seemingly irresponsible children become more responsible when nagging is reduced.

Another possibility is to say directly to your children that you feel you have fallen into a pattern of nagging them (we are certain that they will immediately agree with your assessment). You can add that you're not happy with nagging since it's interfering with your relationship with them and not giving them an opportunity to show that they can handle their responsibilities. You can then involve them in examining what is expected of them and what steps they can take to fulfill their responsibilities. You can also say, "In case you do forget to do something, is there a way to remind you without your feeling I'm nagging you?" If they come up with a way to be reminded then it won't seem like nagging since the idea originated with them. We want to emphasize that if you are able to acknowledge that you are nagging and wish to change, your children may be more willing to change their behaviors.

Question

There is something that really annoys me. I know you talk about giving your children undivided attention when they speak with you. I sit and listen to what they have to say but when it is my turn to speak they will often say, "You just don't understand" or "I don't have time to listen." This makes me wonder why I should be giving them my undivided attention when they don't give me theirs. A perfect example occurred the other night when my thirteen-year-old daughter told me about some problems she was having with friends. I thought she was asking for my opinion. When I told her that some of her friends didn't appear very nice, she responded sarcastically, "That's really helpful!" What did I do wrong?

Answer

Your question touches on a couple of important issues. One concerns how to communicate with our children in ways that address their needs so that they will listen to us. The second issue is how to remain calm when our children seem inconsiderate, especially when we feel we have been sensitive to their needs.

In terms of the first issue, we must remember as parents that sometimes children's goals in communicating with us about their thoughts, feelings, and experiences are not necessarily to seek solutions but to find support and acceptance. It is not always easy to know when to offer advice and when to refrain from such advice and continue to listen to what our kids are saying. In situations such as you describe with your thirteen-year-old daughter, we suggest you begin by acknowledging what you have heard but not necessarily offering opinions or solutions—until the request is made for help. You can let your daughter know that there are some thoughts you have about the matter if she would like to hear them. In this way, you are placing the responsibility on your daughter for deciding if she would like to hear your suggestions.

In a circumstance such as the one you faced, you might respond, "Sounds like this is frustrating for you. What have you thought about doing?" If your daughter says she's not certain and asks what you think, you might still encourage her to come up with possible answers. If she continues to struggle, you can then offer a couple of solutions but only after you feel she is truly stuck. The goal would be for your communications to elicit her ideas. If she should reject your suggestions you can always say, "Maybe we both have to think more about this and talk about it later."

The issue of your daughter seeming insensitive, perhaps even rude, can certainly be hurtful when you spend time with her and she responds that she doesn't have time to listen to you. Although we're not certain why she runs off, possible explanations may be that it is her way of saying that she feels that she is not being heard or perhaps she needs time to reflect upon what you have said. It is understandable that parents would feel frustration and anger when their child cuts off the discussion. However, when your daughter does so it is also an opportunity for you to reflect upon what else you might say or do to engage her. One possibility is to comment, "You might not have time to listen now but if you feel you have time to listen later I will be here" or "Let's figure out a good time for us to talk." In this way, you are expressing your availability to help and keeping the lines of communication open.

Our point is that it is not just enough to listen. You must validate what your children are saying, confirm that they have been heard, and be available within reason to speak with them at different times. Effective communication is derailed when we fail to validate what our children tell us. This doesn't imply that we agree with them, but rather that we are listening and respect their views. If we respond too quickly by telling our children they shouldn't feel a certain way or if we too quickly offer an opinion (e.g., your daughter's friends not appearing very nice), we may unintentionally be robbing them of an opportunity to share more of their thoughts and feelings.

Question

How do you communicate to your children that you may have good opinions to offer them? There are times my kids have made certain choices, such as about the clothing they wear or what they are watching on television. If I suggest there are better choices to make, they become angry. For one thing, I really don't like my nine- and twelve-year-old sons watching wrestling. They say it is the best thing on television and then wonder, "What's wrong with watching wrestling? You just don't like anything we like." By then I get so frustrated that I often yell, "You're right, I don't like it, and wrestling is bad for you." There must be a better way of communicating.

Answer

From your question, it sounds like this isn't the first discussion you have had about the "evils" of televised wrestling or about various choices they have made. At this point your children very quickly hear your communications as judgmental and accusatory. While many parents might argue that their children have to learn that their parents' opinions are important and should not be dismissed outright, we would ask parents, "Is there a way of expressing your thoughts and feelings without your children being poised to feel criticized or judged?" As we noted in Chapter 2 about empathy, parents should always keep in mind the question, "How can I communicate with my kids in ways that they are most likely to hear and listen to me?" It is obvious that at this time your sons are not receptive to hearing what you have to say, immediately becoming angry at your messages and feeling judged negatively.

Unfortunately, in such circumstances, children begin to believe that parents are criticizing them rather than the activity. As we become increasingly annoyed with our children's behavior and choices, as we make assumptions about the meaning of their behavior, we may become more and more accusatory and critical. If we want our children to learn from us rather than resent us, we must minimize the messages that make it appear we are judging them of bad things.

The goal is to minimize your children feeling you are standing over them, ready to tell them what they are doing wrong. To lessen this feeling, you should ask yourself what things are truly important in terms of safety and healthy development and what areas are not worth commenting about. If kids feel every message conveys the belief that they are making mistakes, they are less likely to listen when we do have to set a limit about more important issues. We have found that unless our children's clothing is so outrageous (e.g., a T-shirt that they are wearing with obscenities across the front or attire that is contrary to school rules), it might be best to bite one's lips and refrain from saying anything.

However, we believe you have every right to set limits on certain television shows or movies they watch. When you do so you must be as clear as possible what your rationale is and listen closely to the arguments your kids are likely to unleash when you prohibit the viewing of particular shows (e.g., they may shout that all of their friends can watch, that you are treating them like babies, etc.). Some parents in reflecting upon what their children say, have realized that in fact they may have been too restrictive. Other parents have validated their children's anger and calmly said, "We know that you would like to watch this show. While other parents may allow their kids to watch, we feel these are not shows for nine- and twelve-year-olds."

> Thus, the best way to convey that you might have good opinions to offer is to create a climate in which they hear your messages in a nonaccusatory, empathic way.

It would be wonderful if in response to this validation your children would say, "We can see how loving and concerned you are. Since you don't want us to watch, we won't." Even if children felt that way, we assume that they wouldn't offer such words of endearment (as a matter of fact, without sounding too cynical, if they did it might be grounds for being suspicious). However, by validating their feelings and being clear about your reasons, it will lessen their sense that you are being arbitrary and unfair. If they experience you as understanding their point of view, they are more likely to listen to what you have to say. Thus, the best way to convey that you might have good opinions to offer is to create a climate in which they hear your messages in a nonaccusatory, empathic way. It is for this reason that communication is such a critical dimension of nurturing a resilient mindset in our children.

Question

I was at the park the other day with my two young children. I was sitting on a bench on the playground watching them play. Next to me was the mother of a six-month-old. As this mother was feeding her child a bottle she was reciting the rest of the day's events with the child as well as alternatives to what the family might have for dinner. I couldn't help but ask her why she did this. She responded that it was her opinion that talking to her young child this way helped the child develop good language and communication skills. Is this true? Did I miss out on doing something important with my children?

Answer

Your question raises a good point. Is it possible that by talking to our children from the moment of their birth we set the stage for effective communication? We believe and scientific research has demonstrated that this is in fact true, that children in homes in which parents possess and model good language and communication skills develop more advanced language and communication abilities at an earlier age. Although infants are not yet capable of responding with words, it is our words as parents that help to reinforce our children's language skills. In addition, our tone of voice as well as our smiles and how we hold and cuddle our infant can serve to create a soothing, comforting atmosphere that is conducive to language development as well as to a feeling of well-being and security.

Your question also touches upon an important point we would like to emphasize, namely, that effective communication does not emerge suddenly when our children reach the teenage years. It will be easier to have a dialogue with our adolescents if we set the stage early, if we recognize that the foundation for language development and communication is established when they are infants. Even before our children possess language we have countless opportunities to communicate verbally and nonverbally with them. While one need not "review" the agenda for the day as the mother you observed in the playground did with her child, there are many things about which we can converse. People are constantly talking to themselves so why not include your infant as a silent partner in the discussion?

Many parents feel a bit uneasy when they want to have "a talk" with their kids about such serious subjects as sex or drugs. Attempting to enter into discussions about serious matters with our children without having established a foundation for learning how to communicate is similar to deciding to begin an exercise program with two hours of jogging followed by two hours of weight lifting, having never jogged or lifted weights before. It is common sense for novice exercisers to build up their stamina slowly and consistently over time. We emphasize a similar approach to strengthening healthy communication with our children.

The last part of your question is also very important. Don't assume that if you haven't engaged in this kind of communication when your children were young that all is lost. Certainly the younger your children are when you begin this process of communication, the easier it is for them to develop their language skills. Regardless of the age of your children, however, understanding the components of effective communication and its relationship with developing a resilient mindset allows you to begin communicating more easily, increasing the likelihood that when important topics have to be discussed, everyone will feel comfortable and a system will have been established for doing so.

Question

I have always had difficulty admitting when I make a mistake or saying I am sorry. Now I feel that if I say to my kids I made a mistake, they might feel they can get away with things. I am also concerned what they are learning about mistakes. The other day my nine-year-old told me that his teacher didn't like when children in the class made mistakes. As we discussed it further, my child explained that even if someone apologized for making a mistake it was still not a good thing. I think many people say they are sorry when they make a mistake but really don't mean it. What do you think?

Answer

We will discuss the handling of mistakes in greater detail in Chapter 8. However, your question also relates to how comfortably we express our feelings and thoughts about our own mistakes and the mistakes our children experience.

Let's examine your first question about parents admitting they made a mistake. We believe that there is nothing wrong with acknowledging we have made a mistake and saying we are sorry. Communicating regrets does not imply we are letting our kids "get away with things." Parents can say they are sorry without becoming overly permissive or having their children take advantage of them. If anything, a parent acknowledging and correcting a mistake can serve as a model for becoming more responsible and accountable for one's actions. However, if parents find themselves apologizing every day for the same mistakes, then these apologies are likely to be experienced as insincere and increase the probability that children will perceive such statements as hollow and misleading. If people say they are sorry and then change their behavior, it is a clear sign that they take their apology seriously and learn from their past behavior. We believe that many people are sincere when they acknowledge mistakes, although as we know, some are not.

> If children believe that mistakes cannot be corrected or feel they will be unaccepted or punished for a mistake, they are likely to resort to self-defeating ways of coping.

The second issue you raise about your son's teacher not liking students to make mistakes and your son's belief that even if you apologize for a mistake it is not acceptable, requires you to discuss these views with him. In order to clarify your son's perception you might ask him what his teacher does that indicates she or he does not like students to make mistakes. If, in fact, the teacher has said negative, even demeaning, things to students when mistakes have occurred, you can offer an alternative view to your son and, if indicated, speak with his teacher. A classroom environment should be one in which teachers have communicated that mistakes and failure are part of the learning process and students feel safe when they make mistakes.

It is equally important to challenge in an empathic way your son's opinions about making mistakes. The coping strategies we use to deal with mistakes either enhance or decrease resilient qualities. If children believe that mistakes cannot be corrected or feel they will be unaccepted or punished for a mistake, they are likely to resort to self-defeating ways of coping (e.g., quitting or avoiding certain tasks). We must communicate in various ways that mistakes are teachable moments. Thus, when your son voices the view that even if you say you're sorry, a mistake is still a bad thing, you might say, "I'm glad you can tell me how you feel" (this is a validating statement) and then wonder with him why he thinks it is a bad thing. You might wonder if there are times he has made a mistake and learned from it and share with him similar experiences you have had. You can tell him that a number of people feel the same way he does, but in fact there is another way to look at mistakes, namely, that they serve to help us learn new things. A sensitive discussion can serve as the impetus to change your son's mindset about mistakes and increase his capacity for resilience.

Question

I grew up in a home where everyone always seemed to be angry. I know I have a short fuse and I really think hard about not yelling or screaming. I try to use humor when I am angry since I think humor can help defuse a bad situation. But what I believe is humorous often upsets my children. They think I am making fun of them. I don't know why they can't tell I am just kidding with them. For example, the other day my seven-year-old son spilled a glass of milk. I smiled and said, "I know you didn't want to drink your milk, but did you have to spill it all over the place?" He started to cry. Why can't kids tell when you are being funny?

Answer

It is evident that you have worked to develop coping strategies to help you keep your anger under control and to manage it in a more effective style. We believe that humor and playfulness are important components in communication and can defuse a tense situation. When parents call upon humor at appropriate times, communication with their children is enhanced. Humor has also been found to help children deal with adversity. Humor can be used to break the ice. However, there is often a thin line between humor and sarcasm. As a matter of fact, we frequently advise parents that when they are angry the use of humor may not be advisable with their children since it is often perceived as sarcasm.

Humor should be used to create a warm environment in which parents and children feel comfortable and in which children will more readily learn from us. However, at the current time your children experience your attempts at humor as putdowns. Obviously your intent in expressing humor is to lighten the situation, but given your children's reactions they do not realize your intent. It may be that the nonverbal cues accompanying your words (e.g., tone of voice, facial expression) suggest anger, which would lead your children to feel you are being sarcastic such as your son did when you joked about his spilt glass of milk.

Rather than ask, "Why can't kids tell when you are being funny?" it might be helpful to consider such questions as "When I attempt humor am I actually very angry and if so, should I use humor?" or "How can I express humor in a way that lessens the possibility of my kids feeling I am being sarcastic?" If children don't perceive us as being funny but rather hurtful, then we must examine how we communicate and how we handle angry feelings. Once again, we are highlighting the importance of empathy in communicating effectively.

Question
How can I disagree with my kids without turning our discussion into World War III? I hate to admit this but sometimes I feel like they are baiting me. The other day my thirteen-year-old daughter said that she didn't like what I cooked. I told myself not to respond disrespectfully but then she said it again and asked if we could go out to eat. I lost it and screamed, "No, you eat what I've put out." It didn't help when I added, "You're never satisfied. You should be more grateful for all I do for you." Another time when I was trying on a dress in a store, my eleven-year-old daughter told me I had gotten fat. I glared at her and said she should learn how to speak respectfully to me, that I was her mother. What's going on?

Answer
At times all children test their parents. The reasons for this are varied. Many want to see how far they can go before we set limits, others are expressing anger about other issues, and still others may feel we are critical of them so they will return the favor. While it is often helpful to understand the roots of why our children feel the need to provoke us so that we might

be in a better position to remedy what we are doing, even if we don't understand all of the factors involved, there are still things we can do to avoid taking the "bait."

We want to be clear that we do not believe that parents should permit children to be rude to them. In those instances in which they are, parents should say, "I don't like the way you are talking with me. I don't talk with you in that tone of voice so you shouldn't talk to me like that. It will be easier for me to hear what you have to say if you say it in a respectful way." (Of course, you can only offer this kind of comment if you actually speak respectfully with your children.) If we want and expect others to treat us with respect, it is vital that we model that behavior.

What might you have said in the situations you wrote about? When your older daughter commented that she didn't like what you cooked, you might say that this is what you cooked for tonight but since you want her to enjoy what you cook you would like to talk with her about the kinds of food she would like to eat. We knew one family that involved their children in shopping for different foods for dinner. While some limits were set so that meals were not filled with "junk food," the kids were really rather responsible in selecting healthy foods. They even participated in preparing a meal of their choice a couple of times a month. The important thing is to respond to your daughter's criticism of your meal by turning it into a problem-solving activity rather than a screaming match during which angry, hurtful things will be said.

It is also understandable that you became angry when your younger daughter commented on your weight. One's weight is a touchy matter, especially if extra pounds have found their way onto our body. We're not certain why your daughter said what she did, if her perception was correct, or if she was being disrespectful on purpose (there is the possibility that she was saying it with no ill intent). Many eleven-year-old girls are very sensitive about changes in their own body and being overweight and this may have triggered her remark. Regardless of the reason, it might have been better to have simply said, "You're right, this dress doesn't look good on me" or "I guess I will have to lose a few pounds" (if your daughter's comment was accurate). We should use communication to minimize anger and power struggles with our kids rather than saying things that keep arguments alive.

> We should use communication to minimize anger and power struggles with our kids rather than saying things that keep arguments alive.

Question

We have a lot of tension in our family. My wife and I can go days without speaking when we are upset with each other. I have concerns about my ten-year-old son's poor grades and my fifteen-year-old daughter's lack of responsibility in helping around the home. She stays on the Internet with her friends for hours. We never seem to have the time or the ability to sit down and talk. If I try to discuss things with my kids at dinner, they say that they are eating. What's the best way of talking about important things that are going on?

Answer

Your question is certainly relevant to many aspects of effective communication. Since parents serve as models for their children, let's start with your relationship with your wife. Imagine if we asked your children to describe how you and your wife communicate when the two of you are upset. What would they say? We would guess from your description that they would answer that their parents can go days without speaking so that whatever issue is bothering you goes unresolved. Thus, they are not witnessing communication as a way to solve problems, but rather are learning that one way to deal with conflict is simply not to discuss it. Obviously, this is not a helpful lesson, but the reality is that is what they are learning. Instead of withdrawing from each other at times of anger, you and your wife must learn to express what you are experiencing in a way that will help the situation. You should do this for yourself as well as for your children. You may need the input of a marital counselor to assist with this process.

Your interactions as husband and wife are influencing your children's interactions with you. As you attempt to improve your communication style with your wife, the two of you should adopt a more proactive role with your children. In today's fast-paced world, many parents unfortunately rely on a reactive communication style. They catch their children on the run and barely find time to discuss all the important issues facing their family, let alone engage in constructive discussions. We must strive to adopt a more proactive style with our spouses and children. In addition to taking advantage of spontaneous moments for communication (the dinner table may be a good place to talk about the day but not necessarily about problems), a specific time for family discussion is worth considering.

We suggest you establish a weekly time to discuss family issues and problems, as well as possible solutions. Explain to your children the reasons for such a family meeting, casting it in terms of helping everyone in the family to get along better and to solve existing problems. Consider setting up an agenda ahead of time, asking each of your children to pick topics they feel are important to discuss. We have found that many youngsters experience an agenda as a concrete sign that their parents really want to hear their views. You can use the family meeting to address such issues as your children meeting their responsibilities (and what their responsibilities should be) and your daughter chatting on the Internet for hours. Your son's poor grades can be discussed at the family meeting or alone with him at another designated time.

Keep in mind, however, that we are not suggesting communication should be confined to a scheduled, once a week event. Being proactive means we accept the responsibility of communicating with our children throughout the week about important subjects before they become major problems.

Question

Recently my teenage daughter complained that she was struggling in school and didn't have very many friends. She added that she was "depressed." This alarmed us. With the increasing number of children experiencing depression and attempting suicide, this was a hot button. I quickly said there was no reason for her to be depressed, that she had a good life and a loving family. She told me that I just didn't understand her problems and stormed out. I felt terrible. When I tried to speak with her later she didn't want to speak. How worried should I be about depression? What can I do differently the next time?

Answer

Depression is a very common problem of childhood. However, despite many recent advances, it is often unrecognized and misunderstood. Researchers now understand that even children fortunate enough to not face significant life stress may still be vulnerable to develop depression based upon genetic and biological factors as well as daily life experience. For some children, depression may be chronic. For long periods, often as far back as parents can remember, these children appear unhappy. Yet for some youngsters, depression represents a dramatic change for the worse, often following a particularly stressful life event. You may be surprised to know that struggles in school and poor school performance are often sensitive indicators of risk for depression. Problems with peers represent a second, equally powerful risk. Thus, your concerns for your daughter are justified given her comments about school and social problems.

Without completing an evaluation, we can't tell you if your daughter is depressed. However, we can suggest that if you suspect depression you consider speaking with a school counselor or therapist in your community. A decline in school performance combined with apparent unhappiness and increasing social problems are often key signs that a youth may be suffering from depression. Depressed youth frequently hold a negative view of themselves, their immediate world, and their future. The stronger they feel negatively about these three phenomena the more depressed they are likely to become.

Symptoms of depression include the inability to locate enjoyable activities, excessive sadness or unhappiness, a change in appetite and weight, physical agitation, visible fatigue, feelings of worthlessness or guilt, difficulty with concentration, and, finally, thoughts of death or suicide. The description "lonely, sad, and angry" is often characteristic of depressed youth crying out for help. Frequently by the time a depressed youth begins to exhibit angry behavior, a full depressive episode has set in and parents may be distracted by the disruptive nature of the behavior, believing their children have developed discipline problems. Keep in mind also that depression is episodic. In many cases over a six- to twelve-month period, depressive symptoms may lessen. Throughout childhood and teenage years, however, nearly 20 percent of youth will experience at least one significant episode of depression.

If this sounds familiar, if our description appears to fit your daughter's behavior over the last six months, we suggest you seek professional help. In terms of communicating with your daughter we suggest you begin with empathy. When she expresses feeling "depressed," it would be best to validate what she says. No one wants to hear that they should not feel the way they are feeling. You might say to her, "I'm glad you could tell us how you feel. We've got to figure out what would help since feeling sad is such a difficult experience." You can convey concern about her unhappiness and suggest the possibility of seeing a professional counselor. Many youth (and for that matter adults) may respond to this type of suggestion by indicating that "I'm not crazy." You can agree and then explain a little bit about depression, its effects on people, the fact that most people with help can recover, and that you feel this is an important action to take at this time. Even though many depressed teens enter a counseling situation with some resistance, an experienced counselor is able to create an alliance and trusting relationship with most youth. If you want to learn more about depression we suggest the book *Lonely, Sad, and Angry* by Barbara D. Ingersoll and Sam Goldstein.

Question

While I was growing up my parents didn't want to talk about how babies are born or about sex. I told myself that I would be different and answer my kids' questions honestly. However, I am wondering if I am doing a good job. My four-year-old son has asked me four times in the past two weeks if girls were born with a penis and if it was taken away. Each time I told him that girls were not born with a penis and that boys and girls are different. By the fourth time he asked, I said to myself that I am not explaining things very well. I even said, which I wish I hadn't, that I had already told him that girls are not born this way and he should try and remember what I tell him. I could tell by the way he looked at me that he was upset. What can I say differently if he asks me the same question again so he will remember what I am saying? Why does he do this?

Answer

We believe strongly that communication is an active, ongoing process. Children, particularly younger children, may have to hear a message many times before they understand and incorporate it into their thinking and understanding. Even as adults we sometimes have to hear the same thing several times before we truly understand it. Just think about the number of times many adults have been given directions about how to use a computer or swing a golf club before they finally grasp a particular operation. Adults often fail to appreciate the significance of repetition in learning. It is important for you to be prepared to answer the same questions from your child repeatedly. This does not mean you are doing a substandard job of teaching but rather that posing the same questions represents your child's attempts to understand his world, develop a sense of mastery, gain knowledge, and solve problems. All of these are qualities linked to a resilient mindset.

> If we want to raise resilient children, our words and actions must convey to them that none of their questions is silly or irrelevant.

If we want to raise resilient children, our words and actions must convey to them that none of their questions is silly or irrelevant. We must actively reinforce their curiosity by responding, "That's a wonderful question." When they repeat the same question a few times, we can say, "I'm glad you asked me again. Some things take time to learn." We never want children to feel that their questions are silly; if they feel that way, they may cease asking questions and learning new things.

You appear to have given your son a clear, honest answer about the differences between the bodies of boys and girls, but it is evident that he needs more time to absorb and process this information. As adults, we may feel that the differences between boys and girls involve straightforward facts but for a child attempting to understand these differences, there may be many other issues involved.

Although this doesn't sound like your child, some readers may have a child who asks the same, often simple questions, dozens of times. In many cases, these children experience language or communication problems. Sometimes these children have receptive language difficulties that make it difficult for them to understand what their parents are describing. At other times, children with language difficulties learn that asking a question is a way to engage their parents in communication and thus, they ask the same questions again and again. When the parents of these children finally become exacerbated with the repetitive nature of this interaction, the children often find another question to ask as the same negative script is played out over and over. When these or similar kinds of problems are present we suggest that parents seek the assistance of an experienced speech and language pathologist or developmental psychologist.

Question

This may seem like a funny question. When I was growing up I don't remember my parents ever saying to me that they loved me. I am sure they did, but I never heard it. One time I actually brought it up to them and they said I should know they loved me. I never saw them being affectionate with each other or kissing. They have been married for more than fifty years so I guess they love each other. The problem is I am not sure the best way of letting my three kids, who are between the ages of three and nine, know that I love them. I actually find it a little uncomfortable to express affection. To be honest, it is not that easy for me to show as much affection as I would like. How do you start? How do you know if you are doing a good job communicating your love?

Answer

In Chapter 5 we address in-depth questions dealing with issues of loving children and helping them feel special and appreciated. As you point out, some adults find it difficult to express love and affection based on their experiences or for that matter their temperamental style. We believe it is a problem that is important to address and that you begin with small steps and goals to maximize your feelings of comfort. We would not recommend that parents engage in affectionate behaviors that they find uncomfortable since children can easily sense the discomfort.

Begin by thinking about what displays of affection are within your comfort zone. Perhaps when you read to your children you can have them rest against your body. If you read to them at bedtime, you might lay down with them. A hand on the shoulder may be another way of showing affection. In addition, at bedtime you might say, "I love you" and notice their reaction as well as your own. They may actually be surprised at first, perhaps even uncomfortable since they have not heard you say this before. Don't be concerned. By the next time, they and you may be more at ease. One of the ways of knowing you are conveying your love more effectively is that as times goes by, your children will be much happier accepting your demonstration of love and much more willing to show their own affection.

In addition, remember that there are many other ways you can communicate to your children that you love them. These include creating traditions and special times, not missing significant occasions, and using day-in and day-out interactions with them to build their sense of self-esteem and self-confidence.

We know of many parents who grew up in homes where models of showing affection were not present, where parents assumed that the very act of clothing and feeding their children was enough of an indication of love. We have also seen parents who grew up in such environments become more comfortable in directly expressing their love and affection for their children and not leaving it to their children's imagination to decide if love is present.

Question

How honest should you be with your kids about a serious medical problem? Our kids are six and eight years old. Their grandmother was diagnosed with cancer and the prognosis isn't good. Their grandmother lives across the country. They only see her once, maybe twice a year. It is my husband's mother and he doesn't want to say much since he doesn't want to upset them. But they can see that my husband is upset. Also if he is on the phone with his father and our kids come into the room he whispers things like, "I can't really talk right now." I know they realize something is going on. I don't want my kids to be upset, but I don't feel comfortable with the way we are handling things. What should we say?

Answer

If we want children to become resilient, we must realize that it is important to be honest with them without overly burdening them. Many parents faced with your situation believe as your husband does that to tell your kids about the seriousness of their grandmother's illness would make them upset. We agree that they will probably become upset when they learn of her illness, but they already recognize that something is wrong. When we are honest with children we can help them to express and deal with their distress rather than have them wonder what is happening. When we attempt to hide or minimize the reality of a difficult situation, it actually conveys to children the message that we feel they cannot handle what is occurring and that they should not approach us with questions or concerns. In this scenario we rob them of an opportunity to feel in control and to learn techniques for coping with stressful situations and handling painful feelings.

We suggest you inform your daughters that their grandmother is ill. Answer their questions openly and honestly. For example, if their grandmother's prognosis is not good you can say that the doctors are doing all they can to help their grandmother but that you don't know what will happen. The illness of a grandparent sometimes causes children to worry about the health of their own parents. If they ask if you will be okay, you can discuss how most people lead long lives and that you are still young. What you say should be based on what your child can understand. The most important thing is to be guided by honesty and open communication; these guideposts will help your children to voice their concerns and questions with less reservation.

4

Changing the Words of Parenting
Rewriting Negative Scripts

Question

I was fascinated when you mentioned the concept of negative scripts in your workshop. But what exactly is a negative script? For example, how do you know whether it is your negative script or your child's negative script that has to be changed? I have been reminding my twelve-year-old son to do his homework and not tease his younger sister for several years. It doesn't seem to be working since he still forgets to do his homework and continues to tease his sister. Isn't this his negative script? Shouldn't he be the first one to change? How else will he learn to be responsible?

Answer

First, let's explain a negative script. The words and behaviors we use with our children again and again in similar situations and in similar ways become the scripts of parenting. When what we say and do have positive outcomes we can think of these scripts as being effective. They deserve to be repeated. When the outcomes do *not* lead to the desired results as is the case with your son, then these scripts are negative and should be modified or abandoned. However, in our experience even when scripts are ineffective or counter-productive, many well-meaning parents hold on to them, somehow expecting that at some point their children will respond in a positive way and that these scripts will be transformed from ineffective to effective.

You are correct in noting that a negative script is in full bloom with you and your son. We would guess that you can almost predict your child's response to telling him to do his homework and not tease his sister and that he can predict the words and tone of voice you will use to remind him. Have you noticed that scripts often take on the feeling of a play you have seen countless times with all of the actors repeating the same words as if they were cast in stone? Ad-libbing is not a part of one's repertoire. However, since we believe that we are the "authors of our own lives" we encourage people to change those scripts that lead to increased family anger and resentment.

> The words and behaviors we use with our children again and again in similar situations and in similar ways become the scripts of parenting.

You are also correct in observing that it is your child's responsibility to change. However, we believe that if we want our children to change their scripts it is our responsibility as parents to facilitate that change. If you have repeated the same words over months or even years and they fail to result in the desired outcome, we would suggest that instead of focusing on how your child should change, you must focus on what you can do differently. As one father told us who finally realized that he must initiate a change of scripts, "I recognized that if I did not change what I was doing, my son would never change what he was doing. Actually, I felt he would outlast me."

If we want our children to be flexible, thoughtful, and receptive to new ideas, we must model these behaviors. If not, we fall prey to the seductive trap of negative scripts. By learning to identify and change your words of parenting, you will strengthen your child's ability to understand and identify problems. As a result, when confronted with challenges your child will be more likely to be flexible in his or her approach. If, as you point out, you have been reminding your son to do his homework and not tease his sister for several years, why adhere to the same script hoping that somehow your child will change? These scripts and the scenes they play out will be repeated over and over with minimal change. Every parent can point out examples of repeatedly telling their children to do something with little or no positive response on the child's part. If your child has to change his negative script, you must first have the insight and courage to change your own.

By learning to identify and change your words of parenting, you will strengthen your child's ability to understand and identify problems.

As one possible change in script, you might ask your son if he feels you have been nagging him. Most likely, he will respond with a resounding, "Yes." You can then say that you want to figure out how not to come across as a nag. He might say, "Stop getting on my back." You can say, "I think the two things I nag most about are your homework and teasing your sister." You might ask him if he sees homework and teasing as problems. At this point some parents have stated, "Why would you ask your child if these are problems? Of course, they are problems." However, it has been our experience that what we as parents view as problems may be very different from what our kids view as problems. Thus, in many situations parents are asking their children to change behaviors that the children do not view as problematic.

If your child does view homework and teasing as a problem, instead of resorting to the script of nagging, you can change your approach by encouraging him to come up with possible solutions. If your child does not view these as problems you can say, "I now understand why we have had all of these battles, what I see as a problem, you don't." You can then discuss in a nonjudgmental way why you believe these behaviors are problems. When you first discuss this it is unlikely your son will say, "I've seen the light. All of your years of reminding me have finally paid off." However, it has been our experience that parents engaging their children in this kind of discussion permit their children to be less defensive and more receptive to change.

One final word. Many parent-child or family scripts have been "playing" for years. They will take time to change. So don't get frustrated if your son does not respond in a positive way immediately to your change of script.

Question

We have three sons, eight, ten, and twelve years old. Whenever we tell our eldest two sons not to do something, they stop doing it. If we ask them to help out they typically help out. But our youngest son seems not to hear what we have to say. We remind him over and over again to do his homework, clean his room, put his toys away, and not leave his bicycle outside. The other day he erupted and yelled, "You're always on my back!" We responded, "We're not on your back, it's just that you always forget to do things." We can't understand why our strategies, which have worked so well for our eldest two sons, don't work for him. We feel he just has to learn to listen. Should we punish him more to help him learn?

Answer

Your question points out an important phenomenon: all children are not the same. In our experience it is easy to feel good about ourselves as parents or have empathy for our children when their behavior meets our expectations and directions, as it apparently does with your older two sons. However, when children's behavior does not conform to what we desire, we often struggle in knowing how to respond and what to do. We suggest you begin by asking yourself whether the strategies you have chosen thus far have been beneficial. From your question it would appear they have not. This suggests that if your youngest son is to become more cooperative, you will have to modify at least to some extent what you have been doing. Although your approach works with your older sons, it has not been constructive with your younger child. It is obvious that at the current time, he experiences your requests as impositions on his life so that "You are always on his back."

To begin to change a parental script, you may need to figure out why your younger son is less cooperative than his two older brothers. One possible explanation may be rooted in his basic temperament. For example, while some children find it very easy to follow instructions and complete tasks, others do not. In many cases, when children struggle it is not because they don't want to do what they are asked but because they lack an essential skill or ability to do so. When parents fail to appreciate this fact, they often begin to blame their children. We assume our child could clean his room, put his toys away, and remember to bring his bicycle inside if he just "wanted to or cared enough." In response to a reaction that challenges this assumption we respond angrily or punitively.

Instead, you might wish to sit down with your son and present your expectations and then ask what he thinks would help him remember to meet his responsibilities, adding that you want to avoid seeming to be on his back all of the time. When children are asked what they think will help, some will immediately offer some solutions while others may say, "I don't know." They may truly not know or they may need more time to think. If your child does provide some possible solutions he or she has set the foundation for discussion. If your child does not, you can respond in a couple of ways such as, "That's okay, together we can figure out what will help" or "That's okay, let's take a day or two to think about it" (unless the situation falls under the category of an emergency, this second response gives children a chance to reflect upon a solution without the pressure of providing an immediate answer). You can set up a specific time to discuss the issue. If at this specific time your son is still unable to come up with a solution, you can adopt an empathic stance and say, "It's not always easy to figure out how to remember things" and then suggest one or two solutions keeping with your son's cognitive and developmental level (e.g., if he has difficulty remembering tasks, a sign listing these tasks might be posted in his room and perhaps in one other place).

In our experience, even if your son should reject this first solution, the manner in which you involve your son in the solution to the problem typically creates a climate more conducive to having a calm, productive discussion. Also, it may help you to understand the kinds of difficulties your child has in fulfilling his responsibilities and what strategies might address these difficulties.

Another key point is to avoid comparing your younger son to his older siblings. Many well-meaning parents will say, "Your brothers/sisters did this. Why can't you?" Although we recognize that such a comment is a result of our frustration, it serves only to add fuel to the fire, often prompting the child to be less cooperative and less inclined to work with you in coming up with a suitable solution. What your older two sons do is not necessarily helpful in responding to your younger son's seeming irresponsibility. All three of your sons have different temperaments, learning styles, and organizational skills. Your older two sons' styles appear more similar in nature when compared with your younger son. Rather than spending time comparing the two older boys with your younger son, it will be far more helpful to sort out your younger son's style and to involve him in a process in which he understands your expectations and figures out what will help.

Finally, we want to address the issue of punishment, which we believe is typically not a very effective teaching technique. We certainly think that there should be natural and logical consequences for a child's behavior, consequences that are clearly spelled out so that a child is aware of these consequences should responsibilities not be met. However, if we rely too much on punishment or punitive approaches, we often fall into the trap of communicating to children that what they have done is inappropriate or unacceptable but we do not provide them a plan for what they should do. In essence, for consequences to be effective, they must not be harsh and they must permit children to return to the problem situation and modify their behavior.

And remember, children should not be punished for failing to fulfill tasks that are beyond their capability. One does not punish a child for poor reading if the child has a reading disability. Similarly, punishment may not be an effective intervention for your child if his capacity to plan, organize, and sustain effort to complete tasks is weak. It would appear from your observations that listening is not your child's problem. Your child's lack of compliance may in fact be the result of a specific skill weakness. If you don't understand this weakness, you are likely to be ineffective in helping your child and likely to engage in repeated negative scripts, which, from your comments, have proven to be frustrating for everyone.

To summarize, see if you can sort out the nature of your son's difficulties (sometimes an evaluation, performed by a qualified psychologist or special educator, of a child's learning style is indicated) and enlist your son in articulating the steps that can be taken to help to remember and the consequences that follow if he does not.

Question

The other day I think I overreacted with my eleven-year-old daughter. She lied to us, telling us she was going to a friend's home to study. We found out that she and her friend, as well as a few other kids, spent the afternoon at the mall. She knows she is not allowed to go to the mall alone. When she came home we were so upset by her deception that we told her we couldn't trust her. We grounded her for the next three months. Later my husband and I felt this was too harsh but we are not certain if we lessen the punishment now that she will see it as giving in and believe that she can get away with behavior such as this in the future.

Answer

Many parents have experienced the situation you report. Sometimes at our workshops parents will laugh at the harsh or arbitrary consequences they have set down, consequences that seem to have little basis in reality. One father jokingly said, "I got so angry with my son that I think I grounded him through his college years and maybe beyond." He then added, poking some fun at himself, "That punishment will certainly be easy to monitor." While your question relates to the topic of discipline, which we will discuss in greater detail in Chapter 11, it also pertains to the theme of changing negative scripts.

First, we want to make clear that there should be consequences for your daughter's behavior. She deceived you by going to the mall without your permission and your anger about and disappointment in her actions are highly understandable. Offering a consequence that is reasonable and fits the offense, such as being grounded and losing an opportunity to go out with friends the following weekend, makes sense. Also, the consequences should be part of a discussion (not a lecture) related to trust. However, what we have found is that the more angry we are with our kids, the more likely we are to impose overly strict consequences that serve only to increase resentment rather than learning (the purpose of discipline is to teach, not to fuel resentment). Once we have cooled down, we may realize that the consequence did not fit the "crime" and deserves to be modified.

Yet, some parents assume that once they have proceeded down a certain road of consequences, changing these consequences is equivalent to giving in or perhaps spoiling their children. They worry that if they back away from the initial consequences, even when it would be wise to do so since these consequences are deemed arbitrary and harsh, their children will believe that they can avoid responsibility and easily manipulate their parents. Many parents assume that if they "back off" this will be interpreted as a sign of weakness by their children. There is some validity to this concern if parents find themselves constantly changing their initial consequences. This inconsistency may be interpreted by children in many ways that run counter to effective parenting. Children may perceive the constant modification of specified consequences as a form of uncertainty, as a buckling under, or even as an expression of insincerity. In terms of insincerity, wouldn't parents feel this way about their children if their children constantly said, "We're sorry" only to repeat the same behavior over and over again?

If we realize as parents that our script involves overly harsh consequences, there is nothing wrong with saying to our children that we thought over the consequences and realize that because of our anger and disappointment, these consequences need to be modified but that there will still be consequences. This approach will only be effective if we are careful in the future to use more reasonable, less arbitrary consequences so that we demonstrate we have learned from our past mistakes. Our flexibility can serve as an important model to our children, helping them to be more thoughtful and less rigid. If we change in this way and if we use the situation to discuss with our children why they felt the need to deceive us and what can be done differently in the future, then changing our script will not be seen as giving in. As we have often stated, if we want our children to change certain undesirable behaviors, then as parents we must have the courage to take the first steps.

> If we want our children to change certain undesirable behaviors, then as parents we must have the courage to take the first steps.

Question

I have noticed that in the past year my relationship with my thirteen-year-old son has changed for the worse. We used to do a lot of things together. We both love sports. I coached his Little League team. We enjoyed going to sporting events together, and we could talk, especially about sports, for hours. Now when I ask him to go out and have a catch, he always seems busy. He is willing to go to a big league baseball game with me, but I think it is more to be at the game than to be with me. The other day after we came home from a game he went into his room to speak with his friends without even thanking me for taking him to the game. I got so upset that I told him he should show a little more gratitude. He didn't even seem to know what I was talking about. Shouldn't he be more grateful? Isn't it okay for me to remind him?

Answer

We believe that the fact that he didn't seem to know what you were talking about suggests that his behavior was not intentional. As children enter their teen years there is no doubt that their peer group becomes increasingly more important to them than their parents. The increased focus on peers is not a reflection of a lack of interest or care about parents but rather a normal process of maturation. Although our teenage children may be actively pushing us away with one hand, interestingly, they hold on to us with another hand (it may appear that it is done with a seemingly weak grip but it is still a grip). They want to know we are available even when they sometimes say we treat them like babies. We walk a veritable tightrope as parents, performing a delicate balancing act. We don't want to be overly involved or intrusive in the eyes of our teenagers, but we also don't want to appear detached or excessively permissive. If we lean too much toward one direction or the other, we may fall off the tightrope. Sometimes it seems there isn't a safety net below.

The balancing act also involves our ability to give up the relationship we had with our children and enter into a new one as they enter adolescence. Some parents are able to accomplish this with relative ease. However, other parents experience this change of relationship as a significant loss, setting off a process of mourning that often elicits attempts to maintain the relationship that once existed. Not surprisingly, this attempt to keep the status quo is perceived by the adolescent as a continuation of a negative script by controlling parents and, if anything, will elicit anger and more intense struggles to break away.

Relatedly, one of the complaints or myths we hear time and time again from parents is their perception that their children should be more appreciative of their hard work and effort. This frequently prompts parents to engage in another kind of negative script, reminding their children subtly or not so subtly on a daily basis of their lack of appreciation. This negative script is heightened when parents feel that their children have lost sight of how fortunate they are to have the parents that they do. One thing we must learn as parents is that when our kids enter their teenage years, just as your son has, it is likely that they will want to spend an increasing amount of time with their friends and less time with you. And yet, almost all want to know that their parents are available. And within reason, parents must be available. While some parents might feel that we are suggesting that their teenager direct the entire family script in terms of when parents should be involved, we believe this should not be the case at all and that parents can step in judiciously when necessary.

For example, if your son rejects your offer to play ball or attend a sporting event together you can let your son know that you enjoy spending time with him and would like to plan for a future activity. You can emphasize that you do not want this time to take away from his activities with his friends and thus, would like to schedule your time in advance. You can also engage your son in asking what kind of activity he would enjoy (many teenagers love to attend a sporting event or go out for dinner). Keep in mind that when you do interact with your son, it should not be used as a time to remind him of what he should or shouldn't do. Rather use it as an opportunity to discuss your son's interests. When you change the script in this manner, your son may be surprised, waiting for your "lecture" to eventually follow. Let him be surprised!

And finally, even after a wonderful time together, he might not offer the kind of thank you that you would like to hear. Most likely, someday he may recognize all that you have done for him and convey appreciation but until he does, simply say to him how much you enjoyed the time you spent together. Do not resort to the negative script in which you tell him once again how ungrateful and unappreciative he is. If you do, he may be determined to prove how right you are.

Question

I heard a parent educator say that one of the problems with modern parents is that they don't know how to set or stick to rules and limits. He said that some parents immediately give in when their kids argue with them or yell. He stated many parents quickly give in when their children accuse them of being mean. They may hold their parents' love hostage. Yet you talk about how if something isn't working parents often have to take the responsibility of making the first changes in their approach. You can see how confusing these kinds of advice can be. These two seem to be saying the opposite things.

Answer

Experts can certainly be confusing although in this instance we think we can bring the seemingly two opposing views together. Your question touches not only on changing negative scripts but on the area of discipline as well. When rules and limits are set it is important to consistently stick with them.

You should not be badgered or held hostage by your children when they are unhappy or upset with your decisions. As parents we must avoid the negative script of giving in to our children when they challenge reasonable expectations and consequences. If we do acquiesce to their demands, they will not develop a resilient mindset; instead, they are likely to become more self-centered and less responsible.

However, being consistent does not mean being rigid or inflexible or continuing to resort to ineffective rules and disciplinary practices. When a tense situation about limits and consequences has existed for a long time; when children experience us as nagging, lecturing, or being unfair to them so that our words begin to fall on deaf or angry ears; when resentment rather than learning pervade the home atmosphere, then changing our behavior or long-standing script does not mean spoiling our children.

> Being consistent does not mean being rigid or inflexible or continuing to resort to ineffective rules and disciplinary practices.

It's unfortunate that the modification of particular rules or limits is seen by some as an indication that parents are "wishy-washy" and have abandoned their parental duties. Parents must maintain their responsibility to establish clearly defined, nonnegotiable rules at home, especially those related to safety and security. Rules should be altered when they have become part of an ineffective negative script and replaced by a new set of rules that are guided by the goals of lessening anger and resentment, enhancing your relationship with your children, and encouraging them to change their behavior because you are willing to change yours. We run the risk of spoiling our children only when we do away with expectations and allow children to do whatever they want.

In essence, if we recognize that certain disciplinary practices are not working, we must have the courage to change them. The changes that take place must be ones that teach our children to be caring, compassionate, responsible individuals capable of assuming a greater sense of ownership for their own behavior. Changing negative scripts does not imply abdicating our responsibility as parents. We only abdicate this responsibility when we back away from established rules and expectations because we don't want our children to be angry with us or if we want to avoid their constant nagging. Being flexible and realistic does not mean being weak.

One final thought that may seem quite obvious but that many parents experience: If you find yourself modifying almost every rule and expectation you've established, then it's very important to consider whether your initial decisions need more thought before they are put into practice. Some parents generate rules primarily when they are angry or frustrated. In the heat of the moment such directives are likely to be arbitrary and harsh. Important decisions about limits and expectations are better handled when one is calm. We realize this is easier said than done, but definitely worth the effort.

Question

I think I know my negative scripts. I tend to focus on the negative with my kids and even my husband. Each morning when I wake up I remind myself not to nag my ten- and twelve-year-old kids about brushing their teeth or combing their hair or having their book bags ready for school. I also remind myself to find something nice to say to them to start the day off on a positive note. Once in a while I am successful but most of the time I am not. As soon as I see they haven't combed their hair or the content of their book bags are scattered around, I begin to nag them again. Is there a magical formula for what I can do to change my script on a more consistent basis? How do I begin?

Answer

We admire your intentions and we can certainly empathize with how difficult it is to change a negative script. It would be wonderful if there were a magic formula or as one parent said to us "a magic pill" to facilitate the process of changing negative scripts. While such magic solutions do not exist, the good news is that there are guidelines or principles that can help you to begin to write and maintain positive scripts that will replace the negative ones. But, as you know, the creation of new scripts takes time and effort.

However, think of the alternative—the continuation of ineffective behaviors on our part. We suggest five principles to help you write positive scripts, principles that will help you develop a constructive mindset to solve problems. The first principle is to accept your responsibility to change. Based on what you wrote to us, you seem to have accepted this first principle to a great extent since you asked what you could do to modify your script (even if you are searching for a magic formula). The emphasis is on what you can do differently. If you immediately assume that it is your children who must make the first changes the probability of change is dramatically reduced.

The second principle, which may seem simple at first glance but requires much reflection, is for you to understand the problem and the goal you hope to achieve. In this case you would like your children's hair combed, teeth brushed, and book bags packed neatly. These are very specific rather than vague goals, which will certainly help the situation. As you reflect on these goals, you might ask why you selected them and how important they truly are in the life of your child. We know many parents who have shifted or even abandoned some goals, recognizing that in comparison with other goals these are not significant enough to warrant constant battles. There is an obvious benefit of not attempting to change too many scripts all at once—you will not be as overwhelmed and can concentrate on one or two really important things.

Related to this second point is the third principle, namely, it is important to consider what you have done so far and why it hasn't worked. As you point out, it is difficult for you to step back and wait to see if in fact your children will eventually comb their hair, brush their teeth, or get their bags packed before leaving for school. It appears that instead of sitting down and discussing with your children why these responsibilities are not being met, you immediately jump in and tell them what to do. As we will discuss in greater detail in Chapter 10 about involving our children in problem-solving activities, it will prove far more helpful if you sit down and discuss with your kids the reasons for the behaviors in question and what would help them to remember. This discussion must be done without tension and conflict. Remember, a basic feature of a resilient mindset is for our children to understand why there are rules and how they can solve problems. Right now, you are engaged in the negative script of reminding (nagging) them.

A fourth principle is to be hopeful, believing that there is a solution for the problem. Consider a number of different choices and choose the one that best appeals to you. We suggested one, namely sitting down with your children and explaining why you believe the behaviors in question are important and how best to remember these behaviors. Your children may come up with other attractive solutions.

Finally, without sounding trite, if at first you don't succeed, try again but also have a strategy available to handle any frustration you experience so that you avoid engaging in the old script of nagging. We know one mother who used the time-honored technique of counting to ten before saying anything. She found that it really did help her to calm down and refrain from falling into old traps. It would be unrealistic to believe that in every case the solution you have chosen and the new script you have carefully planned will be successful. If the new script doesn't yield a positive outcome, don't become angry or helpless. In this climate many parents throw up their hands, claiming to have tried everything and lamenting nothing works. If the new script doesn't work, try again. Consider a backup plan. But stick with it, working as a team with your child rather than as a supervisor, bearing your hot breath on his or her neck.

On a positive note, we have been impressed over the years with the ability of parents to follow these guidelines and change long-established negative scripts (even we have discovered this with our own families).

Question

I don't want to be rigid as a parent. I know my fifteen-year-old daughter and thirteen-year-old son accuse me of nagging them, but I have found that if I nag them often enough they soon come around and do what I tell them to do such as cleaning up their rooms. When they do what I ask them to do, isn't that turning a negative script into a positive script? Haven't they learned a more positive way of doing things? I think my way is right but my wife has said that even though they are doing what I asked them to do, there is more tension in the house and they don't really want to be with me as much. I say most teenagers don't want to be with their parents as much. My wife and I keep getting into arguments about this. Who do you think is right?

Answer

First, let's examine your goal. If your goal is to get them to do what you tell them when you tell them, then perhaps constant nagging is effective in reaching this goal (although a little warning: in many homes, after a while constant nagging often leads to children refusing to do what we want).

However, if your goal is to help your children to learn to do these things independently, then we would suggest that reliance on persistent nagging is not turning a negative script into a positive script. You may have gotten your children to do what you want but at a price that may turn out to be more costly than you realize.

Without wishing to sound too technical, your current behavior falls under what is referred to as negative reinforcement. Let's explain. When children do something that is positive and you reward them, there is the likelihood they will do it again as long as they have control over their behavior. In contrast, when they do something negative and you punish them, there is the likelihood they won't do it again, as long as they have control over the behavior in question. In both of these situations parents wait for their children to act and then respond with either a desired or undesired consequence. However, that is not what is taking place between your two children and you. What's happening is what we refer to as negative reinforcement. As a result of your children not doing what you want them to do, you are on their backs. They complete the task not because they have suddenly developed a desire to be responsible but because they have learned it is the quickest way to get you to leave them alone. When the task is completed they earn relief from your aversive attention. Thus, they are working to earn something, namely, relief of something that is negative—your annoyance.

Unfortunately, this model is seductive since it appears to be effective. However, if the goal is to increase independent, responsible behavior, this model is ineffective and in fact makes things worse. The next day or week, your children will not engage in the responsible behavior until once again you pay attention to them in an aversive way.

We don't believe negative reinforcement is an effective long-term solution. Instead we suggest that parents sit down with teenagers and develop a plan so that the teenager understands what is expected and the consequences, both good and bad, that are forthcoming based upon their behavior. Then these consequences should be applied unemotionally and consistently.

Your question raises another important point, however. As fallout from your behavior your children find being with you an aversive experience even when they are not in trouble. There is increased tension in your home. Are you willing to pay this price? We don't believe it is a matter of right or wrong but of desired goal and outcome. You can certainly continue this behavior if your only goal is to have the room cleaned. But if your goal is to help your children develop responsibility while maintaining good communication and a positive relationship with you, your current course of behavior is not likely to do so. We believe a new script is warranted.

Question

I feel that I have gone out of my way to change negative scripts toward my two sons who are seven and ten years old. I show them more affection. I spend more time with them. I help them with their homework. But they still act fresh and will talk back to me when I ask them to help out. They are still demanding when we go into a store. My seven-year-old still has a tantrum if I won't buy him something in the store. I think I have changed my script. When can I expect my children to change theirs?

Answer

Many parents are frustrated when they change their behavior but their children don't immediately respond. Change often takes time, especially if a current pattern of behaving has become relatively entrenched. There are also instances when the changes we make as parents do not result in accompanying changes in our children. For example, some children, because of their temperament, skills, or abilities, either take longer to respond or require different approaches on the part of parents.

> Change often takes time, especially if a current plan of behaving has become relatively entrenched.

It is obvious that you are devoted to your sons and have attempted to show them your love and caring through affection and helping them with such activities as their homework. However, those actions will not of their own accord result in your sons being more respectful toward you or in keeping them from having tantrums. Definitely continue to demonstrate your love but also look at how you respond when they talk back to you. Do you give in to their demands? Do you yell back? Or, do you firmly tell them that family members do not speak to each other in that way and if they do, not only will they not get what they want but there will also be a consequence (e.g., losing a privilege)? We should emphasize that if a positive atmosphere of love exists, it is easier to set limits for our children.

You also mentioned that your sons are very demanding when you go into a store. This kind of behavior will not necessarily stop if you tell them a minute before you go into the store with them that you love them. It sounds as if you have to prepare them in advance for what you expect when they enter the store. You might say that you are going into the store but you will not be buying them anything and thus, they should not ask. This is often difficult for children, especially those who temperamentally are more easily frustrated. If that is the case and you feel your children will not be able to handle the frustration, it might be best not to bring them into the store. Another approach is to tell them that they are allowed to select one of three designated items but they cannot ask for anything else. Many youngsters respond positively to having this kind of choice.

The important point is to appreciate that as you change your script in particular areas such as showing more affection or being more tolerant of certain behaviors, it does not mean your children will alter all of their negative scripts. You may also have to change your script in other areas such as being more explicit about acceptable and unacceptable behaviors and following through on specified consequences. It has been our experience that as parents focus on changing their approaches in two or three important areas, children will become more responsive to modifying their behaviors.

Question
I get so angry with myself for always falling into the same trap. I know that I shouldn't ask questions or say things that I know will lead to arguments with my kids, but I do it anyway. The other day I told myself that when my eight-year-old son came home from school I wouldn't remind him to do his homework. Yet after he was home for forty-five minutes just playing a video game, I asked him if he did his homework to which he responded that all I care about is his homework. Why do I keep doing it? I knew it would only lead to tension between us.

Answer
Almost all parents say and do things that they can predict will increase tension in the household. Their purpose obviously is not to create more fric-

tion and anger. In our workshops many ask, "Why do we keep repeating something that we know is ineffective and actually intensifies battles with our children?" There are several reasons for this seeming paradox, including our feelings of frustration at our children not fulfilling what we see as their responsibilities, our own sense of disappointment and helplessness, and our belief that saying something one more time will make it finally "sink in."

We agree with you that you shouldn't have to remind your son to do his homework. Not only has this approach been unsuccessful but it works against your son developing responsibility and a resilient mindset. If you continue to follow the same script, it would not be surprising if you wrote us in five years and said, "I'm still reminding him to do his homework. Why can't he remember to do it on his own? Why can't I remember not to remind him?"

So what is your responsibility? What should be your new script? We believe it is to help your child set up a system such that homework will be completed without your reminding him. Don't be distracted by your son's comment that all you care about is his homework. Instead we suggest you respond that homework is important to help with learning and that you don't want to nag him about it. Emphasize that it is important for the two of you to develop a plan that will help him to meet his responsibilities about homework. Once you have that plan, make certain that you have a back-up plan or safety net should the approach you agree upon not work. The more you can turn over responsibility to your son, the less likely you will continue to engage in behaviors that compromise your relationship with him.

We want to mention one other factor that should be considered in this matter, although it may not apply in your situation. Some children have undiagnosed learning problems and are easily frustrated by the demands of homework. One way in which they express their frustration is to avoid doing work. We always advise parents whose children forget to do their homework or complain about it to make certain that other issues are not present such as the existence of a learning disability. However, even if your child is burdened by a learning disability, he can still be helped to assume responsibility for his schoolwork.

We always advise parents whose children forget to do their homework or complain about it to make certain that other issues are not present such as the existence of a learning disability.

Question

I find that I am yelling more and more at my kids. The other day my two sons who are eleven and fourteen years old were fooling around in a store and one almost knocked over some merchandise. I started to yell and I could see how angry my sons were getting. I hated it when my father yelled at me and now I am doing it with my sons. How do you break this pattern?

Answer

You may not realize it but you have already taken the first couple of steps to changing this pattern. Recognizing that we are behaving in a particular way and wishing to change this behavior that we "learned" from our own parents are the initial steps toward change. Some people have asked us, "Doesn't everyone recognize what they are doing? Isn't it obvious?" In fact, what may seem obvious to an observer, may not be obvious to the person engaging in the behavior. For example, we know parents who yell at their children in the same way that they were yelled at by their parents. Some don't see the connection. Others don't think about the pain they felt as children when their parents yelled at them. Still others argue that they turned out okay by being yelled at so there's nothing wrong with yelling at their children.

It is obvious from your question that you are aware of the connection between our response and how your father treated you and that you don't want to continue the cycle. To continue your struggle to change this negative script you might wish to ask yourself the following questions: (a) What behaviors of my sons get me angry and why do they get me angry? (b) What behaviors need to be addressed and what can be ignored? (c) What can I do to calm myself before responding to my sons (this is especially important since it prompts us to consider new ways of coping with the stress we feel)? (d) What are some other ways I can express my anger or disappointment without yelling or screaming (this is related to the previous question)?

(e) What do I want my children to learn from their interactions with me? (f) How would I describe my father, how would I like my children to describe me, and is the way I would like them to describe me the way they would actually describe me?

As we have emphasized, changing the scripts that are housed in our excess baggage from the past is not an easy task. However, the more we can reflect upon the questions raised above and the more we can consider alternative ways of responding, the more we can nurture more loving relationships with our children.

Question

I have a thirteen-year-old daughter and she is so much like me, stubborn. We get into power struggles. I want to change a script. I want her to know I love her. If I tell her I love her she just says, "Oh sure, Dad, then why don't you show it." I told her it might be good if we could spend some time together. She said, "Okay let's go to the town dump every Saturday morning when you bring stuff to throw away and recycle." I was surprised and said, "The town dump?" She said, "I knew you wouldn't want to do it." Then we got into an argument. How could I have changed the script?

Answer

We applaud your efforts to change the ways in which you are responding to your daughter. Since you described both yourself and your daughter as "stubborn" we would guess that attempting to make these changes does not come easily but that you are motivated to do so given your wish for a closer relationship with her. We wish that when children saw the efforts their parents were making to improve family relationships, they would say, "Since my parents are trying so hard to improve their relationship with me, I will reciprocate."

Unfortunately, at least initially, this typically is not the case. When parents modify their script, many children "test" to see if this change is for real by becoming less cooperative and more provocative. Some just don't know how to respond to a new script and need time to adjust. It is obvious that your daughter's response to your change in behavior is to become challenging. We would guess that given your daughter's style you could have almost predicted that she would not say, "Thanks, Dad, for telling me you love me and saying you want to spend more time with me. That shows me how much I mean to you. I will be just as nice to you in return."

We often ask parents to consider the possible responses of their children to their change of scripts. Different scenarios are discussed and for each one we ask parents to think about how they might respond so as to reinforce a positive relationship. Let's look at what you might have said to your daughter when you told her you loved her and she uttered, "Oh sure, then why don't you show it." One possible response would be, "I guess I'm not showing my love in the right way but I really want to. Do you have any suggestions?" If your daughter said she didn't have any suggestions, you might turn it into a problem-solving activity by saying, "Maybe both of us can think more about it."

When your daughter mentioned spending time with you going to the town dump, you might have said, "That's great. It's important to recycle and I know you can be of help." You might even add, "After we go to the dump, if you want we can get a snack." If you are prepared for your daughter to follow her negative script for a while, then you will be better equipped not to resort to your negative script when she uses hers. We sometimes jokingly tell parents, "If your kids are driving you crazy, drive them a little crazy. Change the script. Don't do what they expect. It will throw them off balance."

Keep in mind that one of your main goals is to create a more loving, less tense relationship with your daughter. You have taken some important steps in that direction. When she attempts to throw you off course and down the well-traveled, negative path, keep in mind where the new, positive path will take you. This image will help you to strengthen your new script. In our experience, when parents continue to build this new path, their children will follow. Good luck, and have fun at the dump.

5

Parental Love
When Children Feel Special and Appreciated

Question

I know that it's important for children to feel loved. In what way does the feeling of being loved contribute to the development of a resilient mindset? This may seem like a silly question but what are the things a parent can do to help a child truly feel loved? I guess I'm asking since my parents often said that they loved me but yet I wondered if they really did, especially since they were so busy with their own lives that they seemed to spend little time with me.

Answer

Your question is not silly at all. It's actually very important especially since you were told you were loved but felt your parents' actions didn't support their words. Feeling loved by one's parents and other significant adults provides children with the strength to face daily challenges and to develop a resilient mindset. Love and support are the essential ingredients in helping children feel safe, secure, and comfortable in managing the stress and pressure that are a natural part of growing up. One father who felt very unloved as a child poignantly captured his experience by sharing with us the following image: "I always felt as if we lived in a boat that could tip over at any moment and if I fell overboard my parents might not even notice I was gone. I actually had a dream when they saw I was gone and kept on rowing and I just drowned."

We know love is vital and has been conceptualized in different ways by different people. We believe love is not so much a product as a process. Love is not so much the end point of our interactions with our children but rather the daily interactions we have with them that helps them feel special, secure, and appreciated. When we offer empathy, communicate effectively, respond to their emotional needs, and provide them with safe, comfortable environments, we enhance resilience through the process of love. When we provide consistent and appropriate discipline and teach them to handle adversity and develop responsibility, we demonstrate our love to them. When we encourage them to take appropriate risks and they are willing to do so because they know we are by their side, we help to foster a sense of courage and optimism.

> Love is not so much the end point of our interactions with our children but rather the daily interactions we have with them that helps them feel special, secure, and appreciated.

There is no doubt that almost all parents love their children. But yet a number of children feel unloved such as you did or the man we described above. We often wonder what forces operate to derail the feelings of love that a parent has for a child. In our experience the reasons vary from one home to the next. In your situation it seemed that your parents were so busy with their own lives that their words of love were hollow since they were not reinforced by spending time with you, helping you to feel a part of their lives.

We have also worked with many parents whose feelings of love were compromised because their children did not fulfill the expectations their parents had for them. Love was conditional. The subtle or not-so-subtle message was "I will love you as long as you do what I ask you to do (or obtain good grades or do well in sports)." Our love should not be offered on a contingency basis, to be doled out only when children conform to our standards and expectations.

In our answers to the questions below, we will suggest what parents can do to convey love to their children. The answers may appear to fall under that broad category of "common sense" but as we have learned, we often have to remind ourselves of what is common sense.

Question

I'm a single working mother with three children between the ages of nine and fifteen years. My ex-husband lives in another part of the country and is very uninvolved with the kids. When I come home I am often exhausted. Yet I have this feeling that somehow I have to show twice as much love since I am the only parent in the house. But I just don't have the energy or the time to do it. You advocate helping kids develop a resilient mindset. Will that be more difficult in a single parent home, especially in terms of the love and attention a child receives?

Answer

In most instances single parents face greater stress and pressure in their parenting roles compared with homes in which there are two parents. Single parents do not have a spouse or partner to provide the time and support that we all require as parents. When two parents are present, it is easier for one to take a needed break when feeling tired since the other parent is available to care for the children. When a parent is involved in a power struggle with a child, he or she can discuss the situation with the other parent. If there are two or more children in the family, parents can rotate spending time with each and they can also divide household responsibilities. As a single mother said at one of our parenting workshops, similar to the sentiment you expressed, "I feel that I have to be both a mother and father to my two children and have such little support or time for myself. Some evenings I cry myself to sleep, feeling I am doing nothing right." Given the added pressures that come with being a single parent, it may be more difficult for some to help strengthen a resilient mindset in children. However, we don't want to paint too pessimistic a picture since many single parents have done a remarkable job in raising truly resilient, loving children.

Perhaps one of the most important things you can do, and we realize it won't be easy, is to be more realistic in what you can and cannot accomplish. If you attempt to play the role of both mother and father and show your kids twice as much love (we're not even certain how one shows twice as much love), the likely outcome is that you will feel overwhelmed and burned out. Your children need to feel loved by you but it will be more difficult for you to do so if you continue to be exhausted. Given how tired you are when you come home and knowing you should spend time with your kids, you will have to consider the best ways to demonstrate your love and caring without becoming overly fatigued physically and emotionally.

Considering the ages of your children, we believe you can discuss with them the issue of your availability as well as ways each of them can contribute to the household. While we always advise single parents to be careful not to delegate too many responsibilities to their children to make up for the absence of the other parent, we also believe that children should help out (this, of course, is equally true in homes with two parents). Let your children know that you want to spend time with them, but that you frequently find that after working all day, you often lack the energy to do so. Brainstorm with them about possible solutions and ways that they might help. Some parents have set up a "special" time with each of their children alone during the week, a time in which phones are not answered and undivided attention is provided. We know single parents who do not work on the weekends and have used Saturday or Sunday to "schedule" these special times rather than during a weekday evening. Having a special time set aside does not imply that there will be no other times to be alone with each of your children, but rather that there is a guaranteed time for such interactions. Many parents have told us that setting aside this time leads to less pressure and a less frenetic pace.

In addition, if possible, build in time for yourself either alone or with close friends. We all need time away from the children and everyone will benefit. Some single parents have questioned whether they could ever find time away from their children. Most have found ways to do so even for a few hours.

Just remember there is no way that one parent can do all of the work of two. But you can still provide your children with the love that will serve as the foundation for resilience.

Question

At one of your talks you mentioned the importance of a charismatic adult in each child's life. There is almost something spiritual about that term. Can you explain a little more about a charismatic adult? How does that adult help a child become resilient?

Answer

In research studies in which resilient adults were asked what factors helped them to overcome adversity and lead more satisfying, successful lives, almost all attributed their success and optimism to one person who believed in them. The late author and psychologist, Dr. Julius Segal, called the individual who served this purpose a *charismatic adult*, which he defined as an adult from whom a child or adolescent gathers strength. For many people the image of "gathering strength" does have a spiritual quality in the sense of going beyond oneself and helping others.

Children who have many charismatic adults in their lives are indeed fortunate, but in our experience even one or two such adults can make the difference between a child venturing down a path of failure and hopelessness or a path of success and optimism. A charismatic adult need not necessarily be a parent. As a matter of fact, in situations in which parents are neglectful or abusive, the charismatic adult may be a teacher, a coach, an aunt or uncle, or any adult who plays a role in the child's life. Also, charismatic adults may enter a child's life for a brief period of time, leaving an indelible mark of hope or they may be present in a child's life in an ongoing way. We often emphasize in our workshops that we must never underestimate the impact that one adult can have on a child's well-being and resilience.

In terms of what adults do to earn the label *charismatic* and help the child become resilient, several of the most vital factors include that they accept children for who they are and that they convey in their interactions unconditional love and acceptance. They help that child feel special, while not denying the child's problems. They also focus on building up the child's islands of competence or areas of strength. They are there for the child, both in good and difficult times. They are people whom the child can trust.

Think of your daily interactions with your children and at the end of the day ask, "Have I been a charismatic adult in the life of my kids today? Have they gathered strength from me or have I said and done things that have lessened their strength and resilience?" Since we are all human, there will be days when we realize that we have not served as a charismatic adult on that particular day. However, if we fulfill that role on most days we will provide our children with a basic foundation of love and hope and we will communicate the powerful message that we are there for them. It is a wonderful feeling to know that we have touched our children in such a powerful way.

Question

I have often heard that it is important for parents to love their children unconditionally, but what exactly does this mean? When my children do something wrong I get angry with them. I am disappointed in them. Does unconditional love mean not getting angry with them or not letting them know that you are disappointed when they do something wrong?

Answer

Showing unconditional love toward our children is a goal to strive toward. It involves loving our children even when they fail to do what we want or when they do not live up to our expectations. The importance of unconditional love in the parent-child relationship cannot be underestimated. When children feel that parents only love and accept them if they excel in athletics or sports, if they are socially adept, if they always meet their responsibilities, or if they look and dress in a certain manner, then those children cannot feel secure should they stray from the path of acceptance. As one adolescent told us, "My parents would tell you that they love me, but what they don't realize is their love seems to disappear when they are disappointed in me or if I don't come home with good grades."

Unconditional love is one of the foundations for parents helping their children develop a resilient mindset. In an environment of unconditional love, children feel safe and secure. They are willing to take appropriate risks and make mistakes without fear of losing their parents' approval. They more easily learn ways to solve problems since they feel comfortable in attempting different solutions. They gain genuine pleasure in their successes. They feel truly accepted for who they are and not for what their parents might want them to be.

> When children feel that parents only love and accept them if they excel in athletics or sports, if they are socially adept, if they always meet their responsibilities, or if they look and dress in a certain manner, then those children cannot feel secure should they stray from the path of acceptance.

Unconditional love does not imply that parents do not become angry or disappointed with their children nor does it mean that parents don't discipline them or hold them accountable for their actions. Rather, unconditional love embraces the belief that even when parents are angry, disappointed, or frustrated, they still maintain and communicate feelings of love. They do not use their love as a bargaining chip to force their children to behave in a certain way (such bargaining tools often backfire). They do not demean or belittle their children or compare them to others but rather use transgressions as opportunities for learning. We should emphasize that when children feel unconditional love they are less defensive and more willing to listen and learn from others. Unconditional love helps parents to become effective disciplinarians, especially when discipline is understood in its true meaning, as a teaching process.

Since one of the roadblocks to unconditional love occurs when parents have unrealistic expectations, we emphasize that it is important for parents to examine the goals they hold for their children. We have known many parents whose expectations for their children were difficult to meet. When children failed to live up to these expectations they felt a withdrawal of love from their parents, even if this was not the parents' intent. This situation is likely to have negative consequences, not the least of which is a rupture in the parent-child relationship. Parents must constantly reflect upon the expectations they have for their children and whether they say and do things at certain times that turn unconditional love into conditional love. As parents we must remember that love is the strongest nutriment for strengthening a resilient mindset in our children.

> As parents we must remember that love is the strongest nutriment for strengthening a resilient mindset in our children.

Question

I'm not married but I try to spend time with my six-year-old niece and nine-year-old nephew who live close by. Their parents have had problems, including alcoholism. I think because my sister and her husband have had so many of their own problems they aren't able to show their kids all the love and affection they need. I am concerned that my niece and nephew may grow up feeling unloved. My sister and brother-in-law seem quite willing for me to spend time with the kids and they seem to enjoy it. Can the love I am showing them substitute for a parent's love? Are there any drawbacks?

Answer

First we should mention that we admire your efforts in wanting to help your niece and nephew. We also admire the fact that your sister and brother-in-law recognize their shortcomings and are willing to allow you to participate in the raising of your niece and nephew. While we would encourage your sister and brother-in-law to spend whatever time and energy they feel is possible with their children, what is most important is for them to focus on obtaining help for themselves so that they can be more available to their children in the future.

As your sister and brother-in-law face and resolve their problems, we hope that they will still have as much time as possible to spend with their children, although initially their time may be limited. Children can deal with problems more effectively when they have an understanding of what is going on. Thus, it would be important for their parents to talk with them at a level they can comprehend about the problems that exist and what the parents are doing to resolve these problems (given the age differences between the two children, they might wish to talk with each separately but sometimes it's best to speak with siblings together so that they can more easily provide each other support).

While your sister and brother-in-law do not have to share very intimate details of their struggles, they can say to their kids that they are having difficulty, that they are drinking alcohol too much, and that they need time to get healthier so that they can lead better lives and be more effective parents. They can let their kids know how much they love them and that when they are not as available, there will be others who will be there to help, such as yourself. If your sister and her husband have regularly scheduled appointments and meetings to deal with their alcoholism, necessitating their being out of the house, they can draw a calendar of when they won't be home so that their children have a concrete representation of these times. Such a visual aid, prepared in advance, helps children gain a greater sense of mastery of the situation since things become more predictable. After your sister and her husband have done some of these things they can then answer questions and concerns the children have and attend to their feelings.

By following through on the interventions we are suggesting, your sister and brother-in-law will accomplish a great deal toward reinforcing resilience in their children. They will demonstrate empathy and validate what their children are experiencing. They will model that although people have problems, there are solutions even if these solutions take time. They will also demonstrate love and convey to their children that they recognize the importance of adults being there to take care of them and that when they cannot be available as parents, they will ensure that others will be.

While the love you show them as their aunt may not necessarily "substitute" for their parents' love since they may still yearn for the love of their mother and father, the way we like to think about it is that children need love from many people. This is even more important when parents cannot provide all of the time and love that children require. We have been impressed by the number of children lacking strong parental support who have successfully negotiated difficult lives. In doing so, the common denominator seems to be that each of these children locates an adult in their lives or an adult locates them who can offer the time and love children require. An extended family member, teacher, coach, or community member willing to invest time in them, willing to provide them with a source of emotional strength and support can make the difference between children feeling pessimistic and defeated or optimistic and hopeful. We suggest rather than considering your love as a substitute for their parents' love you think of the process as supplementation rather than substitution. Certainly in the situation you describe, these children would benefit from further supplementation, from the opportunity to interact with an adult capable of providing them with additional support, love, and affection.

One final thought. As your sister and brother-in-law take hold of their lives and become more effective parents, we would hope your niece and nephew don't lose you as a supplement but that you continue to supplement the activities of their parents. There is no limit to the number of charismatic adults that children can use to nurture their resilience. At certain points of a child's life some adults may play more of that role than others.

Question

Sometimes I find myself disappointed when my children's grades or achievement in other activities don't meet my expectations. I try to avoid conveying the sense of being let down to my children but wonder if it is conveyed to them in my expression of affection and love. How can I help them set goals and aspirations, some of which they may not meet, while still helping them understand I love them?

Answer

Many parents struggle with the question you raise. All parents share the goals of happiness, success, and satisfaction in daily life activities for their children. However, when our children do not reach these goals we must question how realistic these goals were and how to respond when these goals are not met. We must also keep in mind that the attainment of particular goals involves a process that usually doesn't occur in one large step but rather through many small steps. Disappointments would be avoided if parents could keep in mind the importance of these small steps. As you suggest in your question, your children are seemingly quite aware when you are disappointed in them and they may very well experience a loss of your love when they fall short of your expectations.

Establishing realistic goals for our children is often easier said than done. So many of our own feelings and past history impact on what we expect from ourselves and our children. At times, the excess baggage from our own lives colors our visions of our children so that we do not see them as individuals in their own rights. For example, many parents confuse accepting children for who they are as an excuse for letting them get away with things and not teaching them responsibility. We want to emphasize that accepting our children and appreciating their differences in skills, temperament, and ability doesn't mean we water down goals or excuse inappropriate or unacceptable behavior. Rather we understand this behavior and help to change it in a manner that builds up rather than erodes a child's self-esteem. Thus, acceptance of your child's capabilities is a major step toward maintaining your love and defining attainable goals.

There are four critical steps to help you and then your children learn to set realistic goals as you provide ongoing nurturing and love. Following these steps, which take time to achieve, may help you to be more tolerant and less frustrated with them. First, it is important for you to be educated about each of your children's skills and abilities in the specific problem area. In the case of school, make certain your children possess the capabilities to be successful. Some children would rather let adults think they don't care than believe they lack skill or ability. Some children have subtle or not-so-subtle learning disabilities that unless diagnosed will result in ongoing school failure.

> Acceptance of your child's capabilities is a major step toward maintaining your love and defining attainable goals.

Second, it is important for you to measure your mindset. What we mean by that is for you to reflect upon why you react in a particular way when your children struggle or don't achieve to the extent you would like them to achieve. We suggest that when parents react negatively and convey to their children that they feel they have been "let down" this is usually the result of unrealistic expectations or failure to understand the child's true capabilities or the parents' own self-image tied to the accomplishments of their children. If you continue to follow the pattern you report, your frustration will be intensified and your relationship with your child will be compromised.

Third, it is important for you to make adjustments and establish realistic goals as you understand what your children are capable of doing. Focus on your children's islands of competence and not just on their areas of weakness. Each success your children experience will build confidence for the next challenge. Children who feel accepted and loved will find it easier to learn from their parents.

Finally, and most importantly, collaborate with your children. When children view their parents as working with them, they are much more willing to acknowledge when they need help or more comfortable seeking assistance. Disagreements between your goals and those of your children can be discussed in a respectful manner and compromises can be reached. Action plans to achieve goals can be determined. Such a collaborative dialogue reinforces a problem-solving attitude and also communicates love and respect. When parents convey their expectations in an accepting, loving, and supportive manner, children are often motivated to exceed those expectations.

Question

Given all of the problems kids face it seems many may feel unsafe. I know that after a recent school shooting, my two kids seemed hesitant to go out or even go to school. The shooting took place at a high school. When my son, who is a middle school student, heard about the shooting on the news, he said he didn't want to go to high school when he got older. Are there ways of helping kids to feel loved so that they will feel safe and secure? If children feel loved does that mean they will be less fearful?

Answer

Some events, such as a school shooting, will shake children's sense of security. Even if the shooting occurred thousands of miles away, the immediacy of television brings that event quickly and vividly into one's home. Children as well as parents are likely to personalize what they witness, wondering about the safety of their neighborhood school. In some cases, suspiciousness will reign and a neighborhood child or adolescent who in the past was simply perceived as a "little different" may suddenly be seen as a "potential murderer."

While we must ensure that we protect our children, we must also make certain that we don't create a generation of fearful children who see terrorists lurking behind every corner. It is also important to remember that even children growing up in loving homes will not be free of the anxiety occasioned when events such as school shootings, kidnappings, terrorist acts, or plane crashes occur. However, the more loved and accepted children feel, the easier it is for them to voice their concerns with their parents and for their parents to help them deal with these feelings. Thus, children who have a close relationship with their parents will often have avenues available to help them lessen their fears compared with children who do not have adults whom they can turn to for support.

Typically, the most effective way of managing the anxiety of children is to be available to discuss their concerns. There will be many opportunities for you to do so as a parent. If a school shooting or other disturbing event appears on the news or in the newspaper, parents can mention their feelings. This will often prompt children to bring up their own concerns of safety. Parents can empathize with these anxieties. Once they validate what their children are experiencing and listen closely to their children's worries, they can then introduce what measures have been taken or will be taken to ensure school safety. One boy felt more at ease when his parents and then the school principal openly discussed the issue of school shootings; the principal actively involved the students in how they could create a more caring school environment in which no student felt left out.

While many youngsters may be eager to discuss a school shooting or other disturbing events, others may not. Every child and adolescent is different in terms of his or her ease of entering a dialogue about particular events. We should never force children to discuss these disturbing events, but we should let them know that we are available should they wish to do so. In our experience, when parents communicate their availability in a nonjudgmental, caring manner, children are more likely to approach them at some point to enter into a discussion.

In essence, when you ask the important question of how best to help children feel loved so that they may feel more safe and secure, our answer is to reinforce a resilient mindset by being empathic, being available to discuss troubling events, engaging in a problem-solving approach to decide what might make the situation as safe as can be, and letting our children know that they can bring any concern or worry to us.

Question
You recommend helping kids feel special. Yet I read an article by another parenting expert who said that kids who feel special are often spoiled and think they deserve anything they ask for. So what do you mean when you say that children should feel special? I am sure you don't want them to become spoiled.

Answer
We have always been curious as to how the word *spoiled* found its way into the parenting literature. When a food is spoiled the only thing left to do is to throw it away. The term itself denotes an end point, a product that cannot be fixed, corrected, or changed. We think the term is misapplied and misused when it comes to children. Certainly some children are given everything they want and more. Along the way they may rarely be afforded the opportunity to set their own goals, to work toward success, and to learn

to deal with mistakes and failure. In such situations, children are robbed of the opportunity to develop a true sense of self-esteem, confidence, and competence.

Rather than referring to these children as spoiled, which holds such a negative connotation, we suggest that they be seen as lacking a resilient mindset due to their experiences. By suggesting this change of meaning, we are not simply engaging in word games but rather attempting to define the current mindset of these youngsters. They may come to believe that everything is easy and their wishes and desires equate with success in the absence of hard work. While spoiled food may have to be discarded since it cannot be improved, it is obvious that we believe that children who have not developed a resilient mindset can be helped to do so. We believe that children who have not felt the sense of fulfillment that accompanies meeting responsibilities, working for goals, helping others rather than always expecting others to give to them, can be provided with experiences that will result in tasting the joy that comes from doing these things.

> When children feel special in the eyes of their parents and other adults, they feel accepted and loved unconditionally.

Feeling special involves a very different process from what many people perceive as spoiling children. Feeling special doesn't mean children are given whatever they want or they do not have to meet their responsibilities. Rather, feeling special equates with feeling loved. When children feel special in the eyes of their parents and other adults, they feel accepted and loved unconditionally. They feel that parents recognize and appreciate their islands of competence. They feel a basic sense of security. One way parents can reinforce this feeling of being special is by establishing regular times alone with each of their children. While we believe in family time, we also recommend that parents find time on a daily or weekly basis to be alone with each child. For example, spending ten minutes a night with your young child and saying that this time is so important that even if the phone rings you're not going to answer it, is a powerful way of communicating to your children their importance to you.

A sense of being special has nothing to do with being self-centered or feeling entitled, but instead is a key component for children to believe they are loveable and worthwhile. In our experience, children who are handed everything on a silver platter with few expectations for them to assume responsibilities are not children who feel special. Interestingly, many of these children feel a sense of emptiness and a lack of accomplishment. They often feel unloved or loved conditionally, and many are insecure since they have not been "tested" and are not certain of what they are capable of achieving.

Question
When I grew up it seemed like the way my parents tried to show me they loved me was by buying things for me. I remember they traveled a lot. Once they were traveling when I was performing in a talent show when I was in fifth grade. They gave me a game before they left and said they wished they could be at the talent show to hear me play my clarinet. I remember thinking that maybe they didn't love me. Was I being overly sensitive or critical?

Answer
Your question raises two important issues. First, how parents deal with their own feelings when they miss events in their children's lives that they know are important. Second, how children feel and what they think when their parents miss these significant events. Obviously we don't know your parents or what was going through their minds when they missed your performance in the talent show. However, we feel relatively safe in saying that the game they gave you as a gift was the equivalent of a "peace offering," perhaps as a way of managing any feelings of guilt they experienced. Your parents seemed aware that they would be unavailable for an event that you perceived as important and that by giving you something they hoped to convey that they cared about you.

When parents miss events they know are important in the eyes of their children, we suggest they be as honest as possible. We believe that parents should tell their children they regret not being present and that as much as possible they will minimize absences in the future. We also believe that gifts are not a substitute for missing noteworthy events in our children's lives.

Having said this, we also want to acknowledge that in today's fast-paced world, it is not always possible for us to participate in all of our children's special events but we must make an effort to do so. Children will be more understanding and forgiving if our absence at important occasions is more the exception than the rule. When parents are absent, especially when on a trip, rather than giving children a toy or game, we recommend calling them or sending them a card. Perhaps the event can be taped for later viewing. From your question, it is difficult to tell if your parents missed many important events in your life. If they did, we can certainly understand why you would feel unloved and it would not be a case of your being overly sensitive. We know of one man whose father missed many of his birthdays. Looking back, he painfully observed, "My father knew when my birthday was. Since he could plan his business trips well in advance I don't understand why he couldn't make certain to be there for my birthday. All the gifts in the world wouldn't substitute for his being there on my birthday. I realize how much I resented his absence and how unloved I felt."

We don't want to come across as being overly harsh toward parents since as parents ourselves we appreciate the many demands they face. However, parents must remember that one of the most important feelings for children is the feeling of being unconditionally loved and one of the most powerful ways for parents to reinforce this feeling is to be available for their children and not to miss special occasions.

Question

I have three children, nine through fourteen years of age. I think I love all of them equally but I keep hearing, "You love him or her more." I keep saying, "I love you all the same," but they don't seem to believe me. Is there a way to minimize kids' feeling that you love their siblings more?

Answer

When children voice feeling less loved than their siblings, it is easy for parents to minimize these complaints by saying to themselves, "Sibling rivalry exists in every family." That may be true but it is important for parents to examine their parenting styles and their perceptions of each of their children. Since parents view each child differently and find some children easier to raise than others and since each child experiences love in different ways, parents may think they love each child the same but that is rarely the case (there is even the important question of how one measures love). Trying to convince one child that you love him or her to the same degree that you love a sibling is often an exercise in futility.

When children communicate that they feel parents love them less than their siblings, it is often an indication that they harbor feelings about other issues. Sometimes those issues relate to the amount of time parents spend with one child compared with another. Sometimes they may be jealous, sensing that their parents love a sibling more because that sibling is a better student or athlete or is more sociable. We know of one teenage boy who was relatively shy and believed his parents favored his younger sister since she was in his description a "social butterfly." His perceptions were fairly accurate and his parents eventually had to face their disappointment in him.

Sometimes the comments of feeling less loved may reflect children's sense of vulnerability in their relationship with their parents. Some children, especially those who possess difficult temperaments, are quick to assume that unless their parents are constantly available to them, they are treated unfairly. They translate this sense of unfairness to being unloved or less loved than a sibling.

As parents, we should accept that we do not love each child the same (whatever "the same" truly means). We should recognize that it is easier to be empathic and more loving toward children with easier, less demanding temperaments, children who do not respond to every request with a resounding, "No!" We suggest that rather than telling your children you love them equally, which in this case you have done and, not surprisingly, they haven't accepted, you begin by validating their comment and seek to understand why they feel the way they do, offering to work with them to deal with whatever situation has led them to this conclusion. Thus, if your children say they feel you love their sibs more, you can respond that you're glad they can tell you how they feel. You can add that you want all the children in the family to feel loved and want to talk with each of them to figure out what will help with this situation. Obviously, one discussion is not going to change a child's mindset about feeling loved but it will begin the process.

We have found that when parents reflect upon their actions toward each child, when they validate their children's assertion that a sibling is loved more, and when they enter into a dialogue about how things can be changed, it sets the stage for children feeling more appreciated and loved. We have also found that children will often arrive at sensible, realistic solutions to what parents can do so that they feel increasingly loved and less jealous. For instance, in one family, the establishment of something we typically advocate, namely, special times with each child, significantly eased the problem of sibling rivalry.

Question

I have six- and eight-year-old sons. When I was a boy I don't remember my parents being very affectionate with me. My mom would kiss me but it felt as if it was an obligation on her part. The closest my father came to showing affection was a handshake. Even affectionate words were rarely spoken. I remember having dreams in which my parents hugged me and told me they loved me. I still have those dreams. I told myself I would be more affectionate with my sons but when I go to hug them I feel tense. I think they can tell. Do you think I will ever feel more comfortable displaying affection? What can I do?

Answer

The process of demonstrating love to children is more challenging when one has not been on the receiving end of a loving relationship. As we noted earlier, when children grow up in a home in which the expression of love is minimal, in which they rarely feel special in the eyes of their parents, in which they don't witness displays of affection between their parents and are not recipients of such displays themselves, it is often difficult for them to engage in the process of demonstrating love toward their own children. We acknowledge that some people biologically may be more comfortable with the physical aspects of expressing love and affection. Nonetheless, we believe that we tend to raise our children the way we were raised. Having parents who comfortably demonstrated love and affection provides children with a model of how to relate to their own children in a loving and affectionate way.

At our workshops, some parents have wondered whether they can "overcome" their childhood experiences with their own parents. As the reader is aware from our answers to questions about changing negative scripts, we believe you can in fact become more comfortable displaying affection even if it is very uncomfortable at first. In our workshops and clinical activities we often ask parents to think about a childhood experience in which their parents made them feel special, appreciated, and loved as well as an experience that left them feeling unappreciated or unloved. It is important for you to incorporate into your parenting practices those experiences that helped you feel loved and special, as well as those that did not. In your question you describe your parents as lacking affection, but we wonder if there were any occasions when you felt loved and, if so, what your parents said or did to convey this feeling to you. If you can't think of times your parents communicated feelings of love, then reflect upon when other adults in your life did so. We have discovered that seemingly minor events often convey to children that they are loved and often have a strong personal impact on their lives. By creating traditions and special times with your children, as well as attending important events, you communicate love.

> By creating traditions and special times with your children, as well as attending important events, you communicate love.

It may well be that since little affection was shown to you, you are uncomfortable in expressing feelings of warmth openly to your children. However, it is obvious that you would like to change this pattern. Begin with small steps that help you to move slowly outside your current comfort zone. Think about one action you can take to demonstrate affection, an action with which you will feel comfortable. Perhaps it will involve a hug, or holding their hand while waiting in line for a movie, or sitting close to them and permitting them to rest on your shoulders. Remember that change takes time not only for you but for your children as well. Even as you feel more at ease giving them a hug, they may wonder at first what is going on. If you have not hugged them before, they may not feel as comfortable being hugged. Give them space to change; if they or you are uncomfortable with a hug, then perhaps start with a hand on their shoulder or resting close to them when you read to them.

In our experience, carefully paced expressions of love and affection will, in most instances, become the norm in the house, much to the satisfaction and happiness of all involved. If your discomfort of displaying affection continues, we recommend seeking a consultation from a mental health professional who can assist you in gaining a better understanding of the roadblocks you are facing.

Question

I want my three kids to love me, but I feel when I discipline them it interferes with love. My youngest daughter, seven years of age, is very sensitive. She constantly tells me I yell too much, which I don't think I do. If I have to discipline her by sending her to her room or taking away a privilege, she often says I don't love her. Her older brother and sister often say the same thing. I find I am backing away from following through on consequences since it seems to be hurting my relationship with the kids. My husband says I have to be firmer, but it hurts me to see my children angry with me. What can I do?

Answer

A very common question we hear at our parenting workshops and in our parenting counseling sessions is the question you pose: Will discipline interfere with feeling loved? Just as loving our children should not be confused with spoiling them, so too should disciplining our children not be confused with their feeling unloved. If all three of your children are saying that you yell at them or that when you set limits you don't love them, it would be helpful to think about why this is happening.

We have worked with many parents who are concerned that they will lose their children's love if they set limits or if they hold their children accountable for certain behaviors. In fact, we often tell parents that in their role as parents they may have to tolerate their children being angry with them once in a while when consequences are set. It is rare for children to say to their parents, "Thanks so much for disciplining us. We know your actions are a sign of love." While children may not say this, interestingly youngsters whom we have seen in therapy and who have come to trust us, have shared that they felt more secure and loved when parents set limits and kept them from engaging in activities that could lead to negative outcomes. Yet, even if our children recognize that limits, rules, and consequences serve a healthy purpose, if they should sense that a parent is ambivalent in the role of a disciplinarian, they may reinforce this ambivalence by openly asserting that the parent does not love them.

Thus, helping your children develop self-discipline and responsibility requires that at times you recognize they may be angry with you when you set limits, even if these limits are fair and reasonable. Your seven-year-old daughter, as you note, may be sensitive. She may perceive even normal limits as excessive. Nonetheless, it is important for you to be firm and consistent in your discipline. If you are burdened by feelings of doubt and guilt, you will become paralyzed when you have to set rules and follow through with consequences.

We should note that when our children say we are yelling, one of the best strategies is to lower your voice and say, "Thanks for letting me know I'm yelling. I have important things to say and if I come across as yelling, it will be more difficult for you to listen." This technique, of course, represents changing the script. By validating that your children experience you as yelling and then lowering your voice, you are setting the stage for them to listen to what you have to say. You can be just as firm even with a soft voice.

Finally, we would suggest that you and your husband assume a proactive approach, which focuses on how best to prevent problems from arising in the future. Consider the most problematic areas and ask if there are ways of modifying these situations to lessen the emergence of negative behavior. For example, we know of one family in which the two siblings constantly fought about sharing the computer. This led the frustrated parents to scream and punish both children by placing the computer off limits for the evening. The situation did not improve. Finally, the parents sat down with the children and together developed the commonsense solution of developing a schedule in advance of when each child could use the computer. Much to the surprise of the parents, it worked. If it had not, the parents could have said we need a better plan.

This last example captures a suggestion we typically offer as part of a proactive approach, namely, speaking with your children about the disciplinary practices in the household, including the limits and consequences that exist. You and your husband might discuss this at a family meeting and help your children develop strategies to become increasingly responsible. Taking this action should lessen your concerns about your children not loving you when you follow through on consequences since you have involved them in the process of establishing these consequences.

Question

*The other day my ten-year-old son was in the talent show in school. He prac-
ticed his saxophone for weeks. I had planned to attend but some unexpected
problems occurred at work. My boss called a meeting at the same time as the talent show. I told my son I couldn't go. He was very upset. He said I never go to
his shows, which isn't true and I told him so. I said I had to be at this meeting
at work. But I think I could have handled it better with my son. Also, do you
think he is being unfair by expecting me to be at all of his events?*

Answer

As we answered in an earlier question, we believe that as much as possible
parents should be present at important events in their children's lives. However, this is not always possible. Obviously, if we know in advance that we
will be on a business trip or away for other reasons, we can prepare our child
for this and suggest certain solutions (e.g., videotaping the event for viewing later). In your example, your failure to be there was unexpected and
seemed to be beyond your control. It was not clear exactly what you said to
your son when you told him you could not attend the talent show or if you
voiced how disappointed you were and empathized with his disappointment. Sometimes, in the heat of a discussion what might appear to be obvious statements for us to make are neglected.

You noted that your son said that you never go to his shows, which you
responded is not true. In fact, have there been other occasions when you
have missed such events? Although it may not happen all of the time, our
children often remember the times we did not fulfill our promises. For
some children, the one or two times we disappointed them by not attending their performance or athletic event can offset the numerous times we
were present. Rather than immediately telling your son his statement is not
true, it might be better to empathize with him by acknowledging that you
know he is upset that you cannot be there and that it feels like you often
miss important events. Listen to what he has to say. You can say that he has
a right to be angry even though what occurred was beyond your control and
that you do love him and will do your best not to miss such events. Hopefully, if you have an understanding boss, you can let the boss know well in
advance when you would like to come in a little later or leave a little earlier
or take time during the day to be at your child's next event. Although this

may not always be possible, it may reduce the times you miss out on significant situations in your child's life.

> If we want children to develop a resilient mindset we must make time available for them, particularly for the occasions they deem as special.

If we are not present at the important events in our children's lives, the events they perceive as special, then they are likely to feel we don't care about them. If we want children to develop a resilient mindset we must make time available for them, particularly for the occasions they deem as special. This is particularly true if time spent with your children is limited by daily schedules. Time invested in our children also pays dividends in the time they will invest in us as adults allowing us to share in their lives as well.

Question

I heard you say at a workshop that we have to help our children learn to deal with mistakes. I don't know if other parents face the same problem but when I try to point out mistakes to my kids they see it as criticism. The other day I told my daughter that when I mentioned that she has done something wrong, she always thinks I don't love her. She told me that she feels I only love her when she is perfect. How can a parent teach a child and correct mistakes without them feeling unloved?

Answer

Your question is related to the question we discussed earlier about ways of disciplining our children without their experiencing this as a loss of love. Most people don't like to be told when they are doing something wrong but such feedback is much easier to accept when it comes from someone we know cares about us and has provided a great deal of positive feedback in the past. When our children feel we are overly critical of their mistakes and expect them to be perfect, we must reflect whether their observations have some basis in reality.

We know of many well-intentioned parents who have set very high expectations. When these expectations are not met, they voice disapproval and disappointment. This will typically result in their children believing they are only loved when they meet their parents' expectations, a sign of conditional love. Even if the expectations set by parents are not unrealistic, if a child's failure to meet these expectations triggers noticeable anger and disappointment, then the child may feel whatever he or she does is not good enough.

Unfortunately, in these cases much of a parent's energy is directed at chipping away, attempting to shape the child into something the parent perceives as desirable. Parents must be careful not to begin by always pointing out mistakes, believing that by doing so they are building up rather than chipping away at their children. In fact their children perceive just the opposite. Many parents routinely engage in this chipping process without realizing it. They pronounce what their children are doing wrong rather than what they are doing right. They correct rather than teach. If the majority of our messages to our children follow this pattern, if we believe that the best way to help them improve is to point out their mistakes, it is likely they will come to resent our actions. We believe it is difficult for children to develop a sense of self-worth and confidence and to feel loved if they perceive that their parents are critical and unappreciative.

We would suggest that you examine your expectations and observe how often you use words that build up and how often your words convey chipping down. Perhaps there are times when you can ignore certain mistakes and other times when you can offer a compliment that you have neglected in the past. The ways we offer feedback may make the difference in whether we come across as helpful or critical. For instance, if our child has answered a homework question and asked us to review it, instead of telling her or him that the answer was confusing, one can say, "I wasn't certain about this point" and then engage in a discussion that may help to make the answer more precise. Or sometimes we can say, "I see what you're getting at. I wonder if there are other possible ways of looking at the situation." As we have all experienced, a change in our words or tone of voice will make a vast difference in how our children experience our feedback.

Helping our children to deal more effectively with mistakes and still feel loved is one of the most important tasks of raising resilient children. If your daughter currently experiences your correction of her mistakes as an indication that you are being overly critical and not loving her, then take the following steps: (1) minimize any remarks that may be experienced as critical and increase your positive feedback; (2) engage her in a discussion of possible ways of handling mistakes; (3) share with her mistakes that you made when you were growing up (as long as it does not come across as preaching); and (4) discuss realistic expectations. In addition, if you feel comfortable doing so, you might even say, "When I correct something you do, if you feel I am expecting you to be perfect or if you feel I don't love you, please let me know since that is not my intention." Although your daughter has said this to you already, letting her know you want this feedback serves as an empathic, validating remark that should lessen the tension that currently exists and help her to be more accepting of her mistakes.

6

Words of Acceptance

Stories to Help Children Learn to Set
Realistic Expectations and Goals

Question

We have three children, all boys. They are fourteen, eleven, and nine years old.
My oldest and youngest have been very easy to raise. If my husband and I ask
them to do something they are always cooperative. They listen to what we say
and generally seem happy. Our middle son has been very different. Sometimes
I wonder if there was a mix-up at the hospital. He battles us about everything,
claims we are not fair, has few friends since he is so bossy, and almost never
smiles. He is so different from his two brothers and has been since birth. If they
come from the same "gene pool" how can one of them be so different from the
other two?

Answer

Many parents at our workshops have jokingly (or perhaps not so jokingly)
wondered if there was a mix-up in the hospital, some even dreaming that
their "real" child was bringing another family much happiness and joy. Up
through the 1970s, many educators and mental health professionals believed
strongly that all children were the same at birth. When children behaved differently it was believed that somehow their experiences at home, at school,
or in the community produced and reinforced these differences. The pre-
vailing view was that children came into the world as blank slates. Their
daily experiences with parents and other adults were written on these slates
in permanent marker and led to pleasant personalities and normal behavior

or emotional and behavioral problems. When children turned out well, parents were given the credit. When children struggled, parents were chastised for acting incorrectly. It is little wonder that many parents felt blame and shame for how their children turned out.

> Temperament contains those inborn qualities that unfold as children begin to interact with the world.

However, since the 1970s researchers and professionals have accepted that children are actually different from birth and that there is a strong genetic contribution to a child's temperament. Temperament contains those inborn qualities that unfold as children begin to interact with the world. These differences are evidenced in the ways children respond to their parents and environment. For example, some infants develop self-control with relative ease while for others this represents an arduous task that eventually leads to significant social, behavioral, and educational problems. Some children appear happy and pleasant from the moment of birth and are easy to soothe and please; in contrast, others struggle to manage irritability and are difficult to comfort. Some infants greet new situations with joy and excitement while others seem troubled and bothered. Researchers have noted that to some extent these temperamental qualities can be grouped as leading to easy, slow-to-warm-up, or difficult patterns of behavior for children.

Although children from the same "gene pool" are more likely to have similar characteristics than those from a different "gene pool," even within the same family there are significant variations in genes. Thus, it is the rule rather than the exception that even biological siblings will experience very different temperaments. However, not all children fit neatly into one or another of these three groups. A child may display characteristics of one type of temperament in some situations and different characteristics in others. The lesson we can learn is to recognize and accept that children are temperamentally different from birth. Unless we are aware of and respond appropriately to these differences, we may have a difficult time meeting our goal of raising a resilient child. If we don't learn to appreciate these temperamental differences, we may set goals and hold expectations for our children that they cannot fulfill, leading to stress, frustration, and further conflict.

From your question, it would appear that your eldest and youngest sons possess an easy temperament. They respond consistently and appropriately to your expectations and requests. Such children are often socially adept, quickly learn the rules of behavior, are easy to please and satisfy, are even tempered, make and maintain friendships, and usually perform consistently in school at a level equivalent to their intellect and learning skills. Children with this pattern of temperament typically make parents believe that the process of parenting is a simple one. At our workshops we have said that these are the children parents would like to take everywhere in their neighborhood, perhaps with a sign around their neck that contains the child's name, the parents' names, the home phone number, and a statement that reads, "As you can tell from the wonderful behavior of this child, I am the perfect parent. Don't hesitate to call for free advice." We still recall a father who said, "If my wife and I had stopped having children after the first two, we would have thought we were the perfect parents. And then our youngest child, Roger, came along and we realized kids from the same family can really be different. What a struggle Roger was!"

From your description your middle child is similar to Roger and most likely fits the difficult temperamental profile. Such children are a challenge to raise. In contrast to your other two siblings, children with a difficult temperamental pattern appear to enter the world letting you know that you are in for a roller-coaster ride. Children with this profile are often moody and intense in their daily reactions. They overreact to many situations and feel the world is unfair. They often have a low emotional threshold and a high intensity of reaction. Unfortunately, the very behaviors they exhibit in response to stress and frustration such as outbursts and temper tantrums, only lead to further social, family, and educational problems. Sometimes children with this pattern experience little pleasure in activities. They have trouble developing consistency in sleeping and eating habits. They may be hypersensitive to touch or sound.

Some parents have asked, "Is there hope for my child with a difficult temperament?" The good news is that while these children present many challenges, biology is not destiny. Changes can take place. Many children with difficult temperaments have become resilient and gone on to lead satisfying, successful lives as adults. However, it is critical that parents recognize this temperamental pattern and within reason accommodate it. It will be important for you to adjust your expectations and make modifications in your parenting style with your middle child. You will have to select your battlegrounds carefully lest every issue become a power struggle. Even when frustrated, you will have to find ways to remain empathic and not overreact with your child. One of your primary goals will be to help your child develop skills and abilities to overcome this pattern of challenging temperament and behavioral response, which, as you point out, tends to make things worse rather than better. In our answers to other questions in this chapter, we will offer specific advice on how best to do this.

Question

From a very young age my eight-year-old has complained about the taste and feel of some foods. He limits his diet significantly, claiming that certain foods don't taste good or "feel funny" in his mouth. He also complains about labels in his clothing. He will only wear certain styles of shirts and socks. When we buy new clothes we have to wash them multiple times before he feels they are "soft enough" for him to wear. The other day my husband overheard me speaking to him about a number of shirts he was still resistant to wearing. My husband became angry and yelled at our son that if he didn't like wearing new clothes we could buy all of his clothes at the thrift store. Why does my child do this? Is this a behavior that will cause him problems in life? Should we give in or make him wear these clothes?

Answer

Your child appears to have a problem referred to as tactile sensitivity. For reasons that are not well understood, such children from birth experience much stronger sensations of touch, taste, sound, and sometimes smell. We know, for example, that some people have much better ability to discriminate different tastes and smells based upon research demonstrating that they have more taste buds in their tongues. It may be that some children have a much lower threshold for discerning sensory information related to touch. Other children experience people speaking with them at a seemingly normal volume level as yelling. Often this pattern is accompanied by a difficult temperament. Such children can be very challenging behaviorally and their sensory problems cause added stress and conflict.

One of the things we advise parents is to recognize that these temperamental qualities are part of your children's biological makeup. They did not choose these qualities and if you are to maintain a good relationship with them, you must be aware of the unique qualities of each of your children and realistically adjust what you say and do. When you have a demanding child almost any request or activity can become a battle, much more so than with temperamentally easy children. Consequently, with temperamentally difficult children you should attempt to follow the old adage "select your battlegrounds carefully" and learn to overlook things that may be a little annoying but hold little relevance in how successful your child will be.

For instance, a mother of a son with tactile sensitivity said that every morning she engaged in a loud argument with her son. He found socks to be very irritating and preferred not to wear them. She told him the importance of wearing socks to school (the school did not have a rule about socks) and predictably an argument ensued. When she realized that the issue of socks was becoming a bitter wedge in their relationship, she reflected upon the importance of this issue at this time in her son's life. She decided to change her expectations and told him that if socks bothered him so much, he didn't have to wear them. She reported that her son was somewhat taken back at first and then responded, "I'm glad you're finally listening to what I have to say." Rather than becoming defensive and engaging in an argument, his mother simply responded, "We all have to take time to think about things." Not surprisingly, the morning time became a much more pleasant experience for both of them. Also, given the more positive atmosphere in the home, this son was willing to go shopping with his mother and they discovered socks made of material that were not irritating to him.

Some might argue that this mother gave in to her son, but we would say she was accommodating his temperament around issues that were not of top priority and were interfering with their relationship. Actually, given his mother's flexibility (and eventually his father's), this boy became more cooperative and more willing to listen to what his parents had to say. His mother told us, "He's much easier to live with and there are far fewer arguments."

We want to emphasize one other point. Use empathy to explain to your child that some people experience tastes, smells, and clothing on their skin more intensely than others. Once you are able to acknowledge that your child is not engaging in this behavior on purpose, he may feel less threatened and defensive. In response he may be more willing to accept your suggestion that together you think of a number of strategies that can help your child learn to deal with this sensitivity.

Question

I was a shy child growing up and even as an adult it takes a lot of effort for me to socialize. It was so painful being shy as a child that I promised myself that when I had children I would do everything possible to help them be outgoing and comfortable in social situations. My daughter is friendlier and more outgoing than I was, which is a relief to see. However, my son reminds me a lot of myself. He doesn't look people in the eye, even if it's a kid his own age. He rarely says hello. If someone greets him he often glances down and may say "hi" but in a soft voice, so soft that it's difficult to hear him. His grandmother is always telling him to "speak up," which is what she used to tell me. I feel like she's blaming me for how my son behaves. I try not to do it but I find myself telling him that he must learn to say hello or he won't have any friends. I constantly ask him if he has attempted to make friends at school, especially since he doesn't seem to have any close friends. The other day when I asked him about friends he started to cry and said it makes him feel even worse when I ask him about friends. I told him that I am just trying to help. Obviously I am not. What else can I do?

Answer

First, it is important for you to understand the pattern of temperament we referred to earlier as slow-to-warm-up. As the name implies, these children require additional time to acclimate to new situations, tasks, or people. They often experience a sense of apprehension or discomfort in new situations. It isn't that they are incapable of warming up but they often lose the opportunity of doing so when their initial behavior communicates to others that they seem disinterested. This pattern of behavior often prompts adults to refer to these children as shy, cautious, or hesitant. As preschoolers they remain physically close and hold on to parents when entering new situations. They prefer remaining in the background rather than interacting with their peers at parties or in team sports. As you note, they often look away when greeted by strangers. For some, this creates the impression that they are aloof. In fact, however, as seems evident with your son, this is not the case. Social situations make them anxious. Most desperately desire to have friends but seem unable to overcome this sense of undefined apprehension.

At times, children with this pattern of behavior are often observed to limit their behavior and rarely take risks. Researchers have demonstrated these children show signs of physical arousal in response to minor events in their environment. Thus, a small amount of stimulation or stress leads to an excessive sense of apprehension and anxiety. The arrival of someone at the front door or entering a new store may not cause most children to feel aroused, yet it may trigger arousal in a child with a slow-to-warm-up temperament. It almost appears that these children constantly stand at the threshold of stress and that even the simple act of saying hello to someone pushes them into a sense of anxiety and apprehension.

If you are to help your son, you must begin by accepting the link between his style of temperament and the problems he demonstrates. This will assist you to set realistic, obtainable goals and expectations. Remember, it is not likely your son will change his style regardless of how much you encourage or exhort him. Also, reflect upon the patterns of behavior you had hoped your child would exhibit and those he actually exhibits. As you note, since you struggled with a slow-to-warm-up temperament as a child, you had hoped your child would not demonstrate the same behaviors. Consider how you have responded to your son, which sounds very similar to how your mother responded to you and, in fact, seems to respond to him as a grand-mother. Although it may not be easy, you might wish to talk with your mother about how her comments, while perhaps well-intentioned, are making your son feel more anxious and thus, less likely to interact comfortably with others.

Make necessary adjustments between your expectations and what your son is able to do currently. By doing so you can help him to begin to set more realistic goals and develop strategies to be less shy. Finally, it is important to collaborate and work with your son. Let him know that you had a similar problem when you were younger and that many kids have the same difficulty (this helps to normalize the situation and not make him feel like an outcast). Share with him some of the strategies you used to help. Ask him how someday he would like to respond in new situations or to strangers. Hopefully he will respond positively. Then together you can define steps to reach these goals and explore strategies to help him.

Question

I know that kids are born with different temperaments and that each child has to be parented differently. I know that since each child is different you can't expect the same behavior, achievement, or even responses from each. But I still find it difficult to translate this understanding of temperament into everyday action. I have a child that you have described as difficult. I find that I am excusing behaviors on his part that I would not accept from my other three children. In fact he has received a diagnosis of Attention Deficit Hyperactivity Disorder. The psychologist has explained that it isn't so much that he wants to be difficult but his immature self-control often leads him to respond in impulsive, unthinking ways. For instance, the other day I said he couldn't go out to play until he finished his homework. He said he couldn't concentrate on his homework unless he first went out to play. I decided to give in and let him go out. By the time he came back in, he told me he was too tired to complete his work. I became angry and yelled at him that the next time I wasn't going to let him out until he finished his work. Sometimes I think I am being taken advantage of and I am not certain what I should do differently in this situation.

Answer

We understand that you meant well in letting your child first go out before completing homework. In fact in this situation many children, particularly those possessing good self-control, would have returned and completed the work thankful that they had the opportunity to play before working. However, given that your child has received a diagnosis of ADHD and in fact is delayed in developing self-control, placing what amounts to a reinforcer (i.e., going out to play) before he has fulfilled the required activity (i.e., his homework) is not likely to lead to success, especially since a consequence was not built in. By accepting that your child has ADHD, you accept that his capacity to develop self-regulation and self-control is limited. However, keep in mind, as we have noted, biology is not destiny. With patience your child can develop better self-control.

> Biology is not destiny. With patience your child can develop better self-control.

We are often asked when children don't meet their responsibilities, "Are they doing it on purpose? If they wanted to couldn't they do it?" To be honest, while these are important questions, they are often difficult to answer. It's not always easy to assess whether it's a question of "I can't" or "I won't." Some children feel incompetent so that regardless of what they do they will not be able to succeed. To hide their sense of inadequacy, they don't try, feeling "what's the use?"; in essence "I can't" triggers "I won't." However, we have found that rather than spending countless hours deciding between "I can't" and "I won't" it may make more sense to work with your child to develop realistic goals and strategies for attaining these goals. Once we can engage our children in using these strategies then we will gain a clearer picture of their strengths, capabilities, and vulnerabilities. Let's look at some possible ways of involving children in the process of solving problems.

When your son said that he couldn't concentrate on his homework until he first went out to play, you might say, "I am willing to let you do so but I am not certain that will help. Before I agree I want to discuss what happens if you come in from playing and are too tired to do your work." If he persists that he will do it, you can repeat what you said and let him know that unless you have a back-up plan you will not permit him to go out. By doing this you are engaging him in the process of thinking about consequences. One possible consequence is that if he does not complete the work and complete it carefully, the following couple of days he will have to do his homework before going outside. Another consequence, which represents somewhat of a compromise, is that he will have to do half his assignment before going out to play and the other half when he comes back in. What we are basically suggesting is involving him in the discussion of the best possible strategies for completing his responsibilities and the consequences that follow should he not do so. If you cannot come to an agreement with your son, then you should say to him, "I know we have different views but this is what I expect." If he is having difficulty doing his work successfully, then you can discuss with him the need for additional assistance.

Once you have arrived at a plan of action, you may have to offer explicit, positive directions about what is required. When giving instructions to your son, explain briefly what to do rather than what not to do. Avoid long discussions or lectures. This is especially important when speaking with children with ADHD since they may not be able to listen or remember more than one or two directions at a time. If you are helping your son with his work, break complex tasks into smaller parts and guide each task separately. Act, don't yak. Keep your voice quiet, slow, and deliberate. If the understanding is that homework must be completed before your son can go out to play, then simply say so without engaging in an argument.

When your son is doing his work, offer immediate feedback, especially since children with ADHD experience problems sustaining attention and controlling impulsive behavior. It will be difficult for him to wait for rewards or work for long-term goals. Rewards and punishments must be provided consistently and as soon as possible following the desired or undesired behavior. Thus, if the arrangement is for him to do his work and then go out to play, he should be permitted to go out immediately after completing his work. We should note that since some children may rush through their homework in order to get outside as quickly as possible, many parents will set a minimum time before a child can go out and even if the child finishes in less time, he or she must wait until the minimum time has been reached.

Another intervention that often proves useful is called "response cost." The concept of response cost involves losing as the result of poor behavior, something that has been earned for good behavior. Children will work more consistently when they begin with a full plate and work to keep it rather than when they start with an empty plate and must work to fill it. Thus in your situation let your child know he has between 4:30 and 6:30 P.M. to play. The longer it takes to complete his homework, the shorter the amount of time he will have to play.

In essence, what we are recommending is that you adopt a proactive approach and take time to plan, supervise, and structure your child's activities, particularly in regard to homework. Homework in the elementary school years helps children become independent learners and develop a sense of responsibility toward school that will be very important in middle school and high school. Remember that by the middle school years at least a third of what your children learn they teach themselves through homework. There has also been quite a bit of research on helping children become more efficient in regards to homework. Consider taking a look at the book *Seven Steps to Homework Success* by Sydney Zentall and Sam Goldstein.

Question

I have a nine-year-old son. He is hyperactive and overly sensitive to disappoint-
ment and has trouble with organization. He is never ready on time. Because of
these behaviors most children don't want to play with him. He is often by him-
self and complains that people don't like him. Clearly he is unhappy. I know
there are many different medications to help kids. Can medication help my son?
This may also seem like a silly question but since I desperately want my son to
be resilient, is there a medication that can help him to be resilient?

Answer

Let's start with your last question first. As far as we are aware, there are no
medications currently on the market or in research directed at improving
resilience. However, lest you lose hope for your son improving his outlook,
we can say there are medications approved to ameliorate certain childhood
problems, problems that may in fact reduce a child's capacity to develop a
resilient mindset. Your son's oversensitivity to disappointment likely reflects
his low emotional threshold and high intensity of reaction, typical of many
youngsters with a "difficult" temperament. Problems with hyperactivity and
organization often accompany this profile. Children with these behaviors
typically experience struggles making and keeping friendships since their
interpersonal skills are adversely affected by these behaviors. Some may at
first desperately seek friendships but when they meet with failure, they may
retreat to their rooms, convinced that no one will ever like them. It is little
wonder that many children similar to your son report being all alone and
lonely. One boy told us with tears, "I call other kids to ask them to play but
they are always busy and no one ever calls me."

In clinic settings, children with this pattern are also frequently described
as having problems with sustained attention and impulsivity, frequently
leading to a diagnosis of Attention Deficit Hyperactivity Disorder (ADHD).
When children receive this diagnosis the question about the role medications
may play as part of their treatment plan is quickly raised. Keep in mind that
we believe strongly that pills will not substitute for skills. A pill is not a substitute for an available, caring parent, a set of friends, a competent teacher,
or successful life experiences. Stimulant medications, in particular, however,
are effective in reducing the symptoms and adverse consequences children

with ADHD demonstrate. The use of these medications for ADHD is well established with nearly four hundred studies demonstrating short-term symptom relief. But symptom relief is not synonymous with changing long-term outcome. Thus, there is not a single study suggesting that when children with ADHD take medicine they turn out better as adults than those children who do not. In contrast, however, when they take medicine and it improves their behavior, it is more likely their teachers and parents will appreciate them more and yell at them less.

Studies involving thousands of children treated with stimulant medications have demonstrated that medication is effective more than 70 percent of the time. Other classes of medicines such as antidepressants sometimes are effective but have not proven to be as effective as the stimulants, including methylphenidate (marketed as Ritalin®, Concerta®, and Methylin®), mixed salts of amphetamine sulfate (marketed as Adderall®), and dexedrine (marketed as Dextrostat®).

Parents often worry that these medications sedate children but this is not the case. Instead when used appropriately, these medications increase children's capacity for self-control. Stimulants have been demonstrated to increase self-control in even unaffected children and adults. However, children receiving the diagnosis of ADHD benefit to a much greater degree. These medicines increase the capacity to think before acting, control impulses, and regulate behavior. The exact mechanism of these medications is not well understood, but they appear to stimulate parts of the brain that are understimulated, in particular, the right prefrontal cortex, basal ganglia, and cerebellum. The pathways between these three organs in the brain appear critically important for self-control. These medications don't mask the symptoms of ADHD but directly act on a cause of the problem by adjusting a biochemical condition that interferes with children's capacity to develop and demonstrate self-control leading to impulsive behavior and poor sustained attention.

It is estimated that more than three million children now receive stimulant medication for ADHD. There is no conclusive evidence that treatment leads to chemical dependence or addiction. Nor is there any evidence that it negatively affects a child's potential height or weight or causes long-term personality change or other serious illness. The most common negative side effects for some children are loss of appetite and insomnia as the medicine wears off.

We believe that the use of these medications to treat children with ADHD is important in many cases. But again, keep in mind that the medicine will not magically fix poor classroom or defiant behavior or learning problems, nor will it magically lead children to develop a resilient mindset in the absence of parental care and support. Also, the decision to place a child on medication should be based on a thorough psychological and neuropsychological evaluation, including the completion of checklists about the child's behavior from parents and teachers.

We want to emphasize that even if a child benefits from medication, it should not be used as the only intervention approach. Some children with more mild to moderate symptoms of ADHD often respond well to a consistent, behavior management or problem-solving approach at home and school; some of these children may not have responded successfully to medication. The problem-solving program we advocate is based in great part on the work of Myrna Shure, author of *Raising a Thinking Child* and *Raising a Thinking Preteen*. This approach, in which children are enlisted to identify the problem, think of possible solutions and their outcomes, and then select the solution that appears to have the best possible chance of success, is a program that can be utilized with or without a child taking medication.

More specifically, in terms of your son, it would be important to discuss with him the problem of being organized and getting ready on time. Engage him in a dialogue of (a) the problems resulting from not being ready on time, (b) what interferes with his getting ready, and (c) possible solutions. For example, we have worked with families in which children select the evening before what clothes to wear the next day, and they have their books and homework placed in their book bags before they go to bed. As simple as this might seem, the more that things are prepared the evening before, the less the likelihood of a child frantically running around looking for things the next morning.

Other households will use a list drawn up by the child and parents to remind the child what needs to be done in the morning. One child, concerned he would forget what was on the list that was placed on the door of his room, requested that the list also be placed on a bulletin board in the kitchen and on the door of the bathroom. This child appreciated his difficulties getting organized and following a routine and realized that at present he required as many visual aids as possible. Since he helped to create these visual aids, he felt more empowered and, thus, remembered to check the lists. Very importantly, his involvement in a problem-solving approach nurtured a resilient mindset. But remember, not every intervention will be successful and many will take time before they take hold.

> But remember, not every intervention will be successful and many will take time before they take hold.

The presence of these kinds of behavioral approaches to increase self-control and hopefully, more satisfying peer relationships prompts us to emphasize another point. Many parents incorrectly believe that if children with ADHD take medicine for a number of years, they will develop self-control more rapidly and at some point they can stop the medication and continue functioning well. Unfortunately, the day medicine is stopped for many children appears similar to the day before it was started. Thus, treating many children with ADHD with medication is similar to treating diabetics with insulin. When the medicine is taken, functioning improves. Remove the medication and functioning quickly regresses, even after a long period of successful treatment. Thus, we believe strongly that along with medication we must continue helping children with delayed development of self-control accelerate their abilities to develop self-discipline and problem-solving skills.

Question

I have read a lot about temperament. It is obvious there is a mismatch between my older son's restless, risk-taking, stimulation-seeking temperament and my quiet, reserved style. He is eleven years old. We don't seem to fit together very well unlike my younger son and daughter. How important is it to develop what you've referred to as "a goodness-of-fit" in helping kids develop resilience? How does a parent go about doing it?

Answer

First, we would like to reassure you that it is common for parents who have more than one child to find it easier to relate to and parent one child compared with another. This involves the concept of "goodness-of-fit." Our history as children in our families, our mindsets, interests, and even our personal temperament as adults all contribute to determine how easily or how difficult it may be for us to accept any one of our children. Outgoing, gregarious parents may experience stress and tension raising a cautious, reserved child, not appreciating how a child could be so shy and cautious when they are outgoing. Achievement-oriented parents may perceive a child with a slow tempo or minimal motivation to be lazy when in fact that is not the case.

In your situation, it appears that the temperament of your younger children is more in accord with your own quiet, reserved style while your older son's behavior is quite different. However, it is important to understand the concept of goodness-of-fit is not predicated on similarities in temperament alone. Goodness-of-fit is much more complicated. For example, we know of many parents who are temperamentally shy and have children similar in nature. Since these parents are not happy with their own shyness, they find it difficult to accept the same characteristics in their children. In this situation, similarity does not equate with goodness-of-fit.

Basically, achieving goodness-of-fit is associated with parents being aware of their own temperamental style and how this style impacts on their views of and responses to their children. This awareness serves as a foundation for parents learning to accept and accommodate their children's temperament and helping their children to modify their styles when these styles interfere with the development of a resilient mindset.

Although you may be uncomfortable at times with your son's risk-taking behavior, rather than attempt to alter it completely (an impossible task), your mindset and the behaviors associated with this mindset can help your son shape and develop his pattern of behavior into a functional skill. For instance, you might seek out activities for your son that are action-oriented and stimulating (and safe). As an illustration, we have worked with families who have arranged for youngsters with temperaments similar to your older son's to be involved in karate, wrestling, or outward-bound types of activities. One family encouraged their daughter to go into gymnastics as a way to satisfy and direct her risk-taking behaviors and to help her develop discipline. She became a state champion in the sport. Her proud mother said, "I envy her courage in doing the gymnastics and her comfort in answering questions from the media."

The issue of goodness-of-fit arises in many families. In fact, we are unaware of any research that indicates the percentage of families in which all children and parents possess temperaments that fit well together. We believe that is the exception rather than the rule. Also, as we noted above, similarities between the temperaments of parents and children may result in more friction rather than less, especially when the parents are not happy with their own temperamental qualities.

The mismatch between parents and children can be attributed at times to the failure of parents to establish a goodness-of-fit between their style and that of their child. This often results in anger and disappointment for all parties. In some situations children feel they have let their parents down. This prompts low self-esteem, poor problem solving, and ultimately the feeling of being unloved or unaccepted. Unfortunately, this pattern is one that works against the reinforcement of a resilient mindset. We often advise parents that if we are to avoid this negative pattern, we are the ones that must take the initial steps in appreciating and accepting the unique qualities of our children.

Question

Is difficult *a fair word to use when describing some children's temperament? It sounds so negative. I know that some people describe these children as spirited or challenging. Is it possible by labeling this behavior negatively, parents create more problems for themselves? Is it also possible that parents of some children may not have difficulty raising these children or that in fact this pattern of temperament may some day prove to be an advantage for some children?*

Answer

You pose some very important questions. We would actually like to address your last question first. There are many well-meaning people who argue that what have been labeled as difficult temperaments in children can actually be gifts or advantages. We have heard how risk-taking children are more likely to become successful entrepreneurs than reserved children or how children who are inattentive are prime candidates for creative ventures. Though it has become popular for some writers to suggest that children with difficult temperaments may become great inventors, explorers, or stockbrokers, while children with slow-to-warm-up temperaments may develop greater empathy, there is little if any scientific research to support these contentions. Further, we believe that children aren't dumb. They are well aware of their daily struggles to be successful. However, when confronted with ongoing frustration, they often develop coping behaviors in an effort to save their fragile self-esteem or avoid looking bad in the eyes of others. For many youngsters the coping strategies they rely upon prove to be ineffective or self-defeating. These children are not likely to be fooled when we suggest that although they may be struggling today their patterns of behavior will somehow help them achieve greatness in the future. We want to develop hope and optimism in our children but to do so we must empathize with their plight and teach them more effective ways of coping and behaving.

On the other side of the coin, we agree with you that one must be careful not to take labels such as "difficult" or "slow-to-warm-up" and apply them so that they come to represent the child's entire personality. When this occurs, parents and other adults can fall into the trap of viewing these children as unable to change their "basic personalities" and responding to them in ways that actually increase the negative behaviors. Just as we do not want children's struggles to be minimized by seeing their difficult temperamental styles as assets, nor do we want them to be branded with indelible labels that appear incapable of modification.

Labels certainly play a large factor in our response to children. Do we describe a child as adventuresome or restless, high spirited or hyperactive, destructive or inquisitive? We believe the words we choose to describe our children's behavior do in fact influence what we think about that behavior and how we choose to respond. However, we urge parents to define the problem not in terms of a label for the child's temperament but rather in terms of the desired behavior and goals parents wish to accomplish. Thus, when we have worked with parents who characterize their child as difficult and hyperactive, we ask them to focus on the behaviors they would like to see rather than the behaviors they wish to erase. We also ask them to describe times when their child displays the behaviors they would like to see so that we might learn under what conditions the child is not "difficult." Parents can then discuss with their children the problematic behaviors and possible strategies to change these behaviors. Labels do not even have to be a part of this dialogue.

> We believe the words we choose to describe our children's behavior do in fact influence what we think about that behavior and how we choose to respond.

In terms of another question you raise, we should note that what are troubling temperaments and behaviors for some parents are not for other parents. For instance, while some parents perceive particular behaviors displayed by their children as difficult, others appear more willing to label these behaviors as normal phenomena of child development and find it easier to focus on what to do rather than what is wrong. Nonetheless, we have rarely encountered parents raising difficult or slow-to-warm-up children who do not perceive that their children's behavior is not problematic to some extent or for that matter offers any type of adaptive advantage.

In essence, it is important for parents to understand the unique temperaments of their children. Rather than placing certain temperamental characteristics on a pedestal while labeling others as pathology, it is more important to appreciate the strengths and vulnerabilities of each child and respond in ways that help each child to develop a resilient mindset. Labels should never be used to define the entire child or to place a value judgment on them.

Finally, we joke about the time before parents have children as "BC," which doesn't stand for "Before children" but rather "Before Chaos!" Consider the type of parents you thought you would be and the type of child you envisioned raising. When children don't fit our expectations, parenting becomes a more challenging task. Obviously, when children demonstrate extremes of temperament such challenges are magnified but we believe can be managed.

Question

I have read your description of accepting children but I am confused as to how to tell the difference between accepting children for who they are and what they can do versus giving into them. For instance, our eight-year-old daughter has not been easy to raise. It is difficult for her to accept "no." She challenges our rules and frequently complains things are unfair. Sometimes when she is angry she can say very mean things, often telling us to "shut up" and "you're stupid." She has been this way from birth. I don't believe we have caused this problem but I'm not certain we have done much to help. What does it really mean to "accept your children"? She always says that we love her two sisters more than we love her. I hate to admit this but she might be right since they are so much easier to raise than she is. I begin to feel guilty after she says we love her sibs more and sometimes I let her get away with saying and doing things that I wouldn't tolerate in her sisters. Shouldn't we be setting some limits, even if this is her basic temperament and it is difficult for her to change?

Answer

Many well-intentioned parents engage in a daily tug-of-war to accept their children for who they are and not what they envision or want them to be. Accepting our children for who they are is a far more daunting task than many realize. Some parents claim they accept their children for who they are but don't recognize that there is an unsaid "but" or an "as long as" after the vow of acceptance. For example, "I accept my child as long as he listens to what I say" or "I accept my child as long as she gets good grades in school" or "I accept my child but only when she says hello to people and is outgoing." Children are very aware of these unstated criteria for acceptance and they represent examples of conditional love that we described in Chapter 5.

However, freeing ourselves from a mindset that constantly includes the words *but* and *as long as* should not be taken to imply that we allow our children to do whatever they want or that we give in to them and don't hold them responsible. Acceptance means we understand that certain behaviors are part of our child's temperament and that we still love our child even when these behaviors appear. Acceptance helps parents to set realistic goals and expectations for their children that are based on each child's developmental level and temperament. For example, some parents would feel comfortable allowing their nine-year-old to cross a busy street to go to a store and purchase candy, while others would not, fearful that their child would pay little attention to the traffic light.

> Acceptance means we understand that certain behaviors are part of our child's temperament and that we still love our child even when these behaviors appear.

Acceptance also involves carefully assessing which behaviors of our child are inappropriate or self-defeating and helping to alter these behaviors. Of course, an important dimension of this task is to be selective and not attempt to change all behaviors associated with our child's temperament—an impossible goal. As the old saying goes, "Select your battlegrounds carefully."

Clearly your daughter has been difficult to raise from birth, experiencing a low emotional threshold and a high intensity of reaction. When distressed, she is prone to project her anger and frustration outward onto others. Since she is difficult to please, she is quick to perceive the world as unfair and not meeting her needs. This leads her to question what appear to you as reasonable rules and expectations but to your daughter are perceived as impositions. It is very easy for even the most understanding parents to lose their patience in such situations, especially if they have gone out of their way to accommodate their child's style. Unfortunately, when parents react angrily they often reinforce their child's negative behavior since the child comes to believe that his or her angry response is justified.

What might you do with your daughter given her seeming neediness and her perception of the world as ungiving and unfair? Obviously consequences must be set when she is disrespectful but also think about adopting a proactive or preventative approach. To help offset her feelings of not being loved, you might empathize and say to her that you know she doesn't always feel loved or that you give her enough time. Suggest that you establish a "special time" each night (or every other night) to spend time with her alone (you would have to do the same with your other two children but we have found that when needy children feel they are receiving some undivided attention, they are better able to tolerate the times when their siblings are getting attention).

Also, as much as possible build in some choices for your daughter. This is important for all children but even more so for youngsters who feel they are always being told what to do. Observe what you say when you ask your daughter to do something and when possible, build in choices. For example, "Do you want to put the toys away by yourself or do you want me to help you?" or "Do you want me to remind you five minutes or ten minutes before it's time to get ready for bed?" Many parents of seemingly oppositional children have told us how choices really do help to cut down on power struggles.

Also, let your daughter know that when she is angry she can tell you but she cannot do so by calling you names. You can say, "You have a choice. You can tell me when you're angry and we can discuss the situation or you can call me names but that will result in a consequence or loss of privilege." As a parent you can decide upon what privilege will be lost; it's best if it's something over which you have control such as taking her to the mall rather than asking her to do something such as going to her room. Helping your daughter feel better about herself and improving your relationship with her will not be an easy process given her temperament. However, if you assume a proactive stance, if you select your battlegrounds carefully, and if you help her to see that consequences are based upon her behaviors, in all likelihood the situation will improve.

Question

Our fourteen-year-old son has always been rather quiet but over the last year he has locked himself away from everyone and everything. He stays in his room for hours listening to music, playing Dungeons & Dragons with two friends, or spending time in chat rooms on the Internet. He has made a number of negative comments about himself and his future. His efforts at school have declined. Finally, the other day we found a note he wrote in which he indicated that it might not be so bad to be dead. I am having such confused feelings. At times, I just want to go over and give him a hug and comfort him. At other times, I feel guilty and wonder what I might have done or not done to cause his sadness. And then sometimes I get angry with him and feel he is just letting himself become more and more depressed and not attempting to do anything about it. I feel like telling him, "There's nothing to be depressed about, just snap out of it." I've never said this but I sometimes think my son knows that's how I feel. I think I feel as

confused as my son does, and I know I'm having difficulty accepting and help-
ing him with his sadness. My husband and I are worried that rather than help-
ing our son develop a resilient mindset, just the opposite is happening. What
should we do?

Answer

Parents go through many different feelings when their son or daughter becomes depressed. You have been very honest in sharing your feelings. It sounds to us that unfortunately your son is struggling with a depressive episode. Children, like adults, can and do suffer from depressive illness. It has been our experience that even individuals possessing a resilient mindset may become burdened with clinical depression, which quickly strips away their strength. Depression influences every aspect of a child's or teen's daily life and functioning. Depression has been described as a whole body illness. It involves changes in mood, sleep, appetite, energy, and daily activities, including relationships with friends and family and functioning at school. While not all depressed youngsters think of suicide, many do. Depression often places teens at risk to begin abusing substances as a means of lubricating their unhappiness.

Many parents have asked us how can they tell whether their child is clinically depressed or just feeling a little moody or blue. Understanding the symptoms of depression can provide parents with the knowledge they require to be more accepting and helpful if their child is suffering from clinical depression. There are nine clinical symptoms of depression. We will review these for you so that you can be in a better position to determine whether in fact you should seek professional help. Keep in mind that these symptoms should represent a change in functioning—a change for the worse. Although you describe your son as someone who perhaps has always been "rather quiet," clearly your description suggests a significant negative change over the past year. To be considered clinically depressed, a child must demonstrate a significantly depressed or irritable mood. Depressed teens often display a low emotional threshold and are quick to strike out with angry behavior. They may feel lonely and unsupported. They often complain that life is unfair or no one cares about them.

The second symptom of depression represents a loss of interest or pleasure in nearly all activities. Although you describe your son as still enjoying music, the Internet, and at least one game, does this represent a significant narrowing or restriction of his previous activities? Individuals with clinical depression experience at least one if not both of these first two symptoms. Let's examine the other seven.

To be clinically depressed, one must exhibit at least four of the following: a change in weight and appetite; a change in sleep pattern; physical restlessness or "zombielike" behavior; fatigue or loss of energy; feelings of worthlessness; problems with thinking clearly, concentrating, and making decisions; and finally, recurrent thoughts of death or suicide or a suicide plan or attempt.

Some children demonstrate a few but not all of these symptoms. If these symptoms cause a change for the worse in daily functioning, other minor clinical conditions of depression, one of which is referred to as Dysthymia or minor depression, should be considered. If you suspect, based on these symptoms, that your son is depressed, seek an evaluation from an experienced mental health professional. To introduce the notion of professional help, which many teenagers reject at first, you might say to your son that you love him and that you are very concerned about how he is feeling. If he says he is okay and you shouldn't worry, you can bring up specific examples that suggest he is not feeling fine, including his note that it might not be so bad to be dead. You should be very persistent since the issue is one that may involve a life-or-death situation. It may also help you to be persistent if you begin with the assumption that your son is not malingering and is not capable of simply "snapping out of it." Accepting his depression and being empathic will help both you and your son during this very difficult time.

Question

As I think about my ten-year-old son, I often become depressed. I recognize that some of my sad feelings are related to the fact that he is not the kind of child I dreamed about. I feel guilty about this feeling. Each morning I tell myself to be more accepting of him but that reminder usually lasts for only a few minutes. My acceptance quickly dissolves when I see how disorganized he is even though we have tried to help him. His book bag looks like a tornado has struck. When I see he can't find his homework and when I see his hair is not combed and he looks disheveled, all I want to do is scream. What more can I do? I hate to admit this but I find it embarrassing to be his mother. In public places I worry that people are commenting on what a poor mother I must be. Can I still hold on to some of my dreams for him or is it unfair to him and me?

Answer

No parent wants his or her child to be disorganized or look disheveled. Similar to yourself, many parents believe that if their children do not present themselves in an acceptable way to others it is a reflection of their effectiveness as parents. When the behavior of our children is markedly different from the dreams we had for them, frustration and anger are likely to appear. Some parents find it relatively easy to abandon the initial dreams or fantasies they had of their children when confronted with who their children really are. Other parents have a great deal of difficulty letting go of these dreams and we have found that one of the main reasons revolves around their own insecurities. One nine-year-old boy whom we saw in therapy said something that was very perceptive. He noted, "One of the reasons my father wants me to get good grades and do good in sports is because it will make him feel like a good father."

It's not clear why your reaction to your son's problems is so intense. It's obvious that you recognize that you have to be more accepting but after only a few minutes you are not able to do so. On an intellectual level you seem to understand that your son's behavior is part of his temperament and style and will take time to change, but on an emotional level it is difficult for you to accept him. It's also obvious that you are very concerned about what others will think of you because of the behavior of your son.

> The dreams we have for our children must be constantly modified and in that sense all parents have to give up part of their dream.

The dreams we have for our children must be constantly modified and in that sense all parents have to give up part of their dream. This doesn't mean we give up all of our dreams or expectations but rather that we learn to become more realistic and modify these dreams when indicated. If you find that you are not able to accept your son and if you continue to be overly concerned about the opinions of others, we would suggest that you seek professional help for both your own well-being and that of your son.

Question

My wife and I have two temperamentally difficult children, a twelve-year-old daughter and a ten-year-old son. We feel we are constantly screaming at them to get things done or help out in the house. They tell us we are nagging and we tell them it is not nagging but reminding. If we don't remind them they don't remember what to do. How can we begin to develop a more cooperative attitude? How can we be more accepting and along the way help them learn to be more responsible?

Answer

One of the main characteristics of resilient children is that they possess a sense of responsibility. They are aware of what is expected of them and meet these expectations, typically without having to be reminded. Some children develop this capacity with seeming ease. It's almost as if from birth they communicate the message, "Just provide me with responsibilities and I will fulfill them." In contrast, other children struggle to complete their responsibilities for a variety of different reasons such as their temperament or cognitive style, how clearly these responsibilities are defined by parents, or their perception of what it would mean for them to follow through on what is expected (e.g., some children who are engaged in power struggles with their parents view meeting their parents' expectations as "giving in" on their part).

When you constantly remind your children to do something, they refer to your actions as nagging; as psychologists we refer to it as negative reinforcement. Some children, because of their temperament or environment, receive a large amount of negative reinforcement. That is, parents spend excessive time exhorting, nagging, or cajoling them. Many children comply with requests, not because they wish to complete the task but to gain freedom from the aversive consequence, namely, their parents' angry attention. Negative reinforcement is often seductive. It appears to work when you do it but over time increases the likelihood children will not respond unless "nagged." In addition, constant reminders reduce the opportunity for children to develop a sense of responsibility, and thus, are counterproductive to developing a resilient mindset. One other major drawback of nagging— eventually as children get older, many may just refuse to do what you want, prompting you to use stronger forms of negative reinforcement. Power struggles thrive in such an atmosphere and all parties involved suffer.

We suggest you begin by considering four important principles. First, serve as a model of responsibility for your children. As the saying goes, children don't necessarily do what we say but they do what we do. Children will notice if you fulfill your responsibilities. We have worked with many families in which parents complained about their children's lack of responsibility only to be greeted by a litany of examples offered by their children of the parents' failure to meet responsibilities. One boy told us that his father constantly missed "family time" that he had promised because of work requirements. A teenage girl who was punished for a "messy room," described how her parents rarely put away their own clothes. Another teenage girl rightfully thought it was hypocritical that her parents became very upset when they caught her drinking beer, and yet acknowledged when she confronted them that they regularly smoked marijuana. Their retort was, "We're adults and can make those decisions." This kind of rationale does not sit well with kids.

Another way of modeling responsible behavior is what we discussed in Chapter 4, namely, the courage to change negative scripts. If something we are doing as parents is not working, our ability to change our approach can be experienced by our children not as giving in but of recognizing when responsible behavior dictates a new approach. Thus, as we have recommended in previous answers, surprise your children by saying to them that you think you are nagging them too much. Most likely, they will readily agree. Then turn the discussion into a problem-solving session in which you tell them of your willingness to change but that they also have some responsibility in the process. This kind of dialogue can help articulate expectations and how each family member would like to be reminded should an expectation not be met.

Second, offer your children opportunities in keeping with their developmental level to reinforce responsible behavior through the act of helping others. We will discuss this principle in greater detail in Chapter 9. The basic premise is that when we say to our children that we need their help, they are much more likely to meet their responsibilities than when we say, "Remember to do your chores." We believe there is an inborn need in children to help others and that as parents we should use this need to provide our children with opportunities to assist others and to shine. Resilient people feel that they are making a difference in their world.

Third, make certain you are distributing responsibilities fairly. Not all responsibilities are exciting (some will fall under the category of "chores"). Acknowledge that some activities are tedious or boring, but explain to your children why they must be met if the household is to function smoothly. Divide responsibilities among family members and establish a schedule for changing them every couple of weeks so that all family members, including parents, assist with different activities. Also, as we noted earlier, build in ways to remember responsibilities such as through the use of lists. The less "nagging" the better off everyone will be.

Fourth, we suggest you take a "helicopter view" of your child's life. A helicopter view will provide you with a broader perspective. It will help counteract what we have seen with many parents, namely, placing too much weight on a particular area in which their children appear irresponsible when in fact in many other areas of their lives they are quite responsible. Some parents have told us that their children are "totally irresponsible," but when we have questioned them about this assessment, they begin to offer examples of responsible behavior such as completing their homework, being on time for a job, offering to help an elderly neighbor bring groceries into the house. Ask yourself how your children do in the community or at school. If they function well and demonstrate responsible behavior, we suggest you begin by discussing and reinforcing those examples as you attempt to set in place a system and strategies to motivate your children to demonstrate a similar level of responsibility at home. Use their successes as a starting point to change your perspective and their behavior.

We believe that if you can follow these four steps, your son and daughter will begin to demonstrate greater responsibility.

7

Nurturing Islands of Competence

The Experience of Joy and Success

Question
From a commonsense point of view it would seem that when a child is success-ful at some task, this experience would contribute to the development of a resilient mindset. I know that I want my kids to be successful at what they do but will that guarantee that they will become resilient?

Answer
The answer to your question is actually much more complex than it seems—as are most issues in parenting. The more successes a child experiences the more likely that child will develop a resilient mindset. However, there are qualifications to this statement. Two major factors that determine whether a child's successes nurture a resilient mindset are (a) whether the child believes the successes are based, at least in part, on his or her own resources and efforts, and (b) whether the successes are judged to be important to the child and significant others (friends, parents) in his or her life.

> The more successes a child experiences the more likely that child will develop a resilient mindset.

Let's look at the first factor. Attribution theory provides a framework that examines to what children attribute their success. Children with resilient mindsets who succeed at different tasks such as in sports, academics, or art, while acknowledging that adults in their lives have helped them, also believe that they are major contributors to their own success. They don't do this in a conceited or bragging way, but they do feel a sense of confidence. In contrast, when children with low self-esteem are successful in an activity, they are quick to discount their role and instead attribute their success to outside factors such as luck or chance. For instance, we have worked with many youngsters with learning problems. Some have responded to a good test grade with such comments as "I was lucky" or "The teacher made the test easy." If a child attributes success to variables outside one's control, then that child will not feel the same sense of joy and accomplishment as a child who takes some credit for the success. Also, a child who does not experience ownership for the achievement will not be as confident about succeeding in the future.

The implication for parents is that our response to our children's success must include comments that reinforce their efforts, diligence, and perseverance. If our children offer the opinion they were "lucky," we can respond, "I know that you feel you were lucky but I also think we make our own luck and you shouldn't forget all that you did to be successful." One statement such as this is not likely to change your child's attitude immediately but it can lay the foundation for a more positive outlook. Parents must also be careful that when assisting their children with certain tasks they not do too much lest the children feel the success is really the parent's, not their own. For instance, we know of one young adolescent boy who asked his father to review a paper he had written for his English class. When the father returned it to his son replete with many corrections, the boy remarked, "Now it's your paper, not mine. No seventh grader writes this way." This boy used only a few of his father's suggested changes, wanting to ensure that it was truly his paper, one for which he could take responsibility.

The second factor is also a very important one. If children are successful in activities that they judge to be of little importance or relevance to significant others, then, unfortunately, that success may make little, if any, contribution to the development of a resilient mindset. We know of one boy with learning disabilities. His mother told him that while he struggled with learning, he was a very kind, considerate, and warm child. One night as he was lamenting how dumb he felt, his mother empathized with him but also commented on his strengths of kindness and compassion. Her son responded, "But they really don't give grades for that in school and kids still tease me about my learning." Although this mother did all of the right things in empathizing with him and pointing out his strengths, the pain he was experiencing in school and with peers did not allow him to see his strengths as strengths. Hopefully, at some point he will be able to do so.

In addition, some children are successful at activities that are not highly valued in their families. We know of one adolescent boy who loved to garden and take care of plants. His parents acknowledged that he enjoyed this endeavor and was very good at it, but they basically perceived gardening as a frivolous activity compared with achievements in academics and sports. However, this boy did not like sports and he struggled in school. Unfortunately, he received little, if any, positive feedback from his parents or peers for his gardening talents so that his accomplishments in this area did not bring him the feelings of satisfaction and accomplishment that would nurture a resilient mindset. Imagine what would have happened if the parents had said to their son, "It is amazing what you are able to do with these plants. You really have quite a green thumb. Would you like to go to the plant store to get some more plants to take care of? It would certainly help our house look even better."

As parents, we must recognize that successes in our children come in many shapes and forms and with different timetables. If these successes are to contribute to a resilient mindset we must find opportunities to enjoy and acknowledge what our children have done and reinforce the role they have played in their success.

Question

I've noticed something about my nine-year-old daughter that upsets me and I don't know what to do about it. Even when she does something well, she doesn't seem to obtain any enjoyment. It seems like it has always been that way. The other day she came home with an A— on a test and didn't seem happy. When I said what a nice job she did, she seemed glum. When I asked what's the matter, she said, "Nothing." A couple of weeks ago she scored a goal at her soccer game. I know some kids may be modest and not want to look too happy, but when her teammates congratulated her she didn't even smile. Why wouldn't a child be happy when things like that happen? I told her that she should smile and say thank you when her teammates congratulated her but she seemed to get angry when I said this. Is there anything I can do?

Answer

Your description of your daughter fits a type of temperament that appears to influence a child's feeling of success. Years ago, before we realized how different each child was at birth, it was very easy to "blame" a child's negative outlook on parents (e.g., parents were assumed to be too demanding or not encouraging). However, with greater research about the impact of children's inborn temperament on their perception of themselves and the world, we now recognize that some children from a young age have a more difficult time experiencing the joy of success than other children. These children are not necessarily depressed nor burdened by serious psychiatric problems. They simply view the world through "mud-colored glasses." It is often difficult for parents and other adults to understand this feeling, especially if they haven't experienced it themselves. Imagine, however, how you would feel if your accomplishments, though praised and reinforced by others, simply didn't provide any sense of joy or pleasure. The process by which mastery at an activity fosters a feeling of success and builds upon an island of competence is derailed for these children. As appears to be the case for your daughter, these children are quick to discount their accomplishments and abilities.

Although it is not clear why this situation occurs, the best explanation we can offer is that there appears to be a biological vulnerability that some children bring to the world that impedes but does not necessarily prevent them from learning to experience the joy of success. Often complicating matters for these children is their perception that their actions have little to do with their successes. Thus, they come to view success as something over which they have little control. They may not only miss experiencing the joy of success but perceive whatever successes they have had as simply a function of luck rather than skill, effort, or ability.

At one of our workshops a mother offered a description of her son, which was similar to how you characterized your daughter. While obviously sad about his attitude, she half-jokingly wondered if there was some pill her son could take to give him a more positive attitude. There are no medicines to correct this problem but there are steps parents can take to begin to change their child's negative outlook. As we have mentioned several times in this book, the first step is for you to be empathic and strive to understand your daughter's view of the world. If we are not empathic, our frustrations might lead us to say things that could worsen the problem. One father, annoyed with what he described as his daughter's "constant frown and lack of enjoyment" yelled at her, "You will never be happy if you keep putting yourself down and if you walk around like you have the world's problems on your shoulders." Obviously, this did not help the situation. Based on our therapy work with children similar to your daughter, we know they would love to feel a greater sense of joy and accomplishment; just telling them to "cheer up" is often experienced as throwing salt into a wound, even if the parent did not intend it that way.

If you can maintain an empathic stance, then you can begin the slow process of changing your daughter's perspective. As one example, we ask parents if they notice any occasions in which their child seems to enjoy success. Although some parents cannot think of any examples, most can. One parent of a teenage girl observed that her daughter's entire demeanor brightened up when she was helping younger children with a task. If you can identify such situations of enjoyment, ensure that there are ongoing opportunities for your daughter to engage in this activity and without making too much of a fuss about it, comment on what a nice job she is doing.

Also, when your daughter demonstrates little delight in her accomplishments, rather than commenting on her unhappiness, you might compliment her on her success and don't be concerned if she does not respond with a thank you. If there are times that she looks sad even after an achievement you can ask if anything is wrong. If she answers no, you might say in a supportive way that it looked as if she wasn't happy and if that's the case you wanted to see if you could be of help. By responding in these ways, you are keeping the door open for your daughter to reflect upon and hopefully, begin to change her response to various situations.

Question

I always hear child experts say that you must have realistic expectations for your children or you can rob them of an opportunity to experience success. The problem I have is that I am really not sure what is "realistic." I don't want to expect more than my kids are capable of doing but isn't there a danger of expecting too little? How do you know what is the right level?

Answer

We are often asked what are realistic expectations for children. Without wishing to sound vague, our typical response is "First tell us about your child's temperament, skills, and weaknesses and then we can decide what is a realistic expectation." For each child a realistic goal may be different. If we observe carefully, children provide us with many cues about when the bar is set either too high or too low. If children succeed too easily at the goals that are established, they are likely to finish the task very quickly and even appear bored. If this is the case parents can raise the bar in small steps, knowing that their child needs to be challenged and expectations must be heightened. In contrast, if we see our children struggling and failing at particular tasks, we may have to lower the bar a little until they are able to succeed at the task or we may have to offer them additional support. We should encourage our children to perform their very best but we must also remember that the experience of success is often independent of the level of performance. If we want our children to achieve higher grades we must help them first feel successful with the grades they are earning. If we want our children to remember five things they should do each morning (e.g., brush their teeth, comb their hair), we must first applaud when they remember to do two or three things.

One of our favorite suggestions in terms of gaining a better picture of where the bar should be placed is to involve our children, when appropriate, in the setting of goals and expectations. A problem-solving dialogue can be established in which we discuss expectations with our children about various issues including the number and kinds of responsibilities they have, how late they might stay up on school nights, curfews on weekend nights, and when homework must be completed. While parents still have the final say, this kind of dialogue reinforces a sense of ownership in our children and typically offers a more precise assessment of what our children are cognitively and emotionally able to do.

> As parents, we must learn to appreciate the individual differences in each child and accommodate our expectations to those differences.

One shoe does not fit all. As parents, we must learn to appreciate the individual differences in each child and accommodate our expectations to those differences.

Question

I like the metaphor "islands of competence." You mentioned at a workshop I attended that parents should identify and reinforce each child's islands of competence. I have three children. With two of them it is easy to do. My older daughter is athletic and talented in gymnastics and soccer. My son is a wonderful artist and loves to create things. We have his drawings on the wall and his school does the same thing. I have the most difficulty with my youngest daughter, who is nine years old. She has had learning and social problems. I am embarrassed to say that if you ask me what her islands of competence were I might not be able to identify any. Yet, I can also say she is a warm, caring person.

Answer

We recognize that it is easy for us to suggest you identify and highlight the attributes that help each of your children shine and feel a sense of accomplishment. Yet, as you point out, locating these attributes and helping your children take advantage of them may be difficult. The process of locating a child's island of competence may require some parents to "sail halfway around the world." For other parents little, if any, sailing is involved since the island or islands of competence are in clear view. Even if our search is lengthy and the destination unclear, it is a very important journey for us to take. We must find each child's island of competence since it is through our strengths and abilities that we find joy, pleasure, and success in life.

> We must find each child's island of competence since it is through our strengths and abilities that we find joy, pleasure, and success in life.

We would argue that of your three children, locating an island of competence is probably most important for your youngest daughter given her struggles with learning and social problems. We would guess that she has experienced fewer successes than her siblings. Many youngsters with whom we have worked who have problems in school often perceive themselves as unintelligent because they equate school grades with I.Q. Many of these children appear to swim in an ocean of inadequacy characterized by feelings of diminished competence and ability. Yet we believe that every child possesses at least one small island of competence, an area that is or has the potential to be a source of pride and achievement. As these areas are located and reinforced we have found that they begin to grow.

Although you said if we asked you what your daughter's islands of competence were you might not be able to identify any, you actually provided important information about what might serve as an island of competence. You noted that she is a warm, caring person. Given this quality, your daughter may enjoy helping others. Even at her relatively young age, she might like to teach younger neighborhood children how to play a game, interact with elderly individuals living in nursing homes, engage in an activity that helps the homeless, or participate in charity drives.

We should always keep in mind that being a warm, caring person is an important island of competence that can serve your daughter well. It can become a stable, invaluable port throughout her life, providing her with experiences that will strengthen her resilience and sense of dignity.

Question

Why are some kids embarrassed by their accomplishments? I noticed that when I compliment my eleven-year-old son he seems upset, even when no one is around. If I do it when others are around he becomes angry. I can simply say "nice game" after his Little League game and he looks down and his face turns red. Should I just stop complimenting him since he seems so uncomfortable when I do so?

Answer

Interestingly, many preteens become embarrassed when their parents or teachers compliment them in front of their peers. The reasons for this may be varied. Some kids your son's age may feel too much of a spotlight is being placed on them, making them self-conscious, while other youngsters may not believe they deserve the positive feedback. For instance, one girl told us that her parents praise her so much that "at this point I really don't know what it is that I'm really good at. I almost feel that the reason they keep praising me is because they think I don't feel good about myself."

Some adolescents may feel that compliments are really for younger children, especially if the compliment is about an activity that does not seem very worthwhile in the eyes of their peers. For example, during a family therapy session a ten-year-old boy yelled at his parents that he was angry that they told him in front of a couple of friends what a good job he had done cleaning his room. It's similar to a girl we worked with who became upset with her teacher when the latter complimented her in front of the class for having written one of the best papers the teacher had ever read. Still other kids have told us that when their parents compliment them it is usually followed with a lecture of how much better they could do if they even put in more of an effort. One adolescent boy said, "Whatever I do, they expect more. I cringe when I hear a compliment since I know higher expectations will follow." And, as we noted in an earlier answer, some kids attribute success to things outside of their control so that compliments ring hollow.

We want to emphasize that when children have difficulty accepting compliments it does not necessarily mean that they don't want to receive praise. Many parents who are consistently greeted by a less than enthusiastic response for offering their children positive feedback, might ask the question you raised, "Should I just stop complimenting him since he seems so uncomfortable when I do so?" We believe that when children deserve positive feedback they should receive it, but as parents we must figure out how to provide this feedback in a way that lessens any possible embarrassment or any immediate rejection of our comments.

Many parents have told us that their children more easily accept their compliments when no one else is present. However, from what you wrote your son has difficulty tolerating praise even when others are not with him. We are not certain why that is the case and, of course, we would need a great deal more information to sort out the factors that might be contributing to this behavior. One possible approach you might take is to write your son a note in which you compliment him. The benefit of a note is that he can read it by himself and instead of immediately rejecting what you wrote, he can reflect upon it. We have worked with parents who have written such letters and even acknowledged at the beginning of the letter that they know their child is not comfortable accepting compliments but they felt they really wanted him or her to know how they felt. One parent who adopted this approach called to say that his child was much more willing to accept positive feedback offered through a note and eventually was more comfortable accepting it in person.

If your son had a good game, you can still say "nice game" but if he is self-conscious do not do it with others around. Also, be prepared that he might feel ill-at-ease when hearing your compliment. If it seems appropriate, you might comment that there are times you want to acknowledge his achievements but are trying to figure out the best way to do so. Another suggestion is to notice if there are times when your son is more likely to accept praise and attempt to figure out what factors might be playing a role in these situations.

Our basic advice is that when praise is deserved by our children, we should provide it but in a way they can more easily accept what we have to say. We must ensure that our positive comments do not embarrass them, that we focus on their contributions to their success, and that we don't quickly state that their accomplishments could be even greater if they put in more work.

Question

Whenever my child succeeds at something her first response is, "I was lucky." I keep telling her that she wasn't lucky but that makes her angry. The other day she was playing chess with a friend and she won. The friend, a good chess player, was very nice and said, "Nice win." My daughter's response was predictable. She said, "I was lucky." I think her friend was actually hurt that my daughter couldn't accept her compliment. How do you help a child change that kind of view?

Answer

Your question is similar to many others we have received and one that we especially address in our answer to an earlier question in this chapter. As we noted, some children attribute their success to things outside their control such as luck or chance. They typically do not have high self-esteem or a solid feeling of competence and thus, find it difficult to believe that any success that they experience is based on their own effort or skills or resources. Thus, when they are faced by mistakes or failure they do not have a solid foundation on which to fall back upon, intensifying their feelings of self-doubt and inadequacy. Since we reviewed attribution theory earlier, what we would like to address is how best to respond to your daughter when she dismisses her success.

Although it is not easy for parents to hear their children minimize or make excuses for their achievements, if we are to change our children's mindsets we have to rely upon effective empathy and communication skills. The natural reaction of a parent is to rush in and reassure his or her children, telling them that they are talented and successful. If children do not perceive themselves as successful, then a parent's positive comments are often perceived as false praise and rejected by children.

> If we are to change our children's mindsets we have to rely upon effective empathy and communication skills.

Instead, parents should first validate what their child is voicing. As we have emphasized many times validation does not mean you agree with your daughter but rather that you have heard what she is communicating. When your daughter says that she was lucky, you might say that you know she feels that way and are glad she could tell you; once having said that you can add that you see things differently. We have found that when parents first validate their child's belief, the child is often more responsive to hearing an alternative view. You can offer the opinion that you think your daughter's success is more than luck but rather reflects skills that your daughter possesses. If your daughter appears responsive to at least listening to your observations and is willing to enter into a dialogue, you can share your concern that if she continues to minimize her success, she will not feel as confident.

One father we knew pursued this course of conversation with his son and was pleasantly surprised that after an initial defensiveness on his son's part, the son was willing to talk with him. The father wondered if there were times when his son felt deserving of compliments and interestingly, his son talked about his skill in playing computer games. It was a start to change his son's mindset about success.

One other point we wish to make relates to your daughter's response to her friend after winning at a chess game. In a nonjudgmental way you might wonder with your daughter what her friend felt when she offered a compliment and the compliment was dismissed. We do not want your daughter to feel you are being critical of her or attempting to make her feel guilty but rather that you want her to examine her mindset and behavior in terms of its impact on her relationships with her peers. Changing a child's mindset takes time but it is important to begin lest your daughter continue to be robbed of the experience of enjoying her success.

Question

Can you spoil children by making too much or a big deal out of some of their successes? I believe that kids need praise. I will often yell when my kids score a goal in soccer or get a hit in a baseball game. My wife feels that I am praising them for every little thing they do and that they won't appreciate that true success takes hard work. I think she holds back from praising them because she is worried that she will spoil them. Who is right?

Answer

If you don't mind, we won't engage in a debate about whether you or your wife is right. Instead we would like to offer some comments about the role of praise and positive feedback in a child's development. We hope our comments will serve as a catalyst for both you and your wife to discuss and consider. Perhaps both of you may change your behavior to some degree.

Children deserve and relish positive feedback but like any kind of reaction on the part of parents it should be done in a reasonable way. If our child scores a goal in soccer or gets a hit in a baseball game, we see nothing wrong with a parent shouting, "Nice goal" or "Good hit." However, if that parent is overly exuberant, if the praise comes across as if the child is the second coming of soccer star Mia Hamm or baseball star Sammy Sosa, the praise can actually be embarrassing to the child. Encouraging statements should be commensurate with what the child has accomplished. Children know when a certain level of praise is not deserved and when it occurs it diminishes their sense of success.

If parents praise a child for almost everything, then praise becomes meaningless. We believe that parents can encourage children and acknowledge their commitment to a task or their passion for a game without constantly telling them how wonderful they are. A danger of symbolically placing a child on a pedestal is how far the fall is when the child has a bad game or gets a poor grade. Will the child feel less loved, less accepted?

Obviously we're not present when you are providing your kids with positive feedback. Notice if it occurs "for every little thing" and whether your reactions have to be modified. Also, notice what you say and do after a game when your children have not excelled. We have talked with parents who take their children out for a treat but only if their child's team has won the game or if their child had an especially good game. That kind of parental response is similar to conditional love and will actually lessen a feeling of accomplishment.

Just as we believe there are things you should consider as you praise your children, we also believe that your wife should reflect upon her position. If it is true that she holds back from offering positive feedback for fear she will spoil your kids, then she must be careful lest they feel she doesn't care about or appreciate their successes. In our clinical practices we have heard from many adults that their parents rarely, if ever, gave them positive feedback. One woman could not recall a time when her father said something positive in response to her achievements. She said with sadness and anger, "My mother always said my father was proud of me but if that was so why couldn't he have told me directly?"

Children should know that we love and accept them unconditionally. Our positive feedback should serve to reinforce their feelings of success in a realistic way. Indiscriminate praise or a dearth of praise will deprive a child of this sense of accomplishment.

Question

My eleven-year-old son has reading and math problems. He obtains extra help at school. He attended a meeting we had with his teachers to review his progress and set goals for the coming year. I thought it was a good meeting. However, my son said something very interesting on the way home. He said that at the beginning of the meeting the teacher said he was good in science and social studies and immediately switched to discussing his problems in reading and math. He is a real perceptive kid and asked, "Why do adults spend so much time on kids' problems rather than what they do good?" I was impressed with what he said.

I realized that I often focus more on his problems than his strengths, and I wasn't sure of the best way to respond. What can I do and what can I suggest to his teachers about focusing more on his strengths?

Answer

Your son is very perceptive and raises an important, often underappreciated issue. We believe that while many parents and teachers may mention and acknowledge children's strengths, much of our energy is directed at fixing problems or weaknesses with the mistaken belief that by doing so children will be happier and more successful as they transition into adult life. Unfortunately, we can find little research to support this belief. In fact, it appears to be just the opposite. When children with histories of school achievement problems, such as your son, are interviewed as adults, they rarely describe their early school experiences as the basis for whatever success, satisfaction, or happiness they have achieved in life. Frequently, it is just the opposite. Particularly among adults with histories of learning disabilities who transition successfully into adult life, it is the identification of their strengths and abilities combined with opportunities to reinforce and display these islands of competence that are perceived as the true "secret" of success.

We suggest you let your son know he has made a very astute observation and that in fact not only should adults focus on his problem areas but also on his strengths. Focusing on strengths does not imply that we simply list them but rather that we figure out how to harness them. It is for this reason that we advocate that educational plans begin with a list of a child's strengths and a description of how these strengths will be used. Since your son is proficient in science or social studies, thought should be given to how one might employ these skills to help him to feel more competent. One possibility would be to arrange for him to assist a younger child with a science experiment. When children have opportunities to shine and develop islands of competence, they feel more successful. This feeling of true success will fuel his confidence and increase his willingness to engage in academic areas that require more effort and work.

You can share these thoughts with his teachers. When we have worked with teachers in identifying and displaying a child's islands of competence, teachers have typically reported the increase in motivation they observe in the child. One teacher told us about a boy in her fifth-grade class. "In the past, he denied having trouble with certain academic work and resisted any assistance even when he wasn't doing well. However, he's a wonderful artist. When I asked him to do some posters, which I displayed, and when I asked him to show some kids in kindergarten how to draw cartoon figures, not only was he elated but he became more open to accepting help around his academic subjects."

Question

One of my children responds to any kind of failure or frustration by quitting. He really possesses many skills but since he always quits at things he really hasn't developed what you call an island of competence. How can I help him stick with an activity long enough so that it can become a strength?

Answer

Many youngsters who struggle with issues of self-esteem are quick to quit activities that prove challenging. It is as if they are guided by a mindset that, "If I can't do it by now, I will never be able to do it. So I should just give up." We know that a number of children require extra time and practice to be successful, but from your description your son has difficulty believing that many challenging tasks can be overcome. There are a couple of possible approaches to take. Notice if there are any activities at which he perseveres and begin by reinforcing those. Often if children can experience success in one area, they are more likely to attempt other areas. Use his success in a particular domain to discuss how some things at first may not be easy but that with practice, they often can be learned.

> Often if children can experience success in one area, they are more likely to attempt other areas.

In addition, you might discuss with your son the issue of making a commitment to stick with an activity. For example, you may give him a choice of one of two sports to play and let him know in advance that the commitment is for the entire season. If after a few games he says he wants to quit, you can say that he made a commitment for the season and has to honor that commitment. We knew one boy who wanted to play the clarinet.

Initially, he was able to use a clarinet owned by the school but after a month he had to decide whether to continue playing the instrument, which would necessitate buying a clarinet. He said he wanted to continue. Since he had a history of quitting at things, his parents discussed with him that they would buy the instrument but if they did so, he had to make a commitment to play it for the entire school year. He agreed. About two months later, as he struggled to learn to play, he told his parents the instrument "stunk" and he didn't want to play it anymore.

The parents empathized with him but reminded him of the commitment he had made. He quickly said, "Well, can't people change their minds? Didn't you ever change your minds?" They answered "yes" to both questions but said that they were concerned about how often he changed his mind, that they felt he did not give himself a chance to see what he could accomplish, and that was why they had asked him to make a commitment before they paid for the clarinet. Although he was not happy at first with his parents' position, he did continue to play. It proved to be an important lesson since he became increasingly proficient as a clarinet player and performed a solo in the school's talent show. Most importantly, he learned that skills take time to develop and if you quit too quickly you rob yourself of an opportunity to develop your islands of competence and sense of accomplishment.

Question
After hearing you at a workshop I was intrigued by the notion of islands of competence. It seems obvious that all kids need some areas in which they feel a sense of accomplishment or pride. But could you even make it clearer how the feeling of possessing an island of competence contributes to a resilient mindset? Does it matter what the island of competence is? Is it important that parents or other kids see it as an important skill?

Answer
We believe that for children to develop a resilient mindset they must possess at least one or two islands of competence, or areas of strength. If children do not believe they are competent in any arena, they are likely to feel insecure and vulnerable. Given their low self-esteem and lack of confidence,

they are prone to retreat from challenges or to engage in self-defeating coping strategies such as quitting or bullying to avoid possible humiliation. We must remember that an important feature of a resilient mindset is the belief that we have strengths. Success breeds success. Identifying and reinforcing one island of competence can serve as the catalyst to attempt other challenges and to deal more effectively with mistakes.

You raise several vital questions about whether it matters what a child's island of competence is and whether it is important that parents or other kids view the island as something of value. We answered these questions to some extent in our response to an earlier question in this chapter, but we believe several points deserve to be emphasized again. The reality is that the strength of an island of competence for a child is defined in great part by how others perceive the relevance of that island. The more valued the island is by significant others in a child's life, the more the child gains a sense of pride and accomplishment. Thus, a child who is proficient at the game of marbles but lives in a home and/or community where no one else plays or is interested in that game will not gain as much satisfaction compared with a child whose friends also value the game. As parents, this does not mean we should discourage our child from playing marbles. Rather, we might suggest to our child that he or she invite friends over and teach them the game. We might also think about encouraging other islands of competence that will have greater recognition among peers.

As parents, we must nurture islands of competence even when they are not of great interest to us or to our children's friends. We should do this for at least two reasons. One is to convey to our children that we recognize and appreciate their unique strengths. This sense of acceptance will serve as an important foundation for resilience. The second reason is that while a particular island may not appear to be of relevance now, at some point it may assume greater significance in the eyes of others. We must be careful as parents not to impose upon our children what we think their strengths should be but in the process lose sight of what their strengths really are. We have worked with many youngsters who were steered away from certain activities that brought them a great deal of joy (e.g., gardening) toward other activities (e.g., sports) that the parents saw as valuable but in which the child had little interest. It is very difficult for a child to gain a sense of pride in a particular activity when significant others belittle the importance of that activity.

> As parents, we must nurture islands of competence even when they are not of great interest to us or to our children's friends.

In essence, possessing islands of competence greatly contributes to a resilient mindset; we must nurture these islands in our children and convey to them how proud we are of their accomplishments.

8

Mistakes Are Experiences from Which to Learn

Question

You have suggested that the way children think and feel about mistakes is more important than the mistake itself. Yet, I believe our culture strongly teaches children that they should avoid mistakes. How does making mistakes contribute to a resilient mindset?

Answer

While a number of people may believe that mistakes should be avoided, we believe that there are many who recognize that mistakes, if handled effectively, can serve as a major force for developing a resilient mindset. In actuality, there is no way of totally avoiding the mistakes and failures that are a part of everyone's life. While we do not want our children to face ongoing failure, to attempt to overprotect them and rush in whenever we fear they might fail at a task robs them of an important lesson, namely, that mistakes are experiences from which to learn. It also communicates another subtle or perhaps not-so-subtle message to a child: We don't think you are strong enough to deal with obstacles and mistakes.

We are not advocating that you throw children in ten feet of water if they can't swim and tell them they can learn something from this experience. What we are saying is that we can provide opportunities in which we monitor the kinds of mistakes children make and ensure that how they handle these situations will lead to learning and growth.

The ways in which children understand and respond to mistakes and setbacks are a key component of a resilient mindset. Resilient children persevere in the face of difficult tasks. They typically attribute mistakes, particularly if the task is achievable, to things they can change. They view parents and other adults as available to help them and they don't hesitate to seek assistance when necessary. Thus, when resilient children fail a test at school or strike out in a Little League game, they consider what they can do differently to succeed next time as well as which adults they can call upon for assistance. They might approach their teacher or their parent to gather information about how to study more effectively or their coach about how to become a better hitter.

Resilient children also possess the insight and courage to recognize when a task may present demands that are beyond their abilities. At such times rather than feeling rejected, they direct their energies toward other tasks that are within their capacity. These children possess one of the most important features of a resilient mindset: the belief that adversity can lead to growth. They view difficult situations as challenges rather than as stresses to avoid. Resilience is reinforced each time they confront and master these challenges. If children have not been "tested," then how will they know what they are capable of achieving?

> The ways in which children understand and respond to mistakes and setbacks are a key component of a resilient mindset.

In marked contrast, children who are not resilient typically perceive most mistakes and failures as events that are beyond their control to change. It is as if each mistake reinforces the belief, "I am a failure" or "I am a loser" or "Things cannot get better." One pessimistic child told us, "I was born to quit and God made me that way." When children possess this kind of mindset and believe that they do not have the ability to learn from mistakes, they often try to mask this feeling by relying on self-defeating ways of coping such as quitting at tasks, blaming others, denying responsibility. We use the word *self-defeating* since these ways of responding serve to lessen the possibility of future success and the emergence of a resilient mindset. For instance, we once observed the reaction of a boy at a Little League game who struck out the two times he was at bat. After the second time, he flung his bat down and shouted at the umpire (who was a father volunteering to umpire that day), "You are blind! Has anyone ever told you how blind you are?" The boy then ran off the field refusing to return or talk with the coach. He blamed the umpire but as we watched him we could not help feeling how inadequate he felt.

In essence, as you will see in our answers to the following questions, we believe that as long as children view mistakes as a basis for learning, their self-esteem and resilience will thrive. If, however, they feel trapped by their mistakes, their self-worth and confidence will diminish, making it even more difficult for them to perceive the possible positive aspects of mistakes and failure. Thus, as parents we must reflect upon how we respond to our children's mistakes and ask ourselves whether we are communicating the message, "We all make mistakes. We believe you can learn from these mistakes given your skills and competencies and we are here to assist you in this process."

Question

I am worried that I might be overprotecting my daughter from making mistakes. She is nine years old and I will either tell her something is too hard to try or if she makes a mistake I immediately rush in and try to comfort her. You mentioned the scripts we have as parents. If I could write the best script, it would be for my daughter not to have to feel the pain of making a mistake. Is there anything wrong with that?

Answer

It's a natural response for parents to want to protect their children from pain. If a parent feels that making mistakes will cause their children pain and humiliation, then our protective instincts are aroused and we do all that we can to help our children avoid those situations that may result in mistakes. However, we must remember that while no child joyfully asserts, "I love to make mistakes" or "There is joy in making mistakes," mistakes need not be painful or associated with humiliation. As we noted in the answer to the first question in this chapter, as parents we should step in when we believe that making a mistake places our child at risk for harm, but typically the day-to-day mistakes a child makes are not of this nature. If we believe that mistakes represent opportunities rather than indices of inadequacy, then we will not be as worried when our children fail. It's interesting to note that in the

Chinese language the words *crisis* and *opportunity with danger* are represented by the same symbol. Thus, there is recognition that mistakes can either be viewed as unalterable crises or as opportunities for growth, even if those opportunities are tinged with uncertainty. It is natural for parents to wish to insulate their children, to reduce the adversity, risk, or stresses they may face. On the other hand, too much protection, support, or insulation may deprive children of opportunities to learn to deal with mistakes in affirmative, self-esteem enhancing ways.

> If we believe that mistakes represent opportunities rather than indices of inadequacy, then we will not be as worried when our children fail.

We suspect there are plenty of areas in your daughter's life in which you didn't rush in to rescue her. Did you pick her up every time she was learning to walk? Did you carry her every time she asked to be carried? Did you do all of her schoolwork as she was learning to read? If you did, then perhaps your problem is greater than we suspect from your question. However, if you did not, then we would ask you to reevaluate your mindset relative to mistakes and to appreciate the countless times you allowed your daughter to fall and get up. There are only some areas in the lives of children in which parents have to "rescue" them and those typically concern issues of safety and security.

There is one additional point we wish to highlight. If in fact your daughter feels extreme pain or reacts very adversely to mistakes, if she increasingly avoids certain tasks, it is important to recognize that this may be a sign that her mindset about mistakes is very negative and that she requires additional help learning to cope with stress and adversity. Biologically, some children are overwhelmed with even minor mistakes. However, as you adjust your expectations, even these children can be helped to feel less vulnerable and more willing to view mistakes as challenges from which to learn.

To help you feel more at ease about not overprotecting your child, reflect upon times she made mistakes and you did not rush in. What were her reactions? Was she overwhelmed or did she eventually handle the situation okay? Also, during the next couple of weeks, observe what happens if your daughter knows that you are there to help but that you do not intrude. Observe your reaction if she makes a mistake. The more you can encourage her to attempt new and difficult activities and the more you can respond positively when she does make a mistake with a statement such as, "That's okay, let's figure out what we can do differently next time," the less fearful and pained she will be.

Question

My thirteen-year-old son has always been rather quiet and shy. He had diffi-culty separating from either his father or me when he had to begin attending school. He has few friends, rarely participates in class but has always been well behaved and a good student. As a young child he had an excessive number of fears. Many of the activities children enjoy he has avoided, explaining that he just doesn't like them. We think many of these things make him nervous. He also tends to worry at times about things we don't feel he should be worried about, such as our family's financial status or even if we have enough gas in the car. We are not even certain how he even responds to mistakes since he avoids almost any situation in which he perceives he might not be successful. He has limited himself in social activities and extracurricular activities at school. We feel he is missing out on a lot of opportunities. Why does he do this? Does this represent a fear of mistakes, and what can we do?

Answer

Your description suggests that your son experiences an excessive degree of anxiety or worry in comparison to other children. Problems with anxiety are the most prevalent form of difficulty in adults and they appear more fre-quently in children in comparison with other psychiatric problems. Diffi-culty with anxiety can take many forms but the characteristic features are tension, worry, fear, and apprehension. Some children seem to be anxious from birth, appearing rather shy, quiet, and withdrawn and, as you note, avoiding any situation in which they might fail. Unfortunately, when chil-dren demonstrate early problems separating from parents to attend school they are more vulnerable to lifetime problems associated with anxiety.

Separation anxiety is the most common of the anxiety conditions. The essential feature of this condition is anxiety about being separated from per-sons to whom the child is most closely attached, usually parents. Many children with separation anxiety also experience other fears and worries.

Even as they become accustomed to separating from family members, they continue to demonstrate other problems with worry. This appears to be the case for your son. Given the extent and longevity of your son's difficulties we suggest you seek professional help. Your child may be struggling with what is called a generalized anxiety disorder. Children with this condition can best be described as worrywarts. They worry about present and future events. They often harbor guilt about real or imagined shortcomings. They tend to be self-conscious perfectionists, avoiding many activities because, as you point out, they fear mistakes. Sometimes these children experience physical symptoms such as a stomachache or headache. Other times not.

Based on your observations of your son, he appears to be burdened by an additional problem that has become much better known in the last ten years to professionals—social anxiety or social phobia. Children with this problem appear uncomfortable or nervous in social situations. They often hold back, limiting their social activities as a means of avoiding feeling uncomfortable. Unlike some children who perceive mistakes as bad things and indicative of how inadequate they are, children with anxiety disorders avoid situations in which they perceive they could feel ill at ease. Thus, their problem is not so much a fear of mistakes but an effort to avoid the uncomfortable feeling when perceived difficult tasks are encountered.

We know that from our description of these different forms of anxiety, any parent might become discouraged with his or her child's prognosis. The good news is that anxiety problems in children and adults are the most effectively treated of all psychiatric conditions. You might be surprised to know that the best treatment for this problem is not medication but a course of counseling known as cognitive behavioral therapy. Through this form of counseling, children learn to identify anxiety or situations that provoke anxiety, to develop counter-thoughts to manage their feelings, and eventually to confront and overcome challenging activities.

There is one other point we want to emphasize. Although you didn't mention it in your question, we know some loving parents who become so frustrated (and helpless) with their child's worries that they may say things that make the child feel worse although on the surface the parents want to be helpful. What are these comments? A sample include: "Be a big girl (boy), there's nothing to worry about." "No one likes you because you don't make an effort to say hello to them." "If you keep quitting at things, you'll never be happy." "I can't understand why you're so afraid of everything. There's nothing to be afraid of." "You should try harder." One child told us, "I worry about so many things and then when my parents get angry with me about my worries, I worry even more that they're angry with me and that I've disappointed them."

What anxious children need to hear are empathic statements recognizing their distress and offering realistic hope. As an example, parents might say, "I know that there are a lot of things you worry about and I know that's not easy for you. I know how much you would like to stop worrying so much. There are people who can help with the problem and we will get whatever help is possible." Such a comment, accompanied with a hug, can be very helpful to a child.

Question
Our twelve-year-old daughter really frustrates my wife and me. We don't think we are perfectionistic parents or expect too much from her, but she constantly quits at things when she doesn't succeed immediately. For example, she took violin lessons for two months and said it was too hard to learn so she quit. While she hasn't quit her soccer team, since she worries about what the other kids might say, she really doesn't play with much enthusiasm and has already told us she doesn't want to play again next year. We are worried our daughter can't handle dealing with not being perfect. What can we say to her?

Answer
Years ago it was not unusual for mental health professionals to blame parents if a child was a perfectionist. The first thought was, "Those parents must have placed a great deal of pressure on that child to be perfect." While the style of parents may contribute to a child being perfectionistic, we now know that biologically some children from birth have stronger perfectionistic tendencies than others. One mother told us that when her son was eighteen months old he would build a tower out of blocks. If the blocks didn't line up perfectly, he would knock the tower over and yell, "Bad blocks." This mother said, "He was only eighteen months old and already seemed pressured to have things perfect. He's now nine years old and he still gets upset

when things aren't perfect. If he makes one mistake on a test, it's like the end of the world. And just like he used to blame the blocks by saying 'bad blocks,' now he blames the teacher."

While a child's biological predisposition plays a role in perfectionism, we must be careful not to say or do things that reinforce the belief in our children that perfect is the only acceptable level of performance. It is crucial that we avoid setting the bar too high, or say negative comments when our children make mistakes, or utter demeaning remarks about our children's capabilities (e.g., "Do you ever use your brains?" "Are you that dumb?"). These negative experiences could easily lead a child to believe that being perfect is the only acceptable level of performance.

In terms of your daughter, assuming that undue pressure has not been placed on her to perform, it is reasonable to conclude that she possesses strong inborn needs for perfectionism. You didn't mention how she is doing in school. Often children with good school skills, combined with perfectionism, perform quite well until the demands of school increase in high school and college. Then very few can perform perfectly. In those situations, many of these children struggle, often feeling inadequate despite a history of excellent performance.

In a sense, perfectionistic children need to be desensitized. Desensitization is a term used when individuals, through repeated exposure to a fear or anxiety-provoking event, become more comfortable in facing and dealing with that event. Sometimes parents might be able to do this on their own, but, in our experience, the input of a professional who can counsel both the parents and child is often indicated. The process usually begins by helping children explore their feelings about needing to be perfect and over time confronting and completing tasks over which they may not be able to perform perfectly. In examining the need for children to be perfect, a counselor might ask such questions as: "What happens if you make a mistake?" "How do you feel when things don't go perfectly?" "Have you ever made a mistake and then things turned out okay?" (This last question helps to assess those occasions when perfectionism was not as prominent.) Counselors can encourage children who are perfectionists to take some realistic risks and have them consider the possible consequences. Many children discover that their fears of not being perfect are exaggerated.

For example, we remember a thirteen-year-old boy we saw in therapy who would stay up late into the night to complete all his work and study until he was exhausted. He was able to verbalize that he believed if he did not attain a straight A average, his parents would be disappointed and that he might not get into a good college. In family therapy sessions, his parents reassured him that they did not expect straight As, and that there would be many good colleges to choose from even if he did not have straight As. The parents examined some of their comments that might have reinforced his perfectionism. It might seem ironic to note since we work with many families who come to see us because their children are obtaining poor grades, but an indication of our success in therapy with this boy was when he received a B on his report card and he could joke about not being perfect.

Specifically in addressing your daughter's problems, you might discuss with her in an empathic way the pressure she is placing on herself. Perhaps this will allow her to talk about the worries and concerns she has related to making mistakes. Given how this problem appears to be affecting many areas of your daughter's life, we think it would be helpful to seek a consultation from a mental health professional.

Question

We have two sons, eleven and fourteen years old. Our younger son seems to place a lot of pressure on himself and then becomes frustrated and angry if he doesn't meet his goals. However, we think part of the problem is that the goals he sets are too high. When our older son was eleven he was the top scorer in his youth basketball league. Our younger son is a solid player but is not the top scorer at eleven years old. We notice he blames his teammates for not getting him the ball enough or the refs for not calling the opposing team when he feels he has been fouled. We constantly hear excuses. I guess we have two questions: How do you help children become more realistic about their strengths and weaknesses, and how do you help them handle mistakes?

Answer

Without wishing to sound too technical, your younger child appears to possess what we refer to as an external locus of control. That is, he perceives the events in his life as being controlled by forces outside of himself. When children possess this view, they even have difficulty taking ownership for their successes, frequently attributing their accomplishments to luck or chance. While some children may not verbalize this belief, they do hold it.

Children with an external locus blame others when they fail. As we have noted in earlier answers, typically this occurs because they attribute mistakes to things they cannot alter. Since they believe they are unable to correct their errors, they cope by casting blame elsewhere. As you point out, they are quick to make excuses and find it difficult to accept any responsibility for the events in their lives. This is an extremely important life issue. We can all think of adults whom we choose not to interact with because they rarely if ever accept responsibility for their actions or behavior.

There are a number of steps in which you can engage to help your son develop a more resilient mindset in relation to mistakes. Although it is a slow process to help children modify their perception of mistakes, it is an important one to undertake. Your goal will be to assist your son to recognize that although he can't control every event in his life, he plays some role in the outcome of many events. We would like to review four basic principles that you can follow.

> Although it is a slow process to help children modify their perception of mistakes, it is an important one to undertake.

First, you should serve as a model for dealing with mistakes and setbacks. It may take dozens and dozens of times but if your son hears you dealing with mistakes in a reasonable, responsible way, there is the likelihood that eventually this pattern will be modeled. In our clinical practices, we have been impressed with how closely children observe what their parents say and do when confronted with mistakes.

Second, make certain your expectations are realistic, an area we discussed earlier in this book. When expectations are too high, our children will experience many failure situations that contribute to their feeling that they are not very competent.

Third, it is important to emphasize that mistakes are not only accepted but also expected. As parents, we can do this in a variety of ways. When there is a problem in the family, you can have family members consider alternative solutions and when a solution is arrived at, you can state, "In case it doesn't work, what's our back-up solution?" This question conveys that not all solutions will be successful but when they are not, there are alternatives to fall back upon. In creating this kind of atmosphere in your household it may be easier to say to your son when he blames others, "I know you think your teammates are not getting you the ball or the ref is not doing a good job, but perhaps there are things that you can do differently." Thus, you are first validating your son's perception (remember, validation does not mean you agree with your son's view) and then encouraging him to entertain a more responsible view.

Finally, since your son appears to be comparing himself to his brother, it is important for you to take steps to lessen this behavior. Be aware of whether subtly or not-so-subtly you might be expressing thoughts that reinforce these comparisons. Sometimes as parents we are not even aware when we are doing so. We knew one family that affectionately referred to one brother as "the brain," another brother as "the athlete," and a third brother as "Mr. Personality." While they used these labels in what they considered a loving way, their sons perceived it as casting them into molds. To offset feelings of comparison, make certain that you identify and acknowledge your younger son's islands of competence, especially when these islands are different from the areas of strength of your older son.

Question
I have three children, ages nine, fourteen, and sixteen years old. I think I communicate the message that I love them even when they make mistakes or don't do as well on tests or in other activities. I am always encouraging and often show my faith in them by telling them if they put in a little more effort they could do better. Yet everything I do lately seems to backfire. My eldest daughter really zinged it to me the other night when she said, "Dad, you put so much pressure on me." How can a parent convey support and have expectations without kids thinking we put too much pressure on them to not make mistakes?

Answer
We suspect the problem here is not one of intention but of difference in how the message is perceived. You perceive your comments as supportive, encouraging, and helpful. From your description, your children perceive

your comments as critical, judgmental, and focusing on the negative. While some parents, out of frustration, may "blame" their children for misperceiving the situation, it is at times like these that parents must especially exercise empathy and attempt to see the world through the eyes of their children. As we often suggest to parents, think of what your goals are when you say things to your children and ask yourself, "Am I saying things in a way in which my children will be most responsive to listening to me?" Your goal is to encourage their accomplishments but apparently something is getting lost in the translation.

In interviewing many children and adults, we have discovered that comments such as "you could do better by putting in more effort," while intended as encouragement are typically experienced as judgmental and accusatory. One young man said, "How do they know I'm not trying? Is there a test for trying?" If our remarks are perceived as judgmental, it often triggers anger in our children and they begin to believe that we are always putting undue pressure on them. When we have discussed this issue with parents, we are often asked, "How can we encourage our kids without it seeming like we are being critical and putting too much pressure on them?"

We believe there are several ways of doing this. As we have noted, avoid saying things that may quickly be interpreted as negative. If your children have done a good job, start with a positive comment. If there is room for improvement, you can let them know but only after you have given some positive feedback. Some children have told us that their parents just focus on the negative. When you discuss areas of improvement, avoid words that can be interpreted as judgmental. For example, if your child is struggling with a task and constantly making mistakes, you might say, "That doesn't look too easy, if you need any help I'm here. Maybe together we can figure it out." Or, "I see how much you want to succeed but I think the approach you're using may not be the most effective one." Housed in these remarks are the messages, "We have faith in you, we are available to help, we believe there are different approaches that can be more effective, we feel we can all learn from the mistakes we make." Absent is the implication that our child is not trying or not putting in enough effort.

Relatedly, many well-meaning parents fall into the trap of saying they accept their children for who they are and then add a "but" or an "as long as" that implies some condition for the acceptance such as "I love you as long as I feel you are trying to get good grades" or "I love you as long as you do what I say." What we must realize is that children recognize when they have made mistakes and if provided with encouragement and support, are capable of dealing with those mistakes effectively. Most know when they have underperformed. Pointing it out to them is often experienced as placing salt in the wound, especially if the implication is that the mistake was based on their lack of effort. We suggest you seek words of encouragement. Start with what has gone right. Ask them about their perceptions of their performance, what they might do differently next time. If they report they are satisfied with their performance, even if you are not, it is important for you to allow them to work this through. Simply telling them that they should set the bar higher only conveys to them that you are dissatisfied with the achievements they have made thus far. In our experience, when parents are more low-keyed and less intrusive, children are more willing to examine the ways in which they might improve.

One final recommendation. When your older daughter said that you place too much pressure on her, you might thank her for letting you know this since you do not want to continue to do so. Ask her what it is that you are saying or doing that comes across as too much pressure and engage her in a dialogue of how you might say things that would not feel that way. We continue to be impressed with the ability of our children to provide us with guideposts of how to speak with them. The more we can learn how to communicate in a nonaccusatory way, the more likely our children will develop a resilient mindset.

> The more we can learn how to communicate in a nonaccusatory way, the more likely our children will develop a resilient mindset.

Question
We have four daughters. In looking at their behavior it is hard to imagine that they are growing up in the same household. Two of our kids have always seemed more even-tempered and have handled mistakes in a relaxed but effective way. They just go back to the drawing board, look at what they have done, and try to do something different the next time. The other two are exactly opposite. They

become so upset with mistakes and either say they are stupid or the test is stupid or they blame the adults for the way they are being taught. One of our daughters who plays soccer actually blamed the ball saying it was "an inferior ball" and was not hard enough. If her comment weren't so sad it would have been comical. Why are kids growing up in the same home so different? What can we do as parents?

Answer

As we have pointed out, children coming from the same parents still enter the world with their own unique makeup. From birth children have different temperaments that will influence the ways in which they respond to mistakes. We are not suggesting that parents can't impact this makeup but rather that this makeup influences how parents respond to their children and how their children perceive the world. Thus, it is often the rule rather than the exception that children growing up in the same household demonstrate very different patterns of temperament and responses to stress or mistakes. Some children are born with a predisposition to react more strongly and negatively to mistakes than others. Therefore, they are more likely to experience frustration and engage in self-defeating, coping strategies.

Keep in mind that children will draw their own interpretations and conclusions about what they have experienced. These may be very different from our perceptions. What can you do when this occurs? First, it is important for you to understand how each of your daughters reacts to the stress of mistakes since your response to each will be based on this understanding. Obviously, your daughter who blames "an inferior ball" on her performance is giving what seems to be a clear message, "I can't accept responsibility for my performance, it's the ball's fault." What she is also communicating is the belief that she may not be able to change and thus, has to blame an external object.

In such a situation, it is usually helpful to validate what your daughter is saying (let us emphasize once again that validation doesn't mean agreement) and then suggest a different approach. Thus, you might comment, "I know it seems like the ball is not as good as some others but maybe there are still things you can do even with that ball to help you with your soccer game." If your daughter's feelings about the inferior ball are very entrenched you might say, "Perhaps we can try another ball but it might be that it's still important to learn to play with any ball since we never know what ball will be used in a game."

A second important point, which we have emphasized throughout this book, is to start with the positive. Make a list of those situations for all four of your daughters in which they have persevered and not responded negatively to mistakes. Try to figure out what factors may be contributing to their more optimistic view toward mistakes. This is especially important to do for your two daughters who have difficulty with mistakes. We suggest you begin with these experiences, helping your daughters recognize that there are times when they face challenges without giving up.

And third, observe your comments, not only when your daughters make mistakes but when they offer excuses for these mistakes. Are your expectations in line with each of your daughter's capabilities? If they blame others, do you get angry with them (a natural reaction) and say something that is experienced as negative or do you validate what they are saying so that they will be more receptive to hearing some possible solutions?

As parents we must keep in mind that our children are born with different perceptions about mistakes. While we did not cause these perceptions, we have a responsibility for discovering the most effective ways of helping to change those views that keep our children from learning that mistakes are truly experiences from which to learn.

Question

There is something about our twelve-year-old daughter that is driving us crazy and, to be honest, leads us to be very annoyed with her. When she does something wrong and we try and speak with her about what she can do differently the next time she yells that we only notice the things she does wrong and we don't love her. Yet when we compliment her she tells us we really don't mean it, that we are only saying it to make her feel better. At this point I don't feel like saying anything to her, which I know is not the best approach but I am stymied. I don't understand why a child would act this way or what to do about it.

Answer

Your question is one that we hear from many parents. Your daughter's response seems right out of the book that describes attribution theory, namely, (a) that she attributes mistakes to things that cannot change so that your comments are perceived as criticism and (b) that she cannot accept ownership for her successes. When children hold these beliefs, it can be very frustrating to parents since we all want our children to accept their accomplishments and to recognize that mistakes and failure provide the basis for new learning and more effective approaches.

As we have emphasized throughout this chapter, while our children's beliefs about mistakes are in part rooted in their inborn temperament, as parents we must examine the things we say and do that might contribute to these beliefs. Thus, when you attempt to speak with your daughter about what she can do differently next time, it is evident that she immediately interprets your statement in a very negative way, seeing it as a confirmation that you don't love her and that all you do is focus on what she does wrong. Given the temperament of your daughter, it appears that she is poised to feel criticized since this is what fits in with her self-image.

One approach to lessen the possibility of your daughter feeling criticized is to say to her that you have something to tell her. You can then add, "If what I say makes you feel I don't love you, let me know immediately. I want you to know that I do love you, but if you feel unloved it will be difficult for you to hear what I have to say or to feel that I am trying to be of help." By introducing this comment, you are anticipating what her response will be. While some might argue that this strategy represents a self-fulfilling prophecy for failure, we have found that if it is said in a caring way, it actually lessens a knee-jerk response on the part of children and is experienced as empathic.

A second obvious suggestion to help offset your daughter's negative image is to provide her with many positive comments. However, at this point she is quick to dismiss such comments, questioning whether you truly mean what you say. You can use a strategy similar to the one mentioned earlier, namely, communicate how she might feel before she expresses that feeling. Thus, you can say to your daughter that you have something you want to tell her but that you are concerned she might not believe you. You can emphasize that what you are about to say is true and you hope that she realizes it is.

We know that these interventions will take time to work, especially if your daughter's negative perceptions are well established. However, the more you can reflect upon your own feelings and reactions and the more you can anticipate your daughter's responses, the better able you will be to create an environment in which she will come to realize that mistakes are not the end of the world and that she has strengths.

Question

My child has struggled in school to develop the self-control skills necessary to complete his work at a level consistent with his ability. His teacher uses a behavior management system. He brings home a daily note that earns him rewards. Over time my child has responded to this program with increasing negativity. When I commented that this behavior management program was designed to help him, he answered, "You don't understand, Mom, they don't like who I am. They are trying to fix me." How can I respond? How can I help my child deal with the situation more successfully?

Answer

Even in the best of circumstances, some children perceive that our well-intentioned efforts to help are based upon our dislike of certain aspects of their abilities, behavior, and persona. In these circumstances, children view whatever punishments or rewards that are offered as efforts to fix something broken rather than as processes to help them be successful. In many ways your son is correct. Most educational plans are written for children struggling to learn, behave, or socialize. They tend to focus on what is wrong with the child and pay little attention to listing and building on strengths.

We believe that the problem may not be housed in the reinforcement program but rather in whatever comments have been made to your child as well as his thoughts and feelings about this program. We couldn't tell from your question if your son was an active participant in creating the program. We believe that when a program is developed, a child should be involved. We should discuss with children both their strengths and weaknesses. We should ensure that children understand the nature of their difficulties and how an intervention program will address these problems. We should also build in opportunities for children to give us feedback about how they think things are going and for us to provide them with input. Developing this kind of partnership with children fosters a sense of ownership and control and reinforces problem-solving skills, all components of a resilient mindset.

Not knowing to what extent your son was involved in the implementation of the behavior management program, at this point we suggest you begin by speaking with your child's teacher. Has there been some change in the program at school? Has there been an occasion when a comment was made about the program by the teacher or other students that was responded to negatively by your child? We believe it is also important for you to take a broader perspective, or helicopter view. Has this behavior management program been effective? Is your child doing better in the last couple of weeks than before the program was initiated? It will be important for you to help your child focus on this positive change. We also believe strongly that the ultimate goal of these types of behavior management programs is their removal with the positive behavior change remaining intact. By focusing on gradually reducing the program as your son succeeds, he should be able to recognize the importance of the program; he should also begin to take responsibility for his behavior and develop the internal locus we have spoken about in regard to the positive changes in his behavior and school performance.

There is one final, important point we wish to reinforce that is tied to your son's statement that they are trying to "fix" him. As we noted, too many educational plans neglect to list a child's strengths or specify how these strengths will be used and displayed in school. We believe that your son's program should include a description of his islands of competence and how these might be called upon in the school setting. For example, one child with whom we worked had difficulty with self-control but loved to help out (the wish to help is true of almost all children). He especially liked the custodian. As part of his educational plan he came in each morning and helped the custodian with specified tasks, tasks that served as a good transition into school and provided him with a feeling of accomplishment. This sense of accomplishment soon generalized to his academic work.

Question

At your workshop you mentioned that kids who are resilient believe that mistakes are experiences to learn from and not feel defeated by. You said that they believe that there are adults who can help them—parents, teachers, and coaches. But our nine-year-old son seems to ask for help all of the time. When we say he should first try things on his own, he says he can't do it and needs our help. When a child asks for help all of the time, can that be a sign of low self-esteem and a lack of confidence rather than resilience?

Answer

If a child too quickly requests help it is often an indication of low self-esteem and uncertainty rather than a sign of resilience. When resilient children ask for help they possess a realistic picture of their capabilities and they accept assistance with the belief that it will help them to be more successful in the future. Also, they typically seek help only after they have been unsuccessful at a task several times. In contrast, as you describe your son, his confidence is so shaky that he seeks help without first discovering what he is capable of doing. Often such children fear making mistakes and looking foolish and, thus, will not risk the possibility of this occurring. Instead, they would rather rely on others. While they gain temporary relief if an adult helps them to solve the problem at hand, the relief is short-lived since it does not fortify their confidence and provide them with the courage to attempt new challenges on their own.

> When resilient children ask for help they possess a realistic picture of their capabilities and they accept assistance with the belief that it will help them to be more successful in the future.

In attempting to help your son, notice if there are times he does not immediately ask for your assistance. You might even wish to create a list of situations in which your child acts independently. How do these situations differ from those in which he is hesitant to proceed? When he asks for help too quickly, you might let him know that you are there to assist him but that you would like him to see what he can do on his own. To facilitate this process, you can help him get started, provide him with some hints on how to proceed but then back off. If he seems to resist this, you should be empathic and let him know that some things are not easy to accomplish at first but then point out those situations in which he showed more success on his own. By focusing on the positive, namely, those situations in which your child has demonstrated increasing self-reliance and confidence, you can reinforce the notion that he has shown the capability to work more independently. The reinforcement of this belief is often a long-term process with constant parental encouragement and support. Recognize that it may take a number of years for your son to feel comfortable facing everyday challenges independently.

As you are involved with assisting your son to become less dependent on you, it is important to understand his mindset. Does he feel helpless because he fears making mistakes? Does he perceive that you expect too much from him? We suspect from your question that neither one of these is the problem, but rather his temperament makes it difficult for him to build a reservoir of positive feelings as he faces new challenges. If that is the case, then the more you can place the spotlight on his strengths, the more you can provide him with opportunities to shine, and the more you can provide realistic input, the better equipped he will be to assume responsibilities.

Question

I am feeling upset about something my seven-year-old son told me. He said that his teacher doesn't like it when children make mistakes. He said that she tells kids who make mistakes that they are not careful enough. He actually said that his teacher was nicer to kids who had higher scores on tests. He has some learning problems, and I can see that he is becoming discouraged at school. I really felt bad when he said that he thought his teacher didn't like him because of his poor school performance. I know I have to do something but I am not sure what to do. I don't want to alienate the teacher but I feel she should know how she is coming across. Any suggestions?

Answer

Unfortunately for some children school is an environment that exposes their weaknesses to their peer group. Rather than being a place that fosters self-confidence and the belief that one is intelligent, these children perceive they are inadequate and unworthy. Since self-worth and resilience are linked to a child's response to mistakes and failure, it is important for teachers to find ways to convey the message that mistakes are part of the learning process. They must help students appreciate that mistakes are not the problem. The problem is the fear of mistakes and feeling humiliated.

It is for this reason that we recommend at our workshops that during the first day of school teachers address the fear of making mistakes. We believe the best way to deal with such a fear is to bring it out in the open. Thus, teachers can ask the class, "Who in this class thinks that during this year they are going to make a mistake or not understand something the first time?" Before any student can respond, the teacher can raise his or her own hand and engage the class in a discussion about the fear of making mistakes. We know teachers who have used this exercise in a problem-solving way, raising such questions as: "How can I call on you without your being anxious?" "How should I respond if you don't know an answer?" "How can we make certain that no one puts down another student for giving a wrong answer?" Teachers have told us that this kind of exercise greatly reduces fear and anxiety in the classroom and communicates the message that mistakes are a vital part of the learning process.

We suggest you talk with your son about the importance of your speaking with his teacher about this problem. Although your son may be anxious about your talking with her, you can explain why it is important for you to do so. Then begin a dialogue with his teacher. Rather than suggesting that she is doing something wrong, we suggest you simply convey to the teacher your child's perception that he believes he may not be well-liked or viewed equally in her eyes because he struggles academically. In our experience many teachers are not aware of how students might perceive them. If the teacher says that your son's perceptions are incorrect, you can say that we still need to help him feel differently. Then together with the teacher you can contemplate ways of easing your son's insecurity in the classroom. As we have noted in previous answers, we have found that one of the best antidotes for this problem is when teachers find an activity at which the child can succeed and that will bolster self-confidence and academic self-esteem. We must focus on locating and displaying an island of competence for every student in the classroom.

Question

Our son is a quitter. He blames everyone for his mistakes. He asked us to buy him a model airplane, which we did. He insisted on doing it by himself, which is what he typically does. The wings didn't fit together well and there was glue all over the place. We told him that he is not careful enough and he should have let us help him. He said the glue we bought was bad. The next day we found that he had thrown all of the pieces in the wastepaper basket. I got so angry that

I said something I shouldn't have. I yelled at him that all he does is quit. He stormed out of the room. I wish I knew what to say. I wish I could help him learn to not quit.

Answer

We can understand your frustration. Your description indicates that your son truly struggles with what it means to make a mistake. Interestingly, the way some youngsters cope with this problem is to want to do things by themselves, almost as a way of proving that they are competent and do not need any help. Unfortunately, they often do require assistance as they underestimate the complexity of the task and the end result is that they are unable to succeed. When faced with failure, they become defensive, often blaming others, rather than accepting responsibility for their actions.

One of the challenges you face as a parent is to help your son appreciate that we all make mistakes and that there are people available from whom we can learn so as to overcome these mistakes in the future. If you become too frustrated and convey negative comments, it will add to your son's defensiveness and he will be less receptive to learning from you. As you realize, comments about him not being careful enough or being a quitter work against the development of a resilient mindset since they contain an accusatory tone.

What might help is to begin by reinforcing your son's desire to do things independently, but letting him know you are available to help. You can say, "I'm glad to see how much you want to try things on your own. This may be a complicated task to do so if you need any help, please let me know." This kind of statement communicates that you appreciate the task is difficult and that your son may not be able to succeed on his own but that you are there for support. Such a comment can serve to lessen defensiveness on his part. You can reinforce this message by noting that there are some tasks for which we all need help and then offer examples from your own life. Whether it is repairing household appliances, fixing the car, or visiting the dentist, you can explain that none of us possesses sufficient ability to understand or independently complete many of the complex demands and tasks we face each day.

With this foundation in place, we suggest you keep the lines of communication open. Offer him the opportunity to seek help if he feels he needs it. If a mistake is made, rather than quickly pointing out the mistake, help him problem solve about what he would like to do next. We realize that he may reject your offer at first. It may take many exasperating interactions but eventually your patience, support, and availability will help your son deal more effectively with mistakes and frustration.

Finally, if in fact your child engages in most tasks without sufficient thought or planning, if he appears to act impulsively, and if he has difficulty sustaining attention and effort, part of the problem may be an immaturity in the development of his planning and self-control skills. If this is the case, in addition to your support, skill-building activities such as those offered by Myrna Shure in her book *Raising a Thinking Child* can be quite helpful. In Chapter 10, we will also offer additional suggestions based on Dr. Shure's work.

9

Responsibility, Compassion, and a Social Conscience

Giving of One's Self

Question
I don't want to sound too old-fashioned but I remember as a child having responsibilities around the house and doing what I was expected to do by my parents. Yet it seems today we are raising some pretty selfish kids. Our fifteen-year-old daughter seems to be that way. She will spend two hours on the phone helping a friend with some problem but not help out at home. The other night all we asked her to do was empty the dishwasher. Her friend called and they spoke for a while. Finally, we had to remind her to empty the dishwasher. She said to me that I always nag her. I got angry and said we nagged because she was irresponsible. She responded that all she was doing was helping her friend who has boyfriend problems. I asked why she couldn't be helpful to us, that we were the ones who raised her. How can I communicate with her and help her to be responsible?

Answer
Many parents fall into the trap of equating a child doing chores with being responsible. While completing one's chores is a sign of meeting responsibilities, it should never be used as the sole criterion of whether a child is responsible. As a matter of fact, although it may seem a little strange to say, from your description your daughter is demonstrating responsibility but not in the area of household chores. You mentioned that your daughter can spend hours on the phone helping a friend while neglecting to empty the

dishwasher. While we do not want to minimize that there are responsibilities such as emptying a dishwasher or taking out the trash or cleaning one's room that help family life to go more smoothly, parents should not lose sight of the many positive things a child is doing. Assisting a friend is an expression of responsibility that touches upon such important values as compassion and caring and may be more important than cleaning dishes.

We think it is unfortunate that many parents refer to the first responsibilities they expect their children to meet as chores. Often, despite the fact that their children are responsible members of the school and general community, parents may interpret a lack of follow through with household chores as a sign the child is irresponsible. While we are not against chores, we are aware of no research that indicates that children who complete chores at home turn out to be more caring, responsible adults than those who do not. We are often amused by the amount of time parents spend reminding their children to make the bed neatly or hang the towel back on the towel rack rather than on the door. While doing all of these things may be "socially correct," we have not found that it is predictive of anything important in terms of a child's development.

It is for this reason that we advocate that parents take a "helicopter view" of what their children are doing. A helicopter view will allow you to take a moment and think about your daughter and her behavior within the big picture. When we become preoccupied with the day-to-day responsibilities we expect from our children such as chores, we often lose sight of the many areas in which they are responsible. Rather than quickly labeling your daughter as irresponsible, we suggest you change the script and begin by complimenting her for her concern for, allegiance to, and support of her friend. Once you have acknowledged this, we believe it will be easier to discuss the help that you need from her in terms of family responsibilities. You can explain that you don't want her to ignore her friend but that you would like her to think about some way to balance and meet all responsibilities, including those at home.

> When we become preoccupied with the day-to-day responsibilities we expect from our children such as chores, we often lose sight of the many areas in which they are responsible.

This kind of comment can prompt a discussion of what are the most important responsibilities and what responsibilities may be secondary. For instance, we worked with one family in which the mother insisted that her three children make their beds every morning. This appeared to be the one activity that was regularly neglected. When the parents engaged in a discussion with their children about the issue of household responsibilities, this mother was able to change her script and remove making one's bed from the list of expectations. While this approach may not work with all families, this mother's flexibility led to the three children following through on their other responsibilities and, as you might guess, the household did not deteriorate because the beds were not made. If anything, the mood in the house improved.

In essence, by acknowledging and complimenting the positive activities in which your daughter is involved, she will probably be more receptive to listening to your concerns and actively considering ways in which she can follow through on certain expectations. Her problem-solving skills and sense of ownership will be reinforced.

Question

I think this is more my problem than my three children's. I find that I focus on what are minor problems, such as their forgetting to put the toothpaste cap back on or not completely making their beds. Yet, I sometimes wonder are they minor? If kids don't meet their responsibilities, even for minor things, can they develop a sense of responsibility? It seems that too many kids expect things to be handed to them on a silver platter. I want to avoid my kids developing that idea.

Answer

Your question relates to the first question in this chapter, and it is a question we hear from many parents. There is a popular saying, "Don't sweat the small stuff." It is easy to assume children are irresponsible if for five consecutive days you have to remind them to cover the toothpaste or to hang up their jackets and they fail to do so. It is easy to jump to conclusions that you are raising irresponsible children. We found that when parents focus on what their children are not doing, they often fail to notice the many responsibilities their children are meeting. From your question, we can't tell whether they meet their major responsibilities. If they do, perhaps you are correct in saying that this is more your problem than theirs in the sense that you are making assumptions about what being responsible entails. If, however, they are not meeting most of their responsibilities, then this should be discussed with them.

What might help you to determine if your children are responsible or irresponsible is to notice their behaviors for the next few days. List the things that they are doing that suggest they are meeting their responsibilities and those that you believe are indicators of a lack of responsibility. When many parents have done this exercise, they have been pleasantly surprised to discover how responsible their children really are. For example, one mother noted the following responsible acts engaged in by her supposedly "irresponsible" son:

- He helped me take the groceries out of the car without my asking.
- He helped show his younger brother how to play a computer game.
- He remembered to call his grandfather to wish him a happy birthday.
- He offered to run an errand on his new bike (his mother thought that the main motivation was to ride his bike but nevertheless his actions involved helping others).
- He brought homework assignments to a classmate who was ill and had not been in school.
- He completed his own homework assignments.

To some parents these activities may seem like small things. However, we believe they represent examples of a child who is fulfilling responsibilities, many of which involve helping others.

In terms of him not meeting his responsibilities, his mother listed the following behaviors:

- He had to be reminded to make his bed.
- He didn't clear his dishes after dinner.
- He forgot to put his dirty clothes in the hamper.

While we do not wish to minimize the importance of these "irresponsible" behaviors (okay, maybe we are), as you review the two lists, which do you think is more important in terms of a child developing a resilient mindset? Many parents have actually rearranged their priorities when confronted with the two lists, mainly by eliminating some items from the list of irresponsible behaviors. The mother who created the lists just described decided that it was not necessary for her son to make his bed, just that the top cover be smoothed out. As she noted, "Sometimes in our attempts to raise responsible kids, we lose sight of what we want them to learn."

We hope our suggested exercise is helpful to you as you examine your children's behavior.

Question
The other day I realized something quite interesting. I have two children, twelve and fourteen years of age. It is difficult to get them to help out. They don't usually volunteer unless they perceive there is something in it for them. Yet as I think back to when they were very young all they wanted to do was help. I wondered if there was even a gene that promotes helping behavior in young children. When each of my children was three years of age he would eagerly approach me and ask if he could help mow the lawn, make dinner, and even drive the car. Why does it appear children outgrow this pattern? Is there something I can do to help them continue to act responsibly and in a helpful manner toward others?

Answer
We believe you are correct in your observation that young children appear to be strongly motivated to be helpful. It is wonderful to observe the number of children who take great pleasure in helping parents and love to be complimented and appreciated. While we are not aware of an "altruistic gene," it is almost as if children come into this world with a need to be helpful and valued. Similar to yourself we wonder if our culture fails to reinforce this need as fully as it should, eventually resulting in children who focus increasingly on themselves and less and less on those around them. We also believe that while children can be very self-centered at times, placing their own needs first, most children achieve a genuine sense of joy and accomplishment in reaching out and being helpful.

We should note that one of the most positive memories of childhood we have heard in our clinical practices and workshops relate to times we were provided with opportunities to assist others. Fulfilling these opportunities is one of the most effective ways of nurturing responsibility and resilience. It communicates to children our belief that they can truly make a difference in the world. It also reinforces responsibility, teaches compassion, and helps to develop a social conscience.

There are many things that parents can do to nurture this helping attitude. Using such phrases as, "I need your help" rather than "Remember to do your chores" highlights the important contribution children can make. While our children may not respond by saying, "I am so happy to be helpful," we believe it does bring them satisfaction. Involving children in charitable activities such as taking them with you to a soup kitchen, having them help you deliver meals to the elderly, or going for a walk for your favorite charity are all wonderful ways of teaching your children the value of giving to others and being responsible. We have found that children gain a great deal from these experiences. This sense of responsibility will also reinforce their willingness to accept ownership for their behavior, another important feature of a resilient mindset.

Let's take this seemingly inborn need to help and keep it alive and well throughout life.

Question

At one of your workshops you mentioned that it is important for kids to be given responsibilities at an early age, but instead of calling responsibilities chores you suggested we tell children "we need your help." It seems like a word game. Does that really make a difference? We have a four-year-old son. What can we ask him to help with?

Answer

At first glance, it might seem like a word game but we know that words are powerful forces that shape our thoughts, feelings, and, ultimately, our behavior. For example, you can view someone's behavior as careful and respond affirmatively or you can view the same behavior as slow and respond negatively. We believe there is an important reason to help children interpret responsible behaviors as acts of helping rather than as impositions similar to forced labor. Most of us respond differently when we are told what we must do versus being asked to help out. For example, a father who also coaches a Little League team wrote to us to after he attended one of our workshops. He said that instead of telling his team to collect the equipment after the game, he first mentioned that he needed their help. He observed that "they were more cooperative than ever before." He said, "It's interesting how a change in a few words can make such a difference."

You might wish to do an experiment. During the next week, notice the difference in your son's response if you ask him to do a "chore" or if you ask him for help. We would guess that he would be more motivated when he perceives that he is assisting you.

We believe there are a number of activities in keeping with his abilities that you can request that he do at home. He can place napkins on the dinner table, put things away, and even help wash the car. Outside the home you can involve him in a charitable activity such as accompanying you to bring food to the elderly.

Question

Our son is ten years old and has learning and social problems. He does not have any friends his own age. Younger kids seem to like him, maybe because he acts more like them than kids his age. He even likes to teach younger kids who are six or seven years old how to do things that he is good at doing, like puzzles. Should we let him play with younger kids? On the one hand he seems caring and responsible with them but the downside is that he is not gaining experience with kids of his own age.

Answer

In our clinical practice we have worked with many children with learning and social problems who are more at ease relating to younger children than to their peer group given their cognitive and communication struggles. Many children with learning disabilities experience language problems. Often the same weaknesses that contribute to achievement problems at school make it difficult for children to develop the skills necessary to socialize with children of their age. They have difficulty knowing what to say and how to respond to others. For example, they might talk incessantly about a topic in which they feel they have some expertise without realizing how others are annoyed by their behavior. They frequently misunderstand nonverbal cues so that they might "invade" another child's space or misunderstand a joke. Their attempts at humor often fall flat.

Many children with learning disabilities experience language problems.

From your description it doesn't appear that your son is mean or aggressive. Rather, he is most likely neglected by children his age because of his developmental delays. You are correct that the downside of playing with younger children is that he is not gaining experience with children his own age. However, the upside of playing with younger children is that given your son's language and social capabilities, this is the group of children that he feels most competent to interact with as he continues to develop his social skills. Also, he seems to handle his relationship with younger kids very well and is gaining self-worth by helping them do puzzles. We have found that it is a great feeling to be an "expert" in some activity. Since the children your son is playing with are just a few years younger then he is and these interactions provide him with important experiences relating with and being accepted by others, we are not concerned about this situation.

However, even as he is strengthening his social skills interacting with younger children, you might look for opportunities for him to gain experience relating with a child his age. Perhaps you know of a peer whom your son likes and who would be willing to accept your son's invitation to come over to your house. We find it is typically best to have only one peer visit at a time since if you have more than one it can lead to your son being the "odd man out." You can engage in what we call "environmental engineering" or behind the scenes work to maximize the probability that their interaction will be successful. For example, you might provide certain games or activities with which your son is comfortable and which will be acceptable to his peer. Thus, while your son is benefiting from his interactions with younger children, he may benefit from carefully selected meetings with a peer of his age.

We should note that at times, this scenario of spending time with younger children doesn't work as effectively. This is especially true as children transition into junior or senior high school. In elementary school a sixth grader can find third or fourth graders to play with during recess. However, a seventh or eighth grader cannot easily find younger children to interact with at school. Consequently, these children often become socially isolated within the school setting. We suggest that if you suspect your son is delayed in developing social skills you consider speaking with the school psychologist about involving him in a social skills development program. Keep in mind our emphasis upon the importance of children developing friendships as a resilience factor and predictor of good social outcome. We should also note that in adulthood our friendships are not limited to people our own age.

Question

I really like your notion of a resilient mindset. I also believe strongly that kids should meet their responsibilities. Some kids will do what they are told but almost seem to resent having to do it. How can we help kids understand and accept their responsibilities in ways that help them to develop a resilient mindset rather than develop resentment?

Answer

Your question is a very important one. As you know, we believe very strongly that for children to develop a resilient mindset they must learn to accept responsibilities, lest they grow up feeling entitled with no sense of the importance of helping others. If children do what they are told but resent doing it, at some point they may simply refuse or "forget" to do these things since they have little, if any, investment in the activity. As parents we must figure out how to teach our children the importance of meeting responsibilities so that these responsibilities are not seen as impositions that have little relevance to their lives. That is why we have emphasized the need to help others as a motivating force.

> As parents we must figure out how to teach our children the importance of meeting responsibilities so that these responsibilities are not seen as impositions that have little relevance to their lives.

There are five key principles to helping children develop responsibility, compassion, and a social conscience. First, it is important for you to serve as a model of responsibility. Our children are astute observers of our own behavior and whether we are enthusiastically practicing what we preach. If they see us gaining pleasure from engaging in acts of kindness and generosity, it is easier for them to feel comfortable about doing so.

Second, as we have emphasized throughout this chapter, make certain you provide opportunities for your children to feel they are helping others. The belief that our actions have impact on others is a powerful incentive to meet one's responsibility so that it is not just seen as "busywork."

Third, we believe it is important to develop traditions and become a charitable family. This is closely tied to the first two principles but one that deserves to be highlighted separately. A charitable family develops a tradition of involving the entire family in helping others. In doing so, parents reinforce in their children the belief that they are important, that they have the capability of helping others, that they are appreciated, and that they can make a difference in the lives of others. Also, when families work together in this way, it fosters closer family relationships.

Fourth, we should acknowledge to our children that not all responsibilities are exciting or fun. Thus, it is important to distribute responsibilities (chores) in a fair and consistent way at home. It might even help to have a list of responsibilities that must be accomplished and to rotate this list each week or month so that each family member experiences each activity (unless a certain activity is not within the ability of the child).

Finally, we advocate taking a helicopter view of your child's life. As we have noted, many parents may focus on one unfulfilled responsibility and jump to the conclusion that their child is irresponsible. Assuming a helicopter perspective often allows us to observe the many ways in which our children are compassionate and helpful and to acknowledge to them our appreciation for all that they are doing.

Question

This may be a question you don't hear too often. We actually think our eleven-year-old daughter is too responsible. She gets very anxious if she hasn't completed a chore, even if we tell her it is okay. She will even ask what else she can do to help. The other day we noticed that when her ten-year-old brother had not cleared the table she did it for him. She always seems to be rushing in to help others. Is this healthy? What can we do to help? We want her to help others but not to assume the burdens of the world on her shoulders.

Answer

While children should learn to meet responsibilities and to help others, even positive behaviors can be taken to an extreme. Ideally, we would want children to assist others not because they feel intense internal pressure to do so but because they comfortably feel it is the right thing to do. From your description we are not certain that your daughter is "too responsible." Rather she seems to become overly anxious if a chore isn't completed. It's not clear why this is so but from our viewpoint she seems to have taken on the role of keeping harmony in the family and ensuring everything is in order.

The fact that a child asks to help is typically a healthy phenomenon. However, when this helping role is rooted in anxiety, when a child seems preoccupied with not meeting each and every responsibility, it is obvious that too much pressure is involved and the joy of helping is eclipsed by feelings of worry.

As we read your question there was no suggestion that you might be placing too much pressure on your daughter, but we feel it is always important for parents to monitor what they say and do with their kids. Some children are very sensitive from birth and misperceive normal parental requests as criticism that they are not meeting their responsibilities.

Although you mentioned that you have told your daughter that it's okay if she hasn't done every chore, we would recommend that you discuss with her your concerns that she may be attempting to do too much. You can clarify what your expectations are and you can also set some limits on her rushing in to cover for her brother. If her anxiety persists to the level it has, it may signal the need for professional help.

Question

When I comment to my son that I appreciate his meeting responsibility as a chore is completed or he follows through on some activity, he usually responds that I am just making a big deal out of little things to try and make him feel good. The truth is I comment on these things because I want him to feel good and repeat these behaviors. Why does he respond this way and what can I say?

Answer

Without wishing to sound too simplistic, we suggest that you answer very honestly and directly. Let your son know that although he feels you are complimenting him just to make him feel good, in fact you are doing so to ensure that he knows you appreciate even the small things that he does. Emphasize that by thanking him for being responsible, you don't necessarily believe you are making a "big deal out of a little thing." You might add that you feel too many parents neglect to let their children know how appreciative they are and that you don't want to be one of those parents.

You might also consider asking him how he would like to be acknowledged when he meets his responsibilities. One father told us with a smile that when he posed this question to his daughter, she responded, "How about some money?" He asked her for her second choice. When she answered she didn't know, he said that he would continue to say "thank you" unless she thought of some alternative. She still has not offered such an alternative but continues to help out.

Question

I know that you like the word responsibility *better than* chores. *However, whatever we call it there are some things that have to be done in the house that are not thrilling. How do we get across to our three kids that they have responsibilities to meet but do it in a fair way? I guess another way of asking the question is, how do we distribute these chores or responsibilities fairly?*

Answer

This is certainly a question we receive from many parents. You are correct when you note that even if we are careful to express to our children that we require their assistance for the household to run smoothly, many jobs fall in the boring and tedious category. We know of very few individuals who enjoy cleaning. Household chores are the kinds of activities about which we all procrastinate, or "forget."

So what can you do to encourage your children to meet their responsibilities in a fair and equitable manner? First we suggest you discuss why certain activities are important and what would happen if they were not completed. Second, it is helpful for you and your family to sit down and make a list of the responsibilities that are necessary within the household. While differences of opinion may arise about what responsibilities are important, these differences can serve as a basis for further discussion during family meetings. Some chores that at one point are deemed important may later be discarded. Once a list of responsibilities has been created, your family can review which items can be done by any member of the family and which require particular skills that only certain family members can meet.

> While differences of opinion may arise about what responsibilities are important, these differences can serve as a basis for further discussion during family meetings.

Third, when a list of responsibilities and responsible parties has been generated and prioritized, your family can then develop a system for how these responsibilities should be delegated and for how long. Some responsibilities are more tedious than others. Many families create a rotating schedule so that chores among family members change every week or every month.

Fourth, recognize that even with the aid of a list and rotating chores, children may forget to meet their responsibilities. Thus, the final step in a family discussion of the distribution of responsibilities is to raise the question of what the family should do if anyone, including parents, forgets to meet a responsibility. Whatever strategy you choose, a guidepost for parents is to involve children in understanding why it is important for everyone in the family to help and how the work can be distributed equitably. It is important for your children to believe that they are being heard in this process. When this occurs they are more likely to develop a sense of responsibility and ownership.

Question

Increasingly schools are requiring students in middle school and high school to complete a certain number of hours of community service. Some schools have actually used community service as a consequence or, perhaps I should say, "punishment" for bad behavior. I know that you believe in students learning to help others but when you force kids to do community service as part of their curriculum or when you use community service as a punishment, does that help to teach them compassion and caring? Does it promote resilience?

Answer

We applaud the direction most schools are taking to include community service as a curriculum component to teach children compassion, responsibility, and a social conscience. We think that it is important for staff in charge of such a program to discuss with students the significance of community service so that it is not simply seen as a course required for graduation. Staff might ask students about previous experiences they have had helping others. If possible, choices of different kinds of community service activities should be offered. Also, students should have an opportunity to discuss their experiences on an ongoing basis with staff and other students.

We know that some schools as well as our courts use community service as a punishment for transgressions. In general, we are wary of community service being used as punishment when school rules or laws are violated; we believe that other consequences should be employed. We are aware of some instances in which a youngster benefited from community service as a punishment, especially when the activity was well supervised and the youngster could truly experience the benefits of helping rather than hurting others. However, we believe it is important for community service activities to be motivated and driven from within rather than directed externally. When community service is used as a punishment, it often loses the power of internal motivation. Thus, when using community service as a consequence, it should be carefully planned and when possible should be tied directly to the violation (e.g., having a youth paint a wall that he has defaced with racial remarks and writing a paper about racism that involves interviewing students from different races).

Question

My husband and I show our ten-year-old son and twelve-year-old daughter respect. We think we model respect and compassion. Yet we notice that they sometimes say pretty mean things about some of their peers. For instance the other day our son called a kid "dummy" and it almost started a fight. We don't know why he said it. He didn't want to talk about it. Why would he be so mean to this other kid? Will he be that way when he grows up? What should we do?

Answer

Even seemingly compassionate children growing up in homes with caring parents may at some point say or do mean things to a peer. While insensitive behavior should not be ignored by parents, we must also be careful not to overreact or assume that this is indicative of our child's future behavior. If most of the time your children are compassionate, don't let an occasional slip cause you to be concerned about their becoming insensitive, inconsiderate adults. We know many caring adults who have sometimes "slipped" and said things that they later regret.

When your children slip, take advantage of a teachable moment. In the example you offered involving your son, you did the right thing by asking him why he called another kid a "dummy." It's important to obtain a child's perception of an event. Since your son didn't want to talk about it, you might say that you hope at some point he can let you know what triggered his comment. You can add that whatever the reason, it's okay to get angry but he has to think about whether calling this other child a "dummy" was helpful, especially since it almost led to a fight. You can encourage him to think about other possible responses.

> If most of the time your children are compassionate, don't let an occasional slip cause you to be concerned about their becoming insensitive, inconsiderate adults.

In addition, you and your husband should continue to serve as models of respect and compassion. Your children will learn a great deal from observing you.

10

Teaching Our Children to Make Decisions and Solve Problems

Question

In your workshop you have really emphasized problem-solving skills as a basic part of being resilient. That certainly makes sense, but it would help me to understand in what ways these skills contribute to being resilient. Can someone who lacks good problem-solving skills still be resilient?

Answer

Let's begin with the last part of your question. The process of resilience, as we have pointed out, is contributed to by many different skills. Thus, it is certainly possible that someone with limited or poor problem-solving abilities can be resilient. However, it has been our experience that problem-solving and decision-making skills are such basic components of a resilient mindset that someone lacking in these skills would have an overwhelming time meeting challenges and overcoming adversity.

> By learning to solve problems competently and confidently, children feel empowered.

It is difficult to imagine a day passing that does not involve children making choices and decisions. By learning to solve problems competently and confidently, children feel empowered. They learn to trust their capabilities when faced with challenges. They come to understand what they can and cannot control. They learn to anticipate possible obstacles to the choices they make and treat setbacks or mistakes as experiences from which to learn.

If children do not possess these skills, they are more likely to act before they think, to make choices and decisions that do not lead to the effective resolution of problems, and to continue to engage in negative scripts and self-defeating behaviors. Very importantly, this failure to solve problems will interfere with the development of a sense of control over their own lives, one of the most important features of a resilient mindset. Problem-solving and decision-making capabilities are an essential ingredient of resilience.

Question

I have a problem with my preschooler. She is three and a half years old. I know you should let kids do some things on their own but she doesn't want help with anything. The other day she was having trouble getting a dress on a doll. I came over to help and she had a tantrum, screaming, "I can do it." This happens constantly. I think it is important to help her and show her the correct way to do things but she won't accept this. Then when she can't do it on her own she becomes frustrated but still doesn't want my help. I am not sure what to do.

Answer

Most preschoolers relish the opportunity to do things on their own. It is their way of becoming more independent and displaying their competencies. Parents typically have to walk a tightrope in deciding how much and when to step in to help their preschooler. If we rush to help too quickly or if we attempt to assist our children in a way that conveys the message, "I don't believe you have the ability to do this on your own," we rob them of experiencing genuine success. On the other hand, if we remain on the sidelines while our children become increasingly frustrated at not being able to accomplish a task, we risk the possibility that they will not only give up but that they will feel we do not care about them. It's a delicate balancing act, especially when our children say that they can do something on their own but discover that they need assistance.

As we walk this tightrope we must keep in mind that with support and encouragement many young children will display impressive problem-solving skills. We must also build in ways for them to accept our input without feeling we are intruding or that we believe they are incapable of managing challenges. Many parents may not fully appreciate the capacity of young children to solve problems. We are not advising that you let your daughter have the final say in all decisions but that when appropriate, you honor her request.

> Many parents may not fully appreciate the capacity of young children to solve problems.

In terms of your daughter, we suggest you leave it to her whether to ask you for help but that you let her know you are available. Thus, when she is putting the dress on her doll, you might say, "It's not always easy to put a dress on the doll, but I'm glad you want to see if you can do it. If you need any help, just let me know and I'll see what I can do." We believe that such a statement will make it easier for her to ask you to help her since it will still permit her to feel in control. Also, if you do help her, be careful not to do more than is necessary. Remember, your goal is to reinforce her problem-solving skills and sense of ownership.

Even if parents follow through on what we are suggesting, some children may be so entrenched in their wish to go solo that they still will not ask for assistance. Unless the situation is one of safety, it is best to leave the decision to request help with your daughter. If you are patient even in the face of frustration, your daughter will be more likely to seek your help. Help offered in this type of exchange is almost always accepted. Be careful, however, not to offer assistance in a critical or judgmental way. Don't remind your daughter that she struggled or that she could have asked for your help earlier and saved herself frustration. Simply compliment her on her efforts and offer the assistance she requests.

Question

I have a ten-year-old son. I am happy to let him make decisions but I have realized something. I am really happy when he makes decisions that I agree with. The other day we went into a bookstore and he wanted a book I thought was very educational. I told him what a good choice that was. Then we went into a store to buy a sweater and I thought the one he liked was a terrible color. I told him that I thought he would look better in another sweater. He responded that I had told him that he could pick the sweater. I let him get it anyway but I was upset. I am sure he knew I was upset. Any suggestions about what I should do if a similar situation comes up in the future?

Answer

Your question raises an important point. Most parents genuinely maintain that they want their children to be independent thinkers, particularly when it comes to important decisions during the teenage years. Yet without realizing it, many parents also adhere to the following view: "I want my children to be independent thinkers as long as their independent ideas agree with my ideas. As a parent I really know what is best."

We advise parents that they should not provide their children with choices with which they do not feel comfortable. While the selection of one color sweater versus another may not seem like a major event, it still represents a choice that has been offered. If you allow your son the opportunity to pick "any sweater" you must be prepared with "any choice" he makes. As logical as this point appears, we have found many parents are uncomfortable with some of the possible choices they offer their children, yet offer them, hoping that those choices won't be taken. In this scenario the results can be quite negative, including children feeling that they have been deceived and that you do not trust them. In turn, they will learn not to trust you.

Many problems will be avoided if we do not have hesitations about the choices we provide. If we do have reservations, we should examine the reasons for our feelings. It may turn out that the reasons are not very important and that we are overreacting. In that case, we must focus on changing our mindset. However, if in reflecting upon our choices we become even more convinced that one of the choices is not in the best interest of our child, we should remove it from the list of possibilities. If our child asks about a choice we don't feel is appropriate we should explain why. Children are more likely to accept certain nonnegotiable items if we also provide them with many items from which to choose.

Question

I really struggle with the parents' role in helping children solve everyday problems. What I mean by everyday problems are those that come up in any kid's life.

Problems like their relationships with other kids, meeting household responsibilities, and studying effectively. How do you know when you should step in and when you should not?

Answer

We wish we could say there is a precise, easy answer to your question. Unfortunately, there is no one formula or proven, golden path to follow in terms of when to step in and help your children and when to encourage them to be active participants in the problem-solving exercise. This is not surprising as every child is different and each faces a variety of situations each and every day. What we can provide you are some general guidelines as to when to step in but these guidelines must be fitted to the child and the situation.

First, we want to emphasize that a foundation for helping youngsters learn to problem solve begins with parents serving as models. As we have noted many times, children are astute observers of our behavior. If they see us engage in effective decision making, they are more likely to do so themselves. In contrast, if as parents we tend to procrastinate or act impulsively, we do not provide our children with the opportunity to learn good problem-solving skills from us. How do you think your children would answer the following two questions?

1. "How do your parents solve problems and make decisions?"
2. "How do they teach and involve you in decision making?"

Not surprisingly, there are some families in which effective problem solving appears to be a natural part of everyday activities, while in other families most decisions are made arbitrarily with little input from children.

Second, it is important for you to provide your children with choices at an early age. Remember, don't offer options with which you are uncomfortable. Even if your children suggest other options, stick to the options you have offered unless their options make sense.

Third, as your children get older, move beyond simple choices to engage them in decision-making skills. If the situation is one that involves safety and health issues, you may have to step in and let your children know that this is a nonnegotiable issue (e.g., staying up very late on a school night);

however, since most situations are not of this nature, you can involve your children in thinking of at least two or three solutions to problems and deciding which one will be best.

It is important for you to model and teach your children a problem-solving sequence, which we describe in greater detail in response to the next question.

Question

I know we should give our children choices but I had quite an experience the other night. I have a seven-year-old daughter with learning problems. She gets into power struggles over almost anything. The morning time is especially difficult because she never seems to be ready for school on time. She can become paralyzed thinking about what to wear. I heard you say that when kids have this kind of problem you should have them choose the evening before what to wear the next day. I wasn't sure how to go about doing this. I gave my daughter the choice of six things to wear but she still couldn't decide. Will she ever learn how to problem solve and make decisions?

Answer

With patience and support even children experiencing difficulty making simple choices can learn to become more confident in their ability to choose. Although we don't know a great deal about your daughter from your question, we would urge you to consider whether your daughter experiences worry or anxiety in the face of other situations besides choices. Has she been excessively fearful? Is she a worrywart, worrying about most things that the rest of us don't worry about? If this is the case, then in addition to helping her learn to solve problems she is going to have to learn to deal with the excess worry or anxiety she experiences in the face of even simple decisions. A program such as described in *Seven Steps to Help Children Worry Less*, by Sam Goldstein, Kristy Hagar, and Robert Brooks, may offer some very helpful assistance.

A problem-solving sequence follows a logical set of steps. The important features of this sequence include:

1. *Articulate the problem and agree that it is a problem.* It is important for problems to be clearly defined and for children to agree with

parents that it is a problem. It will be important for you and your daughter to agree that her difficulty getting ready in the morning poses a problem leading her to be late for school.

2. *Consider two or three possible solutions and the likely outcome of each.* This step requires you to engage in a discourse with your daughter. As much as possible encourage her to generate solutions. Be cautious not to dismiss any suggestion unless it goes against nonnegotiable family rules. In this case you offered your daughter a choice of six things to wear. We believe that providing her with choices is the right approach but six may be too overwhelming. For some children, especially those with learning problems, two choices may be the maximum number they can handle.

3. *Develop a way to remind each other if someone forgets to follow through.* Many children may forget to do something they have agreed upon. When we remind them, they often become defensive (especially since if we're honest, we must admit that our reminders often sound like criticism) and tell us we are nagging them. However, if we ask them how they would like to be reminded should they forget to do something, they are less likely to hear our reminders as nagging since they were the ones who came up with the idea.

4. *What to do if it doesn't work.* We suggest you also set in place a number of back-up strategies if the agreed-upon strategy proves to be unsuccessful. We feel this is a critical step. It helps children understand that not every solution is effective. It further enhances their capacity to deal with challenges and mistakes.

Thus, more specifically with your daughter you can empathize with her and discuss how selecting clothes each morning seems to be a problem. You can engage in a problem-solving dialogue and find out what she feels might help. If she seems stuck, you can say that it is not always easy to think of solutions and then offer a couple for her to consider. One might be for you or her to select two sets of clothes early in the evening. Before she goes to bed she can select one of the two sets to wear the next day and put the other clothing back in the closet or drawer. You can let her know if this doesn't work you can fall back upon a second agreed-upon plan. The goal is for your daughter to become more active in making decisions on her own with limited input on your part.

Question

As a parent, I can't help but be disappointed when my child makes a poor deci-sion, particularly when there are adverse consequences. When I was a child and my parents expressed their disappointment in these situations, it motivated me to try harder and do better. Yet when I express my disappointment to my child, he responds negatively. What am I doing wrong?

Answer

As we have noted throughout this book, every child is different. You recall using your parents' comments about how disappointed they were in some of your decisions as a motivator to change. Yet, when you express similar statements to your son, he becomes negative. Why the difference? There could be several reasons, each of which may be interacting with the others.

One possibility is that your son has a more sensitive temperament than you had growing up so that he is more predisposed to hearing feedback about poor decisions he has made in a negative way. Also, we always ask par-ents to reflect upon the feedback they give their child and how it might be different from the feedback they received. Did your parents offer you more encouragement to make decisions than you do your son? Did they offer more positive comments than you find yourself giving your son (children are more likely to hear even more critical feedback as helpful when parents have given an ample dose of positive feedback)?

> When children quickly experience our comments as negative, we should ask ourselves what can we do differently so that our children will be more likely to hear what we have to say in a positive way.

When children quickly experience our comments as negative, we should ask ourselves what can we do differently so that our children will be more likely to hear what we have to say in a positive way. We must become more aware of times that our children have made good decisions and compliment them. If we engage in the problem-solving sequence we outlined in the pre-vious answer, then there is a structure in place in which to provide feedback that is more neutral and less negative in nature.

Also, if you're comfortable doing so, you might ask your son if he feels you are being too critical and negative. We would guess that he would answer, "Yes." You can then respond that you really don't want to come across in this way and you might ask, "Is there a way we can talk about things that you've done without my seeming to nag?" Don't worry if he says he can't think of any way or if he responds, "Just don't say anything." Whatever he says, you should remain calm and use it as an opportunity to enter into a dialogue with him.

Question
When we were kids, we weren't taught "problem solving" at home or school. Yet I think we did fine in life. Now as parents it seems like we always have to give choices to our kids or let them come to their own decisions. Sometimes I think we are giving our kids too much say. What they are learning is how not to be responsible. Don't you think we may be giving too much control to our kids?

Answer
Although we don't know what it was like in your house when you were growing up, we would hazard a guess that there were actually a number of situations you faced as a child that required you to solve problems and make decisions. We would also guess that your parents, teachers, and coaches were there at times to provide some input. Thus, we're not certain that we agree with your statement that previous generations weren't taught problem solving. We think that it is likely that many families, overtly as well as through everyday living, modeled problem solving for their children.

We believe that given the changes in our society and the complexity of our culture it may be even more important than it was thirty years ago for children at young ages to learn to make good decisions; this is especially true in light of the increased risks they face even sitting at a keyboard on the Internet within their homes.

> Teaching children how to solve problems and providing them with choices are not synonymous with giving them too much control or depriving them of experiences in which they will learn to be more responsible.

Teaching children how to solve problems and providing them with choices are not synonymous with giving them too much control or depriving them of experiences in which they will learn to be more responsible. As parents, we still provide structure and guidance. The choices we offer and the problem-solving process we outlined in an earlier answer are in the service of helping our children to become more competent and more responsible. By giving children choices, by modeling problem-solving behavior, by allowing them to experience success or failure as a consequence of their choices within a framework of support, we nurture and protect them while they are learning to be more responsible, setting in place a key component of the resilient mindset.

Question

Lately I noticed that when my twelve-year-old daughter arrives at a solution that isn't successful she doesn't consider an alternative. If I should make the mistake of approaching her to think about another solution she becomes angry and resistant. She tells me that I can't accept anything she does and I am always trying to boss her around. Is this part of being a young adolescent, or am I doing something wrong?

Answer

While part of being an adolescent is to at times reject a parent's comments, we're not certain that this explains all of your daughter's behavior. Actually, as we reflected upon your question we wondered what your daughter does when her solution is not successful. Does she quit? Does she continue pursuing the unsuccessful course? Does she ever come to you and ask for help?

Though it is not your intent, it would appear your daughter perceives your behavior as criticism of her decision-making skills and a lack of confidence that she can arrive at a successful solution. She seems to feel that you are attempting to impose your beliefs on her, a situation that will prompt most adolescents to push us away.

A first step to improve your relationship with your daughter is to think about how you might be coming across to her. Also, if there are times when she asks for your opinion, when does this happen and how is it different from other occasions? Are there times when she more easily accepts your input and why do you think that is so?

As you ponder these questions, you might find a quiet time to say to your daughter that you do respect her ability to make decisions but sometimes the decisions we make may not work out and it is wise to have back-up options. Also, tell her very directly that you don't want to come across as trying to boss her but would like to figure out how to offer support and input without appearing as critical or trying to control her life. We have found that discussing openly with an adolescent the issue of how we are perceived and how we would like things to improve sets the tone for a more positive dialogue. It also models a problem-solving approach.

Question
Isn't it the parents' responsibility to make decisions for their children? My four-teen-year-old son says it is his life and if he wants to get an earring he should be able to do so. He also says that it is his room and whether or not it is neat is not our problem. When is it okay for a parent to limit choices and tell children what they should do?

Answer
One of the most common questions we receive from parents pertains to what decisions we should allow our children to make. While we believe it is important to involve our kids as much as possible in making decisions about their lives, we also believe it is the parents' responsibility to make the final decisions when matters of safety and security are involved. Of course, our children may have a very different opinion about what constitutes safety and security than we have. To ensure that our children do not feel deceived even as we give them choices, we should make certain that they understand that there are certain parameters or limits to what they can choose. Some issues should be nonnegotiable such as attending parties where there is no adult supervision.

What decisions our children should be allowed to make becomes less clear when they involve issues of personal preference or style. Without wishing to sound trite, we often advise parents to select their battlegrounds carefully. Providing our kids with some choices in which safety is not an issue (e.g., wearing an earring or particular clothes) often makes it easier to set limits on more important issues such as curfews and alcohol use. If our children feel we are depriving them of making any choices, they are likely to fight us over every decision and even resort to going behind our back.

> To ensure that our children do not feel deceived even as we give them choices, we should make certain that they understand that there are certain parameters or limits to what they can choose.

Some families have no difficulty with a son wearing an earring (as long as the ear is pierced by someone with a license) while others do. We know some parents who have permitted their sons to get an earring but not before their sixteenth birthday. We suggest to parents that they examine not only what their reservations are to a particular decision but also how their child is doing in other important areas in life.

For instance, if your son is a good student, behaves appropriately, has solid friends, and generally follows society's rules and limits, then we believe the two issues of an earring or the neatness of his room (as long as it doesn't look like a pigpen, where sanitation issues may be involved) should not become a reason to initiate World War III. On the other hand, if these two issues are but the tip of an iceberg reflecting a child struggling to comply with the expectations of school and the community, then you are likely facing much bigger problems than simply an earring or a clean room. In such a situation, you would want to look closely at all that is going on in your son's life and in what ways you can help.

Question

My ten-year-old daughter came home from school and said she heard from one friend that another friend was saying some nasty things about her. My daughter asked what she should do. Since she asked, I immediately said she should call the other girl and find out if she was saying nasty things. My daughter said she couldn't do that. I became angry and said, "Then why ask me what to do?" I know I could have handled it better, but how?

Answer

As parents, we typically want to step in and help our children with problems they are facing. This is even more so when they ask us for our advice. While our natural instinct is to offer solutions, we must be cautious about how quickly we do so. In the situation with your daughter we believe it might have been more beneficial to empathize with her plight and then engage her in the problem-solving sequence described earlier in this chapter.

More specifically, you might let your daughter know how hurtful it can be when a friend says nasty things about her. When your daughter asked what she should do, one possible approach would have been to say, "I'm not certain; let's think of a couple of possibilities." If your daughter was unable to think of any solutions (we have actually found most kids will come up with some solutions), you might offer a couple of suggestions. If you raised the possibility of her calling her friend to find out what was going on and your daughter said she couldn't do it, instead of getting angry with her, you might wonder why she felt she couldn't do it. For example, some children feel uncomfortable confronting a friend since they're not certain what to say; once they are provided with some guidance, they feel more confident in making the call. You could have explored whether there were other ways to communicate with this girl or if in fact alternative solutions needed to be considered.

> Sometimes when it appears children are asking for our advice, what they are really doing is seeking our comfort, empathy, and support.

What we are suggesting is to use difficult situations such as that faced by your daughter as opportunities to reinforce problem-solving skills. Keep in mind that sometimes when it appears children are asking for our advice, what they are really doing is seeking our comfort, empathy, and support.

Question

My eight-year-old son knows that his bedtime is 8:30 P.M. Yet every night is a battle getting him to bed. We end up arguing for an hour so he usually doesn't get to bed until 9:30 P.M. I am exhausted and he is too. Bedtime has become a real power struggle. How can we solve this problem?

Answer

Books have been (and many more will be) written about getting children to bed at night. Power struggles are commonplace. There are several things to consider as you deal with your son. Is he a child who needs less sleep than other children his age? If he goes to bed late, does he have trouble getting up in the morning? How much time does he need getting ready for bed? Is any choice built into the bedtime routine to minimize a nightly power struggle?

We believe that there should be a set time for bed but, if possible, we should provide certain choices. For example, if 8:30 P.M. is your son's bedtime, you might ask him if he would like you to remind him ten or fifteen minutes before bed that it is time to get ready. Or, you might have him get ready by 8:15 P.M. and then ask if he would like you to read him a story or if he would like to read a story to you. If it seems that he is not very tired, you can permit him to read until 8:45 P.M. but then it's lights out. If he goes beyond 8:45 P.M. he does not have the privilege of staying up beyond 8:30 P.M. the following night. You can also establish a rule that when he is staying up until 8:45 P.M., he cannot get out of bed or become involved in different activities.

In addition, we know of several families who have given their children a choice of selecting one evening during the week to stay up fifteen or thirty minutes beyond their usual bedtime. The children are allowed to do this as long as they adhere to their regular bedtime on the other evenings. Some parents may worry that soon their children will argue to have this extra time on every evening; however, interestingly, most parents report that this has not occurred and that a power struggle has been avoided.

Question

When I offer my assistance or help in solving problems, my children complain that either they want to do it alone or I am picking on them. How can I be helpful without appearing critical?

Answer

Unknowingly there are times when our words of assistance, guidance, or education are counterproductive. We correct our children under the mistaken belief that if we tell, show, or direct them they will listen, observe, and improve. How else can they learn, we wonder, if not shown the errors of their ways? We would like our children to learn life's lessons without mistake or blunder. The problem is that when we take this approach, we actually minimize the opportunities for our kids to learn how to master difficult situations. To help our children learn to solve problems without our appearing critical, we suggest the following four guidelines:

- **Guideline One: Let empathy be your guide.** Take the time not just to understand but make an effort to experience your children's perspective. This is a key component of resiliency since it permits you to assume a helping rather than "fixing" posture. For instance, rather than immediately offering a comment or suggestion, begin by observing your child's struggles and introduce the idea that together maybe solutions can be found. Empathy is a good starting point for problem solving.
- **Guideline Two: Bite your tongue, watch, and listen.** Too often when we help our children we quickly express our point of view and tell them what to do. You must first learn to watch and listen. Too much advice, even if well meaning, may easily be interpreted as criticism or may deprive our children of developing the ability to solve problems on their own.
- **Guideline Three: Understand before you respond.** Closely tied to the first two guidelines is this third one, namely, respecting what our children desire in a certain situation. Sometimes they don't want our help, perceiving it as an intrusion into their lives or an indication that we don't trust in their abilities. Other times the help we offer is inconsistent with the problem that they perceive. When our attempts to assist are met with anger or rejection, it is easy to become annoyed and either withdraw or become more forceful. Instead, we suggest you offer comments such as, "Is there any way I can help?" or "If you need me, I am here." Children are more likely to approach parents for guidance and support when we create an atmosphere in which

children perceive we are genuinely interested in understanding their point of view and don't come across as telling them what to do. We must think before we act as parents. We must understand before we respond.

- **Guideline Four: Compliment and be patient.** *Opportunities will present themselves.* As obvious as it may seem, it is better for you to compliment and reinforce children before pointing out inadequacies or problems. Developing problem-solving abilities and learning from mistakes is a process that takes time and practice. It can be difficult to be patient given the level of emotional energy and investment parents have in their children. In the end, it is important for you to use these opportunities as teachable moments in which you replace fixing with helping and guiding. This is a basic aspect of raising resilient children.

11

Self-Discipline and Self-Worth

The Keys to Success

Question

I am constantly becoming angry when I have to discipline my son and daughter. I feel that I spend most of my time as a parent screaming and yelling at them. This isn't how I envisioned parenting. We never seem to have the time to discuss what is happening in our lives. We do seem to have plenty of time to become angry with each other. They are only seven and nine years old. My husband and I are frightened to think about what things will be like in our home when they are teenagers. What can I do to start really helping this problem?

Answer

You are not alone in your questions about discipline. Discipline is probably the number one topic of books for parents. It sounds as if discipline in your home is crisis-oriented. What we mean by this is that you are constantly responding to your children once a problem has emerged rather than adopting a proactive approach and looking at what can be done to minimize problems from appearing in the first place. This may not be very helpful but we can tell you that the majority of questions we receive about discipline fall in the category of crisis intervention rather than crisis prevention.

To complicate matters even further, it appears to be a rare occasion when three "parenting experts" agree on disciplinary practices. It is little wonder that many parents seem confused and perplexed about the most effective ways to discipline their children. Obviously, discipline is a very important issue in parenting. Lack of discipline among our youth is frequently cited by political, religious, and law enforcement agencies as responsible for the dramatic increase in community-based problems among youth in the last thirty years. One thing is certain, one of the most important roles you play as a parent is to serve as a disciplinarian. However, the way you go about meeting this responsibility can either diminish or reinforce your child's self-esteem, dignity, hope, and, ultimately, resilience.

> In the dictionary the word *discipline* finds its roots in the word *disciple* so that it may be understood as a teaching process.

In the dictionary the word *discipline* finds its roots in the word *disciple* so that it may be understood as a teaching process. As a form of education and as a corrective process, it is important for parents to realize that intimidation, humiliation, physical force, and embarrassment are not effective disciplinary techniques. It is also important to appreciate two of the major functions of discipline. One is to provide a consistent, safe, and secure environment for our children. The second, equally important, function is to nurture self-discipline or self-control. You are correct when you worry that if young children fail to develop self-discipline they may create significant problems for themselves and their families during their teenage years. Self-discipline implies that a child has internalized the rules of the community so that even if you or other adults are not present your child will act in an appropriate and thoughtful manner. Self-discipline comprises a significant component of a sense of ownership and responsibility for one's behavior.

Becoming an effective disciplinarian requires you to be empathic, communicate effectively, be open to modifying negative scripts, and appreciate the unique temperament of each of your children. The process of discipline should strengthen a responsible and compassionate attitude and help your children develop effective decision-making and problem-solving skills. Discipline should teach your children to use past experience to effectively guide their present and future behavior.

Yet as you point out, even with knowledge in hand, discipline for some children may be a difficult process. Once you understand your role as a disciplinarian we suggest you use a number of guiding principles, including acting in a preventative way; working together with your spouse; being consistent; serving as a calm, rational model; selecting your battles carefully; understanding your children's capabilities; and, most importantly, understanding that positive feedback and encouragement are often the most powerful forms of discipline.

Even more specifically, to move from a crisis-intervention to a crisis-prevention approach, we recommend that you initiate a regular family meeting each week to discuss different issues in the family and to articulate expectations for your children and yourself. Your children should also have the opportunity to share their thoughts and views. These meetings, hopefully taking place in a calm manner, will provide a structure by which effective family rules and consequences can be developed, minimizing the anger that presently takes place.

Question

My wife and I are miles apart when it comes to discipline. I believe my wife is too lenient. She thinks I am too strict. The kids don't bother asking me if they can get something or go somewhere anymore. They just go right to my wife. She seems to let them do whatever they want. The tension between my wife and myself when it comes to parenting issues is always high. Because of my wife's actions, I feel my kids see me as the bad guy. Though I am angry at my children, I am even angrier at my wife since I think she has created this distance between myself and the kids. Because things have been so tense, my wife and I often argue in front of the kids about discipline. This only makes matters worse. I am not sure where or how to begin to solve this problem.

Answer

Although courtship often provides prospective marital partners with opportunities to learn about each other's likes, dislikes, and behavioral styles, it is not until children arrive that issues related to child rearing become an important topic. It is not unusual for a husband and wife to disagree about disciplining children. Each of us forms our thoughts and ideas about discipline based on our background and experience. Thus, even very compatible couples may disagree on this subject. As you point out, divergent views about discipline typically cause noticeable tension between parents. This is especially true when these differences are played out in front of children. This tension takes parents further away rather than closer to developing a set of strategies that will help their children learn clear-cut rules and consequences.

We don't believe parents have to be clones of each other and agree about every parenting decision and practice. But when differences in discipline styles become pervasive and begin to disrupt family functioning the issue must be addressed. As you point out your children have become experts in what professionals call "triangulating," or "splitting" each of you. In a triangulation your child brings an issue to each of you knowing full well that you will argue about the issue, ultimately increasing the probability your child will get to do what he or she wants. Your children don't engage in this behavior because they are bad but because children often possess the desire to get what they want. It is not unusual in this process to observe children going from one parent to the other as they seek to persuade one parent to go along with something even if the other disagrees.

Obviously, arguing in front of your children further reduces the possibility of a compromise because with children present issues such as giving in, losing face, or being viewed as inadequate or unfair are magnified. If you have differences we suggest you discuss them alone and arrive at a mutually acceptable position before talking to your children.

In your situation we strongly suggest that you and your wife sit down and agree that you both want what's best for the children despite the fact that you disagree as to the most efficient means to reach this goal. Begin by making a list of the most important issues that appear to cause conflict. In some situations it may be reasonable to divide these issues and agree that each parent will have the final say over certain topics. In other situations you may find it better to negotiate until you can come to an agreed upon set of strategies. It is important, however, that when strategies are agreed upon each parent consistently follows through as agreed.

In your family, it appears that the issue of "triangulation" is a significant one. We suggest when issues such as discipline arise, rather than being placed on the spot you tell your children that what they are bringing up is important but a decision won't be made until the other parent is consulted. And don't worry if they accuse you of not being able to think for yourself, which we have found is a common response by children when their parents say they have to consult with each other.

Finally, we suggest you consider different beliefs about discipline as opportunities to reflect upon parenting practices. As you point out, intense arguments, unresolved conflicts, and two sets of discipline strategies within a single family not only cause tension and conflict but lessen the probability of a child developing a resilient mindset.

Question
I know that you have reservations about spanking, but our eight-year-old son just doesn't seem to listen. We try to reason with him but the only thing that appears to get a response is spanking. When we ask him to do something he will scream at us. Then I end up spanking him. After a spanking he will do what we ask. The problem is he is a "repeat offender." He does the same thing again a few days later. I have a few questions. Is there anything wrong with spanking, especially since it seems to be the only thing that works with him? How come I have to keep doing it?

Answer
Before we get to your questions about spanking, we would ask you to consider that if you attempted a solution to any problem and found that time and time again the problem reemerged, just how many times would you continue using the same solution? Many parents initially believe that spanking works since it often brings about the immediate desired result, namely, having children stop what they have been doing. However, the true question is whether spanking is effective in helping your child behave more appropriately and consistently in the future.

> The true question is whether spanking is effective in helping your child behave more appropriately and consistently in the future.

Your description of the problem indicates that spanking is not leading to long-term change. Thus, we would argue that your continued spanking of your son represents the physical equivalent of a negative script, which we discuss in detail in Chapter 4. Negative scripts do not necessarily have to be represented by words but can in fact be reflected in actions. We don't know your child's temperament. However, if your child has struggled to develop self-control, an issue we discussed in Chapter 6, your interventions will need to provide a teaching component along with any form of punishment you choose to use. Assuming your child possesses adequate self-control, it is likely that the lack of change in behavior reflects what we discussed in Chapter 4 as "negative reinforcement." Your child engages in the requested behavior, not because he accepts his responsibility to do so, but because it is the quickest way to avoid your anger and a spanking. Once the task is completed, there is little likelihood your child will act responsibly in the future.

Many parents believe that the threat of a spanking or corporal punishment "should be" sufficient to help children behave differently. However, this doesn't appear to be the case. In many cases, when parents rely primarily on punitive measures to teach, when their actions are typically spur-of-the-moment responses often fueled by anger, little change occurs long-term in children's behavior. If parents rely primarily on spanking when disciplining their children, what children typically learn is resentment rather than the reasons for which they are being hit. Spanking robs children of an opportunity to learn how to solve problems and change their behavior.

What you didn't tell us in your question is whether your son's behavior makes you angry, although we must admit that the tone of your question suggests that this is the case. Many parents lose their temper and become angry when children don't do as they are asked and when the problem persists. Unfortunately, even for well-meaning parents, discipline can, at times, end up being characterized by harshness, whether physical or verbal. In many cases, the reasons for this outcome are complicated. They often reflect parents' histories, their level of frustration and anger, as well as their mistaken belief that children learn best when fearful or intimidated.

When discipline is riddled with anger and physical punishment, children are more likely to remember the punishment than the reasons they are being punished. In such a situation there is little opportunity for a resilient mindset to develop since children are unlikely to experience unconditional love, to learn how to solve problems and make decisions, or to learn from mistakes. What they do learn is that if someone bigger than you doesn't like what you do that person can hit you rather than help you figure out how to resolve the problem. When children are spanked they typically stop their behavior but only temporarily. What many parents don't realize is that in the negative reinforcement paradigm, children often resume the behavior parents want them to stop once the parents' proximity to the child changes.

Many parents who believe that spanking is effective assume the child requires more spanking if its effects don't last. What they don't realize is that spanking typically causes more anger. This escalating cycle only leads to greater conflict and emotional distance between parents and children. The results would be far better if the parents relied on natural and logical consequences, something we discuss in greater detail later in this chapter.

Question
I think most parents are concerned about the issue of discipline. These may seem like obvious questions, but what do you see as the main goals of discipline and how does the way we discipline our kids relate to the development of a resilient mindset?

Answer
As we noted in an earlier answer, but it deserves to be highlighted again, we believe that there are two primary goals for discipline, both of which facilitate the development of a resilient mindset. The first goal is to create an environment that is safe and secure, an environment in which children are capable of learning reasonable rules, limits, and consequences. Ideally, the first environment in which this occurs is the home but eventually it generalizes to outside settings such as the community and school. While children may not thank us for the rules and limits we establish, it has been our experience that if these rules are fair and if children understand their purpose, then they actually feel safer and more loved. An environment without rules or one with arbitrary rules feels unsafe to children and leads them to question how much we truly care about them.

> An environment without rules or one with arbitrary rules feels unsafe to children and leads them to question how much we truly care about them.

The second major goal of discipline is for our children to develop self-discipline and self-control. These are characteristics that are essential for success in all aspects of life. Parental input must help children comprehend the rationale for limits and consequences. Involving children in the disciplinary process assists the development of problem-solving skills, which ultimately will help them attain a sense of ownership for rules, increase their ability to recognize that these rules are reasonable as opposed to arbitrary, and use these rules to guide all aspects of their lives.

The process of effective discipline reflects many of the principles we have discussed thus far in nurturing a resilient mindset. These include problem solving and decision making, effective communication, and the setting of realistic goals. We believe that even very young children can be engaged in examining problems and arriving at solutions. How well we handle the role of disciplinarian significantly determines the extent to which our children develop resilient mindsets. Remember the word *discipline* stems from the word *disciple* and is a teaching process.

A major goal that parents should have is for their children to develop self-discipline and self-control rather than to use anger and resentment as the primary fuel when responding to problems. To accomplish this task, we must involve our children in the disciplinary process by helping them understand the reasons and importance of limits, rules, and consequences. We must help them to recognize they can make appropriate choices and decisions, gain increasing control of their behavior as they mature, and eventually possess the confidence and resilience to deal with whatever adversities they encounter in life. It is difficult to imagine a resilient child who has not developed all of the skills associated with self-discipline.

Question

Our only child is a nine-year-old girl. We talk with friends about the problems they are having with their kids. My husband and I look at each other in disbelief. Either we are missing something in our daughter's behavior or she really doesn't require much discipline. She always seems to know what to do, doesn't have to be reminded or punished, and is always respectful. Are we missing something?

Answer

We have come to the realization that it is very easy to feel like a competent parent and to believe that parenting is an easy process when we have "good children." We are not suggesting that some children are "bad" but that, as we have pointed out, children come to the world with different skills, abilities, and temperaments. They mature and develop at different rates.

Not long ago while having dinner in a local restaurant, we had the occasion to sit near two young families, each with a single child approximately a year of age. From the moment the first family sat down at the table, it was as if their child was announcing to the room that he was a great kid and had great parents. Everyone in the room appeared drawn to this child. His smile and eye contact were infectious. His parents beamed and clearly enjoyed the experience of taking their young child to a public place. In contrast, a number of tables away, from the moment the second couple sat down their dinner was disrupted. Very quickly they had a pained look on their faces as their child began screaming and knocking things down on the table. Multiple times these parents took turns taking the child out. Though they worked very diligently to try and comfort their child, it was clear this was not a good situation for their child. Except for the first few moments of sitting down at the table, they never sat together during the course of their meal. We were struck by the difference in what these two sets of parents were experiencing about the process of parenting and the ease or difficulty of raising children.

By your description you have been blessed with a child possessing an even or "easy" temperament, a pleasant personality, and good self-control. The fact of the matter is you are not missing anything. It is important for you to realize that while children are very different from birth, these differences don't diminish your important role as parents. We have had the occasion of working with families of children who probably would have been like your daughter but were unfortunately born into families experiencing multiple problems. The lack of consistency, nurturance, and support within the family environment eventually led these children to experience problems. Though your daughter may not require much in the way of punishment or reactionary discipline, the principles of being effective disciplinarians are still important to keep in mind. It is important for you and your spouse to work as a parental team; to be consistent; to serve as calm, rational models; and to employ natural and logical, rather than arbitrary and punitive, consequences. Even when minor issues arise concerning rules or activities, these can be valuable opportunities to help your child mature and take advantage of her temperamental gifts.

It is important for you and your spouse to work as a parental team; to be consistent; to serve as calm, rational models; and to employ natural and logical, rather than arbitrary and punitive, consequences.

Question

Though the world is very different from what it was when my husband and I were growing up thirty years ago, he insists that we discipline our children the way we were disciplined. What that means to him is that kids should do what they are told because "we are the parents and we know best." If they don't then they lose certain privileges such as watching television. They might even be spanked. My husband believes that since this was good enough for him, it must be good enough for our five- and seven-year-old children. I grew up in a home and received discipline similar to my husband's and didn't like it, so I think we should discipline our children differently. What's your opinion?

Answer

The assumptions that each of us holds about raising children influence the ways in which we understand and interact with them. To be an effective disciplinarian requires that we understand the assumptions and obstacles that may serve as roadblocks to reaching this goal. Your question highlights an issue about one of these significant roadblocks. Many parents repeat the same forms of discipline that they experienced as children even in those cases in which they resented the disciplinary practices of their parents. Such a pattern would be fine if parents grew up in homes in which the disciplinary practices of their parents nurtured a resilient mindset. However, if this is not the case, if discipline did not promote self-discipline and problem-solving skills, then parents may be mirroring ineffective forms of discipline without realizing it.

We want children to do what we ask them to do simply because we ask. Certainly this is an important starting point. But is it a good ending point? We think not. We believe that ultimately the development of self-discipline allows children to follow the rules, limits, and guidelines of the society in which they live, not necessarily because they are forced to but because they accept that system and choose to do so. The restriction of privileges when rules are violated is certainly an appropriate parenting strategy. As we noted in a previous question, however, we believe that corporal punishment is an ineffective strategy.

We suggest you and your husband attempt to understand why each of you, though raised in a similar disciplinary environment, has drawn a different conclusion about the effectiveness of that environment. It is likely through this understanding that a compromise can be reached. Perhaps you didn't like what your parents did to you. Perhaps you felt it was unfair or unreasonable. One helpful exercise is for you and your husband to reflect on the disciplinary practices of your parents and consider if you could rewrite the script, in what ways would you have liked them to have handled things differently.

For example, one couple with whom we worked talked about how inconsistent and arbitrary their parents were in punishing them for different behaviors. We discussed with them that although one of the most important components of discipline is consistency, sometimes the behavior of our children makes consistency a difficult task. We also emphasized that consistency is not synonymous with rigidity or inflexibility, but rather a consistent approach to discipline invites thoughtful modification of rules and consequences, such that when children reach their teen years they are permitted more opportunities to guide themselves. When these parents became more consistent, less arbitrary, and less punitive, they were pleasantly surprised that their children, rather than taking advantage of them as they feared, actually became more cooperative. Their children were learning self-discipline and respect, and the parents learned that for discipline to be effective it should not be associated with constant anger or fear.

Question

I am very frustrated with our thirteen-year-old son and his failure to complete homework assignments. I don't believe our response has been punitive. If he hasn't completed his homework he loses watching the ninety minutes of television he is allowed each evening. As soon as we take away television for the evening he responds that we don't love him. Will our son develop the feeling he is unloved if we keep taking away television when he doesn't complete homework? I would hate to think that he will go through life feeling his parents didn't love him. It would make my wife and me feel that we weren't very good parents.

Answer

Some parents find it difficult to set and stick with consistent limits and consequences because they worry that their behavior will make their children angry with them and not love them. Many children are very sensitive to picking up on this fear and using it to their advantage by saying things similar to your son, such as "I don't love you" or "if you loved me you would let me watch television." The importance of setting firm and consistent limits and consequences should not be sidetracked by this phenomenon. It is unrealistic to believe that when you provide a consequence your child will respond, "I know you're doing this because you love me. I appreciate that you are not letting me watch television so that I will develop better self-discipline."

> Being an effective disciplinarian requires that you develop the ability to tolerate your children being temporarily angry when limits are set, especially if you understand that these limits are fair and reasonable and your child has the capability to complete the assigned task.

Being an effective disciplinarian requires that you develop the ability to tolerate your children being temporarily angry when limits are set, especially if you understand that these limits are fair and reasonable and your child has the capability to complete the assigned task. We want to emphasize the word *temporarily* since most youngsters actually welcome rules if they are consistent and fair. We recommend that you discuss with your son the problems he is having with homework and engage him in a discussion of what he feels would help.

However, we want to bring up another issue that concerns whether your son's not doing his homework reflects struggles he is having with his work. We suggest you begin by making certain you understand the reasons your son has difficulty completing homework. At thirteen he is probably attending middle or junior high school. Often the homework demands increase dramatically from elementary school. Many children experience struggles making this transition. Thus, your child's problem could result from a lack of skill with a particular subject matter or ineffective learning strategies rather than a purposeful attempt to avoid doing homework. Homework, in fact, is a hot button in many families. Reflect upon whether your son experienced problems completing homework in elementary school. Has he experienced difficulties in specific subjects and not others? Does he possess the skills necessary to complete his work in a consistent, responsible, and independent fashion? Obviously, if children are having difficulty mastering the subject matter, punishing them is not the answer and will not improve the situation.

By the middle school years, a significant percentage of what your child learns in school is reflected or completed through homework. Thus, the importance of homework by middle school is not so much to practice and rehearse but to learn independently. It is important for you and your child to understand that time spent on homework from this point forward has been shown to contribute to school success. At the end of this chapter is a seven-part Inventory of Homework Skills questionnaire we use to help parents identify why their child may be struggling to complete homework and a framework to begin planning effective intervention. This is a questionnaire that you and your teen can complete together. We also use a second questionnaire, Positive Parenting Homework Practices, that is also included. We suggest you complete this questionnaire independently. Once these questionnaires are completed, you can then begin to identify specific skills for your teen as well as behaviors for yourselves that you can utilize to help the process of homework move from a source of conflict and anger within the family to an activity that enhances achievement, self-reliance, and resilience.

Question
I have heard that as much as possible parents should rely on natural and logical consequences when disciplining their children. Could you explain exactly what is meant by these terms, and why you feel they are effective forms of discipline? How do they promote resilience?

Answer
Natural and logical consequences can be very effective in helping children understand there are consequences for their behavior that are neither harsh nor arbitrary but based upon consistency and logic. Natural consequences are those that follow naturally from a child's actions. You don't have to enforce them. For example, if your child leaves his bicycle outside overnight

after you have taught him it should be put away and it is stolen, the loss is a natural consequence. As a parent you didn't have to do anything. Hopefully, your child will learn not to leave the bike out overnight again.

While logical consequences sometimes overlap with natural consequences, logical consequences involve some action taken on the part of parents in response to a child's behavior. For example, had you noticed that the bicycle was left out you might have taken it into the garage and locked it up for a day, explaining to your child that since he couldn't remember to bring in the bicycle, the logical consequence is loss of the use of the bicycle for a fixed period of time.

> Natural and logical consequences are forms of discipline that reinforce a resilient mindset.

We believe consequences should fit the behavior. As much as possible our children should be aware of rules and consequences in advance. Natural and logical consequences are forms of discipline that reinforce a resilient mindset. They involve articulating with your children the behaviors in question that require modification, searching for possible solutions, and highlighting that they have choices in what solution to select but that each choice may lead to a different consequence. This process reinforces feelings of responsibility and ownership as well as a sense of self-control.

Question

Our five-year-old daughter is one of those temperamentally difficult kids you have talked about. We have read many books that suggest that time-out is a good technique to use with misbehaving children. When our daughter begins to scream and shout, we tell her to go to her room. But she just screams louder and tells us she won't go. We have dragged her into her room and actually held the door shut but then she starts to throw things around and destroys the room. Should we use time-outs with her? What else can we do?

Answer

First, we should tell you that we don't believe it is necessary for you to abandon time-out. Time-out can be a very effective intervention for children with limited self-control. It offers them an opportunity to gain control and return to the situation for a second opportunity. In fact, when a time-out is used the message to your child should be "you need time to calm down." We suggest that you add, "You can let me know when you feel calm." This statement places control and responsibility in the hands of your child. Time-out typically involves removing children from a certain setting to another setting when they misbehave. The rationale is that separation from desirable activities as well as from other people as a consequence for misbehavior, helps a child learn to change whatever behavior led to the time-out. Time-out is one of the most frequently used techniques by parents as well as teachers. As such, it is likely to be overused or misused. Although a brief time-out of a few minutes can exert a positive influence on a child's behavior, many parents apply time-out ineffectively as often as effectively. If you are going to use time-out, it is important for you to:

1. Make certain your child understands when time-out will be used.
2. Offer a warning that if a certain behavior is not stopped, a time-out may follow.
3. Consistently use time-out when the behavior reoccurs.
4. Locate a specific place for time-out and explain that to the child.
5. Determine a specific duration of time-out. We suggest a very brief period of three to five minutes for your child.
6. Make certain your child understands the behaviors that will lead to time-out.
7. If you are going to use the "calm" criteria for leaving time-out, make certain your child understands that this is the key to end time-out.
8. Remember, most importantly, that for time-out to be effective your child must return to the problem situation and comply.

We believe that time-out may lose its effectiveness by the time most children reach ten years of age. This is particularly true when children are temperamentally stubborn. In these cases, as with your child, the direction to go to time-out is responded to by the child drawing a line in the sand and saying, "You can't make me." At this point the consequence of time-out becomes a lightning rod for further confrontation. We usually recommend that other interventions be explored when children are defiantly resistant to time-out. Restriction of a desired privilege or parents' leaving the room can be just as effective as time-out. You can say, "Either you go to time-out and calm down or you will lose a particular privilege" (you should name the privilege). When applicable you can add, "If you continue to scream and shout, it's still not going to get you what you want. It will also lead to not watching television tonight. It's your choice."

> It is important for children to view time-out as an opportunity to calm down and think of alternatives to their misbehavior.

It is important for children to view time-out as an opportunity to calm down and think of alternatives to their misbehavior. When this occurs, time-out can be a very effective consequence. However, if time-out leads to greater frustration and confrontation, other strategies may be warranted.

Question

Our sixteen-year-old son just obtained his driver's license. He has a 12:30 A.M. curfew on Saturday night. He came home at 1:00 A.M. telling us he was late because he drove some friends home. I responded that it was nice that he wanted to help his friends but then reminded him that he broke curfew and didn't call. He responded that he was just trying to be helpful. I told him he couldn't use the car the following weekend, which was the agreed-upon consequence if he came in after curfew. He argued that he was just trying to help his friends and didn't have a chance to call. My wife thought I was too strict. Was I?

Answer

This is one question we feel comfortable answering briefly. We do not feel you were too strict. From what you wrote there were agreed upon consequences for breaking curfew. While the reason for your son's lateness was to be helpful, he had several choices. He could have said to his friends that if they wanted a ride home they would have to start out earlier so that he could get in before curfew. Or, he could have called and explained the situation and perhaps you would have allowed him to come home late on this occasion but let him know that this kind of situation would not be permitted again. The key issue here is that your son had control over being late. While it might have been easy to excuse his lateness since it was based on his helping his friends, we applaud you for adhering to the established rules about curfew.

Question

We have a real discipline problem with our seven-year-old daughter. Whenever we go into a supermarket or department store she wants me to buy her something. I have read that you should tell your children in advance that they shouldn't ask for things. I do that and she agrees. But then the moment she is in the store and spots something she likes she asks for it. When I say no, reminding her of what I said and what we agreed upon, she has a tantrum. We end up leaving the store, much to my inconvenience, and often I am so angry as we leave that I give her a spanking on the rear, which I hate to do. I am feeling so frustrated but don't know what else to do at this time. Do you have any suggestions?

Answer

Your question raises an important obstacle to effective discipline. One of the key issues is whether it is realistic for you to expect that your daughter will be able to resist the temptation to ask for things simply because she promised to do so before entering the store. When children fail to meet our expectations, especially if they have promised to do so, we usually respond with anger and punishment. But some children make promises that they are not capable of keeping. If this is the case, is it fair to punish children for actions over which they have little, if any, control?

Your description of the problem suggests that your daughter is in need of assistance in developing self-control. To do so you must adjust your expectations. Although it may not be a perfect parallel, how would you feel in the workplace if you were punished for not being able to do a task that you had agreed upon but that turned out to be beyond your ability? We would guess you would be very angry. You would probably contend that if you didn't understand how to complete a certain task you should first be provided with instruction and opportunity to learn before consequences are set in place.

At the present time it appears that it is too stimulating for your daughter to go into certain stores. The "bar" may be set too high. We always recommend that as our children's cognitive skills improve, we can raise the bar or our expectations in a reasonable fashion. But if our children demonstrate difficulty with the height of the bar, then we may have to lower it for at least a short time until they are able to succeed. We suggest you begin by not taking your daughter to places that she cannot handle. Since you said it becomes inconvenient to remove her from the store when she has a tantrum, it probably makes more sense to go by yourself and have someone watch her. As a next step, you can select opportunities in which she can enter stores and develop reasonable self-control. For example, a quick stop at the convenience store while getting gas is a good place to begin. Slowly, over time your daughter should be able to develop the necessary self-control to visit a large store and adhere to the agreed-upon plan that she is not to begin making requests or demands.

Use the forms below to identify your child's skills and your behaviors as parents to help with the process of homework. See the question and subsequent discussion on completing homework on pages 227 to 229.

Inventory of Homework Skills

Name of Child _____ Date _____

Answer each question by marking a check in either the "Yes" or "No" box.

1. **Writes down the correct assignment given by the teacher and brings home the proper books and supplies.**

☐ Yes ☐ No 1. Do you know *when* your teacher(s) typically give homework (e.g., every day, certain days, before class begins, at the end of class)?

☐ Yes ☐ No 2. Do you know *how* your teacher(s) typically give homework (e.g., verbally, on the board, written on pieces of paper)?

☐ Yes ☐ No 3. Do you write your assignments in an assignment book or a homework planner?

☐ Yes ☐ No 4. Do you get the materials (books, assignments) you need from school to home?

☐ Yes ☐ No 5. Do you keep track of all your assignments and their due dates?

2. **Chooses an appropriate place in which to do homework.**

☐ Yes ☐ No 1. Do you have a favorite "homework place" where you can concentrate?

☐ Yes ☐ No 2. Do you have the proper school materials (paper, pencils, rulers, etc.) available in your "homework place"?

☐ Yes ☐ No 3. Do you have a way of keeping your school work/materials organized?

☐ Yes ☐ No 4. Do you usually start your homework at a specific time each day?

☐ Yes ☐ No 5. Do you change things around in your homework place from time to time to see if you study better under different conditions (e.g., with and without music playing, lighting changes, sitting at a desk)?

3. **Starts assignments by reading directions and following them carefully.**

☐ Yes ☐ No 1. Do you usually read directions before starting an assignment?

☐ Yes ☐ No 2. Do you ask for help when you do not understand what to do?

☐ Yes ☐ No 3. Do you have the phone number of another student (or a teacher) in each class to call if you need help with an assignment?

☐ Yes ☐ No 4. If you are stuck on an assignment and cannot get help, do you try to figure it out on your own or ask a teacher for help the next day?

☐ Yes   ☐ No   5. Do you look for examples in the book or from class notes to help you understand how to do an assignment?

4. Manages difficult or long-term assignments.

☐ Yes   ☐ No   1. Do you write down long-term assignments and the steps to complete these assignments on a calendar or list?

☐ Yes   ☐ No   2. Before beginning a difficult assignment, do you underline or use markers to highlight key words in the directions, computational signs and key words in math, or main ideas in reading and social studies?

☐ Yes   ☐ No   3. Do you take breaks so you don't get too tired on difficult or long assignments?

☐ Yes   ☐ No   4. Do you have ways to remember important information such as writing down key ideas, drawing pictures, or making diagrams?

☐ Yes   ☐ No   5. Do you make up questions for yourself or write brief summaries while preparing for a test?

5. Maintains attention when assignments are boring.

☐ Yes   ☐ No   1. Do you spend enough time on homework even if it is boring?

☐ Yes   ☐ No   2. Do you usually finish your homework even if it is boring?

☐ Yes   ☐ No   3. Do you take breaks from boring assignments and come back to them at a later time?

☐ Yes   ☐ No   4. Do you reward yourself when you reach certain goals?

☐ Yes ☐ No 5. Do you try to make a boring assignment "fun" (e.g., make a game out it)?

6. Checks work for thoroughness and accuracy.

☐ Yes ☐ No 1. Do you check your assignment book to make sure you have completed all the homework assigned for that day?

☐ Yes ☐ No 2. Do you put the appropriate headings on your papers?

☐ Yes ☐ No 3. Do you write neatly?

☐ Yes ☐ No 4. Do you check each problem or question to make sure you have answered it correctly?

☐ Yes ☐ No 5. Do you ask someone else to check your work to make sure you have done the assignment correctly?

7. Returns homework to school when it is due.

☐ Yes ☐ No 1. Do you take your completed homework back to school?

☐ Yes ☐ No 2. Do you have a place in your desk, backpack, or locker to keep completed homework?

☐ Yes ☐ No 3. Do you know how and when your teachers collect homework?

☐ Yes ☐ No 4. Do you usually turn in your homework on time?

☐ Yes ☐ No 5. After your homework is returned to you, do you keep it to use at a later time to review for tests?

Source: *Seven Steps to Homework Success* by Sydney Zentall and Sam Goldstein. Used with permission of the publisher and authors.

Positive Parenting Homework Practices

Name _____ Date _____

☐ Yes ☐ No 1. Do you volunteer time at your child's classroom or school?

☐ Yes ☐ No 2. Do you go to school conferences or meetings about your child?

☐ Yes ☐ No 3. Do you ask the teacher about your child's homework practices and policies?

☐ Yes ☐ No 4. Are you aware of your child's whereabouts after school?

☐ Yes ☐ No 5. Do you monitor your child's homework after school or by using a trusted individual or tutor?

☐ Yes ☐ No 6. Do you monitor your child's homework after school with a written or taped list and with a phone call?

☐ Yes ☐ No 7. Do you or your child have homework times established?

☐ Yes ☐ No 8. Does your child follow these times and do you enforce these homework times?

☐ Yes ☐ No 9. Do you limit TV time or make sure it is given after your child has worked on homework?

☐ Yes ☐ No 10. Have you helped your child experiment with different places to study and different home conditions (with music/TV on, at a desk, on the bed, etc.)?

☐ Yes ☐ No 11. Do you provide healthy homework snacks for your child after school?

☐ Yes ☐ No 12. Have you helped your child identify activities or breaks that are rewards for completing a certain amount of homework?

☐ Yes ☐ No 13. Does your child have or have you helped your child develop a way to plan for a long-term project, with checks and reminders?

☐ Yes ☐ No 14. Do you ask about what your child learned at school that day and about his/her interests?

☐ Yes ☐ No 15. Does your child have a system of putting homework in a specific place?

☐ Yes ☐ No 16. Do you help your child practice skills using games or flash cards?

☐ Yes ☐ No 17. Do you help your child understand directions by asking your child what he/she reads?

☐ Yes ☐ No 18. Do you allow your child an alternative way to demonstrate what he/she knows (e.g., drawing pictures instead of typing, talking)?

☐ Yes ☐ No 19. Do you read to your child when the objective of the lesson is not reading but understanding the content (e.g., social studies, math problem solving)?

☐ Yes ☐ No 20. Do you provide ways to make homework faster or more fun (colorful folders, pencils, organizers, choice, getting them started, positive statements)?

☐ Yes ☐ No 21. Do you provide tape-recorded messages, check sheets, tours of the public library, references, choice, and goal setting to develop independence?

☐ Yes ☐ No 22. Do you help your child prioritize homework tasks?

☐ Yes   ☐ No   23. Would you hire a tutor if your child's skill level is significantly below the homework requirements?

☐ Yes   ☐ No   24. Do you find ways to praise your child for good work and homework?

☐ Yes   ☐ No   25. Do you help your child study for tests by quizzing your child on material to be learned?

Source: *Seven Steps to Homework Success* by Sydney Zentall and Sam Goldstein. Used with permission of the publisher and authors.

12

The Alliance Between
Parents and Schools

Question

Our son is eight years old. We moved this summer and he will start a new school in September. At his previous school he experienced problems getting along with other kids. He becomes frustrated easily if he doesn't get his way, then he becomes angry and even more bossy than usual. I wanted to discuss this problem with his new teacher before the school year begins so that she will be prepared to handle it. My husband feels that maybe the problem won't even come up with a new group of kids and if we bring it up with the teacher she might see our son as a disturbed child even before she meets him. Any ideas about how we should handle things?

Answer

The idea of a "fresh start" is appealing to all of us. We all like to believe that whether it is our golf game, relations with others, or performance at school or work, a fresh start without knowledge of our history by others is beneficial. However, we know of no research that has put this theory to the test. We agree that in some situations at school, personality clashes between a student and teacher may bias the teacher toward the student and vice versa. In this scenario, other teachers observing this child's problems may immediately respond to the child more negatively when he comes to their classrooms.

In our experience it usually takes "two to tango." What we mean by this is that in most situations children bring with them a set of coping strategies and behaviors that have been shaped by their previous experiences. Thus, a fresh start really isn't so fresh. In some situations it is easier to make the decision to inform teachers, particularly when children have experienced significant problems with academic achievement or behavior. When children's problems appear less severe and when parents believe that an unfortunate set of circumstances significantly contributed to these problems, then the decision to inform a new teacher about previous issues becomes a debatable point.

> Parents and teachers must strive to form a respectful, working partnership, one that will enhance the process of education and thereby assist children to develop a resilient mindset.

We believe strongly, however, that in most situations teachers should be informed, especially if the information shared will facilitate the teacher's understanding of the child. Parents and teachers must strive to form a respectful, working partnership, one that will enhance the process of education and thereby assist children to develop a resilient mindset. Parents and teachers are partners. For a partnership to be successful, each partner must trust the other. Parents must be active and respectful in their interactions with teachers, willing to trust teachers with important information. This creates a relationship based on mutual respect rather than blame or shame. We must remember as parents that regardless of how tough a time our children may have at school, school personnel are our allies, not our adversaries. Educators must view parents in the same way.

It will be important for you to work closely with your son's teachers, particularly since he has a history of difficulties in the school setting. We have found that most teachers are sincere, caring individuals who entered and remain in the profession because they like to teach and love children. We suggest you communicate with the teacher before school begins. Let the teacher know that one of your goals this year is to help your son develop better self-control, particularly in frustrating social situations. Seek the teacher's input. Has she worked with students experiencing this problem before? Does she have some ideas that can be set in place, even as the school year begins? Establish a way of communicating with your son's teacher throughout the year. The danger of not informing your son's teacher of his difficulties is that his problems may quickly emerge and set a more negative tone for the year before the teacher has an opportunity to place things on a better track.

We also suggest that you sit down with your son, first focusing on his strengths, the things he has done well, and the areas in which he has succeeded in school. Then define those goals and strategies related to helping him develop more effective techniques for handling frustration and anger. We believe it would be helpful for your son to attend a meeting with you and his teacher to discuss strengths, weaknesses, and goals. Hopefully in this way your son will be a motivated, active participant and his teacher will track his behavior during the first few weeks of school, setting in place assistance as needed and keeping you informed in the process.

Question

I experienced learning problems at school. I can remember dreading receiving my report card and always worrying what teachers would say to my parents at parent-teacher conferences. Not only that, because of my school problems my parents had conferences about me much more often than they did for my brother and sister. Now as an adult I find that I dread parent-teacher conferences, even though most of the time I hear good things about my children. When I go into a school it brings back so many unpleasant memories from my own school years. I worry that if my kids begin to have problems in school, my anxiety will interfere with my being able to help them or to work closely with their teachers to come up with successful solutions. I want to try and overcome this anxiety. What can I do?

Answer

Your feelings are shared by many parents who struggled in school. Your recollections of your school history can and will affect not only how you feel when you enter a school but also your relationships with your child's teachers. Some parents experiencing some of the same feelings as yours have told us that when a teacher discusses some difficulties their child is having, they immediately sense that the teacher is judging them harshly or thinks they are not doing enough to help. Others are concerned if a teacher doesn't understand their child, negative judgments may affect the child's confidence and self-esteem. Finally, because you feel anxious during conferences you may be reluctant to ask reasonable questions or assert your opinions.

> Effective communication is the key to planning successful programs.

For all of these reasons it is important for you to develop an effective line of communication with teachers. We recognize that given your feelings about school, it may not be easy to initiate communication but we believe that if it is done thoughtfully and slowly, it can serve to ease your anxiety. Effective communication is the key to planning successful programs. Besides notes and phone calls, face-to-face conferences are the primary means by which parents and teachers can communicate effectively. They are often the only opportunity for more comprehensive discussions to take place. To lessen your anxiety and to make the most of parent-teacher conferences we suggest the following:

- Be on time and respect time limits.
- Be prepared. Inquire beforehand who will attend the meeting, collect your thoughts, take along samples of work, and write down questions you would like to ask.
- Begin the conference with a positive comment. Something your child likes about school. Make a point of expressing your appreciation for the teacher's efforts.
- Be a good listener. Make certain you understand what is being said. Don't hesitate to ask questions.
- Be honest. Even if you feel defensive, remember that you are your child's primary advocate.
- Keep the focus on issues and concerns about your child's performance rather than on the teacher's performance. Ask for specific suggestions as well as how you might be of help at home.
- Before the meeting ends, there should be a review of what was discussed, any recommendations that were made, and the best way for you to offer and receive feedback about the planned interventions. It is helpful to schedule the next meeting at this time.
- Most importantly, keep in mind that everyone wants what is best for your child.

Question

Our daughter is a freshman in high school. She has never really enjoyed school but this year things have gone downhill. She has always complained that we are on her back about schoolwork and homework. We told her at the beginning of the year that we wouldn't ask her questions about school or homework but that her responsibility was to make sure all of her work was completed. We just received her first-term grades. She had one F, two Ds, and two Cs. We found that one of the main reasons for her F and Ds was her failure to complete homework assignments. When we confronted her with this she said that we are always on her back. We reminded her that we weren't on her back for the entire term, assuming that she was doing fine. We said that we didn't ask her about school but given her first semester grades and her comments from her teachers we are obligated to do something. We are just not sure what to do at this time.

Answer

To attempt to answer your question, there are several points we wish to raise and questions that we have. It is important for you to make certain that your daughter's increasing problems are not the result of an undefined learning disability or emotional problem. You mentioned that she has never really seemed to enjoy school. Is that because school has been very difficult for her? Has she developed an island of competence at school? Is there a subject at which she has always been able to succeed? If not, we can't help but wonder if her self-esteem and resilience relative to school are weak.

Certainly high school is much more demanding in regards to work and responsibility than the earlier grades. If in fact your daughter has a learning disability, it is important to address that issue before you implement a strategy for homework. We also wonder about the quality of her class work and how adequate it is. If it appears sub-par, this may indicate that your daughter is struggling with a learning disability or some other problem besides a failure to complete homework. We also wonder if your daughter has had problems sustaining effort for tasks that she perceives as repetitive, effortful, or uninteresting. For example, some youth struggle to complete tasks in which they are not truly engaged. At the extreme, these youth experience significant problems developing self-control, often exhibiting impulsive, inattentive, and hyperactive behavior. This problem, sometimes diagnosed as Attention Deficit Hyperactivity Disorder, can be effectively treated with a combination of educational strategy, skill building, and, at times, medication.

In your daughter's case we suggest from this point forward you become proactive and adopt a problem-solving approach. You might say to your daughter that you know she wants you off her back and that she wants to do well in school but sometimes certain problems interfere with success. Discuss with her and her teachers the possibility of undertaking an evaluation to assess if any learning problems do in fact exist. If a specific skill weakness or problem is identified, make certain it is addressed. Once this happens then it is important for you to sit down with your daughter and work out an agreed-upon plan relative to school and homework. This process should include the following steps:

1. Make certain you and your daughter understand the nature of her academic strengths and weaknesses. Classes that tap into her academic vulnerabilities will require additional time as well as possible tutoring and support.

2. Agree on what type of assistance your daughter would like from you and how that assistance will be provided.

3. Discuss the consequences if each party fails to meet its part of the agreement.

4. Consider strategies that may assist your daughter in becoming more effective at completing schoolwork and homework. Ask your daughter some of her thoughts about what would be helpful. We continue to be pleasantly surprised by the number of students who are able to articulate what they need to improve their performance in school. Make certain any strategies that are developed are guided by the goal of developing a resilient mindset.

5. Finally, don't forget to use empathy in your discussions with your daughter. From your description we suspect she is even more frustrated than you are about her school performance but feels unable or afraid to communicate her concerns. Make certain she understands that you appreciate that she would like to succeed but

has struggled. Ensure that the two of you work together in solving this problem.

Question

We recently read a book that was quite provocative. The author claims that homework doesn't help a child's academic performance in school and if anything interferes with family life. The author claimed that in many families battles about homework become a daily routine and are not worth fighting about. This seems to go against educational practices. Does homework have a positive effect on learning? If it does, how can we help kids do homework without it destroying the family?

Answer

As far as we are aware, no one has written the definitive history of homework. We don't know when the first homework assignment was given. We suspect, however, whether it was a hundred or five thousand years ago, the very first homework assignment was received similarly to homework assignments given to children today. Additional activities assigned to students outside of school are not typically responded to in a positive or enthusiastic manner. Even as adults, very few of us enjoy being told to take work home.

Recent studies indicate that at younger grade levels there is little relation between the amount of time devoted to homework and a student's achievement. On the other hand in the upper grades the more time spent on homework, the greater the achievement gains. In our experience there are several constructive purposes for homework. Homework allows for practice and participation in learning tasks. Homework helps children develop personal skills, such as responsibility and time management. While this may surprise some parents, homework can serve as a positive experience for parent-child relations if parents turn it into a cooperative effort, encouraging the input of their children and offering assistance when indicated. Finally, homework helps parents to be informed about what their children are learning and can foster closer school-home relationships. Keep in mind that over the last hundred years—although children are being asked to learn much more each year in school—the amount of time spent in school has not increased. Thus, as children progress into the higher grades, more and more time is spent self-teaching through homework. In the early grades, the primary purpose of homework then is not so much practice and review but to help children become responsible, independent learners.

While we have questions about the book you mentioned that minimizes the importance of homework, we believe that if homework is to be effective, there must be regular parent-teacher communication. We agree that homework does interfere with family life for some families but not all families. Further, when homework becomes a family battleground, it typically occurs when parents and teachers are not communicating well or when each begins to blame the other for the homework problems. For example, some teachers believe that parents are not doing their part when their children do not complete their homework assignments. On the other side, some parents may not understand the purposes of homework and are confused about the specific role teachers expect them to play. All the while students resist homework, seeing it as an encroachment on their free time. They often complain that homework is a repetition of what is done in class and is too difficult, too long, or too boring.

The best way to resolve these different viewpoints is for teachers and parents to have a clearer understanding of the purpose of homework. Teachers should always ask if homework leads to greater learning and more enjoyment with learning or if it creates more negative feelings about school. If the latter is true, it is important for teachers to consider in what ways they can change the homework requirements.

Similar to other problems we face with our children, it is important to begin with empathy; create a working, effective relationship through good communication; and use a problem-solving method to deal with homework issues and problems. All of these strategies foster a resilient mindset. But even more importantly they help to create a homework alliance with your child. *Seven Steps to Homework Success: A Family Guide for Solving Common Homework Problems*, written by Sydney Zentall and Sam Goldstein, offers a step-by-step program for creating this working alliance.

Question

You often talk about identifying and reinforcing a child's islands of competence. There is a problem we are facing in terms of our seventeen-year-old son. His island of competence is basketball. He is a leading scorer on the varsity team in his high school. However, in order to be on the team you have to maintain a C grade point average. Our son has never been a great student, but he has never had a behavior problem. We feel he might have some learning problems. However, when tested a number of years ago the school psychologist indicated he couldn't find any learning disabilities. Our son just came home with his report card. He earned two Cs, two C−s, and a D in math, his weakest subject. He is now ineligible to play on the team. He is talking about quitting school. We think one of the things that kept him motivated at school was basketball and the dream of playing basketball in college. We are really worried he will quit school. Why take away one of the main things that has kept our son in school? We don't understand the school's philosophy.

Answer

Although the policy followed by your son's school is similar to that found in most schools, we have major questions about its effectiveness or fairness. We want to explain our view, recognizing that many educators hold differing opinions and believe that our view would serve to weaken expectations and standards.

We begin with the assumption that we are all motivated to work harder to maintain or obtain something we want if we perceive that working harder will lead to the desired results. Parents and educational systems routinely hold out pleasurable, enjoyable, or extracurricular activities as "reinforcers" that are available only when required goals are met. In a simple behavioral model, we have no complaints with this philosophy. However, your son's situation points out two very serious problems with this approach.

First, if students are incapable of meeting the goals set by a school then the outcome of their efforts will be failure, depriving them not only of the reinforcing activity they enjoy, but also confirming their perception that they are inadequate and can't meet expectations. In addition, they may come to believe that the school's expectations are unrealistic. Consequently, in future situations their efforts may be reduced, even for tasks that are within their abilities to achieve. It is as if they have come to believe, "What's the use?"

Second, in your son's case what is being held out is not just any reinforcer but an island of competence. As we have mentioned before, an island of competence is important for many reasons. It is an activity that we engage in, feel good about, are successful at, and can use to display our competence to the world. In response we receive reinforcement and support of our worth and capabilities. By gambling your son's island of competence, the educational system hopes to motivate him to work harder and obtain C or better grades. Yet, this is a dangerous gamble. It is equivalent to taking all of your money and putting it on one number of the roulette wheel. Certainly there is a chance to hit the jackpot. But there is a much greater chance to lose everything you have.

This problem is best exemplified in your son's case. His access to athletics, which represents an island of competence, has been made contingent upon his scholastic achievement. While this model may work for many youth, for some it may prove counterproductive. For those who struggle scholastically the loss of the athletic activity deprives them of the one significant school activity that has nurtured their self-esteem and sense of competence.

Several questions can then be raised. "How do we know if students are capable of meeting certain expectations?" "If they are not, what kind of help are we offering as a school to ensure that they can meet these expectations?" "If we are not providing them with the support they need, then is it fair to say you cannot play sports if you don't meet these expectations?" Obviously, these questions are not always easy to answer but they should serve as guideposts as we attempt to motivate students to perform in school.

As a first step we recommend you seek out a community-based specialist in learning disabilities and neuropsychology. We are not suggesting that the school psychologist's evaluation was inaccurate but keep in mind that many evaluations completed at school are not necessarily done to define strengths and weaknesses, but instead have as a main focus the determination of eligibility for special services. Eligibility for special service is based upon a discrepancy between where the school believes your son should be academically and where he is achieving. There are many weaknesses that impact school performance that may not be best understood or defined through this type of discrepancy model.

From your description we are assuming in fact your son likely is burdened by a weakness or weaknesses in skills essential for effective school performance. Once these areas of weakness are identified, you can use this assessment to advocate not only for supportive services at school but to explain to school administrators that there was a reason besides the assumed lack of effort or motivation for your son's struggles. Make certain you also enlist the aid of the high school coach. From your description we suspect that teachers and the coach will likely be supportive because your son has not been a disruptive influence at school. In these situations we have been successful in creating a contract with school administrators working forward, that is, setting in place assistance and support for your son if he agrees to maintain a certain grade point average from this point forward in exchange for continued participation on the high school team. Though it is our preference that grades not be tied to athletic activities for students such as your son, most schools still adhere to this policy, believing that to make any exceptions, such as in the case of your son, will open the floodgates for other requested exceptions.

Question

Our daughter is in third grade. She has always loved school but this year really dislikes her teacher. She wakes up each morning with stomachaches and says that her teacher talks too loud and always looks angry. Our daughter is a sensitive child but it seems that this teacher is much too negative. We are not sure how to handle the situation. Our daughter told us not to say anything since she believes the teacher will become angry with her. We don't want that to happen and we don't want to be seen as overly pushy parents. But we also don't want to see our daughter so unhappy about school. What should we say to our daughter and to her teacher?

Answer

Your question touches upon many issues. It is never easy for parents to observe their children waking up with stomachaches and feeling very unhappy in school. Obviously, something should be done but any interventions that are initiated will be most successful if we understand what might be occurring.

To begin with we wondered what information you were relying upon when you wrote, "It seems that this teacher is much too negative." Are you aware of additional information about this teacher's style, teaching strategies, or feedback from other parents? You mentioned that your daughter is a sensitive child. One of your first goals will be to understand how much of the difficulty in school results from your daughter's sensitivity versus the teacher's behavior. We want to make certain that you understand we are not saying your daughter's observations are misleading. Rather, when children are temperamentally sensitive they often possess a very low emotional threshold. Minor stresses, even an adult pointing out a mistake in a supportive manner, may be perceived as harsh and critical. Also, such children are often hypersensitive to sound and experience a teacher's voice as loud when to other children it is not.

Let's first deal with the issue of your daughter's sensitivity. Does your daughter worry excessively? Does she appear to be anxious or overwhelmed in many situations that other children appear to handle without difficulty? Did your daughter experience problems separating when she began school? Many anxious children experience somatic symptoms such as stomachaches in response to their worries. In these situations such children perceive school, in particular the teacher, as the source of their worry. Unfortunately, often these children may refuse to go to school as a way of avoiding a stressful situation.

We find it interesting that your daughter doesn't want you to speak with the teacher, perceiving that this may make the teacher even angrier with her. This paradox is often characteristic of anxious children. Without wishing to sound too technical, they perceive that if the anxiety-provoking stimulus is confronted, in this case the teacher, it will increase rather than lessen the stress. If our description appears accurate for your daughter we suggest you seek consultation with the school psychologist or a community-based child clinician. Although there may be a biological basis that contributes to some children being more vulnerable to this type of sensitivity than others, there are therapeutic interventions that can teach children to think differently and use a variety of different thoughts to change their behavior.

In regards to your daughter's teacher, we believe that it is important to be empathic with your daughter's wish for you not to talk with the teacher but to let your daughter know that you think it is very important to do so. You can discuss with your daughter what you might say so that the teacher will not feel criticized. Although your daughter may remain worried when you speak with her teacher, it is a meeting that should take place. In addition, there may be ways for you to collect additional data. As we pointed out, how do other parents feel about this teacher and her style? Are other children experiencing problems or does this appear to be a caring teacher whose behavior is overreacted to by your daughter? In our experience, when parents speak with a teacher about their child's concerns but do so in a nonaccusatory, problem-solving manner, effective strategies can be set in motion. For example, we know of one teacher who told her student that she was glad the student's parents had informed her that she was being experienced as speaking loudly. She said to the student she would watch the volume of her voice but if it seemed loud, it would be okay for the student to tell her. After this was said, the student's relationship with the teacher became very positive.

Question

Our son is in the second grade. He is big for his age but he has always been immature socially and struggled learning to read. We just had a school conference and were taken back by the recommendation that he be retained. My husband and I were so surprised that we weren't sure what questions to ask. We told them we had to think about it. On the way home we felt being held back would hurt his already low self-esteem even more. But at the meeting his teachers said that he would not be able to catch up to the other kids and would fall further behind and that he needed a year to mature academically. My husband even wondered about sending him to a private school, although I am not sure we could handle the cost. We have another school meeting in two weeks. What are the kinds of questions we should be asking?

Answer

The question of retention is a very complicated one that requires a great deal of information and thought. Although retention is typically suggested when it appears that a child simply needs a year to mature, in our experience it is not just a question of maturation but rather the kinds of learning and social struggles that a child is experiencing as well as the kinds of support services that should be initiated. Retention has often been an ineffective strategy when the child requires more than just a year to catch up and is not provided with support services. We suggest you ask the following questions:

1. **By being retained in second grade, will my child enter second grade performing academically at an average level in comparison to the other students?** This is an important issue. By entering second grade a second time your child for the first time may experience the ability to work at a level and rate consistent with the other students in the classroom. This is an important resilience-building experience.

2. **From this point forward, will my child be able to keep achieving at this pace?** Think of a horse race in which your horse is running 10 percent slower than the others. After a mile you are only a tenth of a mile behind. However, after a hundred miles you are ten miles behind. The rate at which most children achieve remains fairly constant throughout school. Thus, if teachers cannot explain the rate your child has been achieving thus far and are uncertain or uncomfortable predicting how he will achieve from this point forward you have reason to be concerned that although he may be equivalent to other students entering second grade the second time around, by fourth or fifth grade he may again be a year behind. Retention every three years is simply not a viable means of helping children benefit from their school experiences.

3. **Will my son require special education assistance when he repeats second grade?** If the school team responds that he will not and believes that he can keep pace from this point forward the retention may be a viable option to consider. The limited research on retention demonstrates the small group of children who truly benefit from this activity are capable of keeping up when given an additional year to develop basic skills. This usually occurs in first or second grade. Beyond that point, retention appears to serve as little more than a punishment.

4. **Are there academic areas in which your child is ready for third grade?** If your child is ready and capable for third-grade work in areas of science and social studies then repeating a grade simply to reinforce basic academic skills must be weighed against the lack of intellectual stimulation he will receive by doing the same science, social studies, and related projects during the repeat of second grade.

5. **How does your child feel about retention?** While this may not be a question to ask the teachers, it is an answer that you should bring

with you to the next meeting. It has been our experience that some children welcome this opportunity and don't have to be "talked into it." Yet most children feel quite overwhelmed, distressed, and embarrassed.

6. **You comment that your child is "somewhat immature socially."** We are not certain what this means. If your child has developed best friends in the classroom then being retained does have a liability in causing the loss of these peers. Also, if he has difficulty with peer relationships, rather than retention, he might benefit from a social skills group.

7. **What are the alternatives?** It is important for you to ask the educational team what the alternatives are besides retention. If your son moves into third grade will he qualify for additional special education or related support? Might a social skills group be beneficial whether or not he is retained? As you consider the alternatives, also consider your husband's suggestion of a private school. The idea of a private school is attractive in that it may give your son a chance to "start over." On the other hand, many private schools have only high-achieving students and may not be the best match for your son.

Once you have considered answers to all of these questions, you will be able to make a more educated decision about retention.

> Although retention is typically suggested when it appears that a child simply needs a year to mature, in our experience it is not just a question of maturation but rather the kinds of learning and social struggles that a child is experiencing as well as the kinds of support services that should be initiated.

Question

There has been so much about bullying in the news lately it seems that every story about kids who have shot their classmates talks about how the kids who did it were bullied. It is scary since our eleven-year-old son is constantly being bullied. He didn't even want to tell us about it but one day he came home crying and his book bag was torn. We asked what happened and he couldn't hold back any-

more. He told us about four boys in his class who have been tormenting him. We were stunned since these are kids he has known for years and one was even a close friend in third and fourth grade. We spoke with our son and told him that we wanted to discuss the situation with the principal. At first he didn't want us to say anything but then he said okay. We were shocked by the principal's response. He said that the four boys our son mentioned are all good kids and that our son is too sensitive. He also suggested that our son stay far away from them, leading us to believe that somehow he thought our son was provoking them. What do you think of the principal's response? What should we do now?

Answer

We have serious concern about the principal's response. While the four boys who are bullying your son may be "good kids" that does not excuse their behavior. Good kids may sometimes do hurtful things without realizing the pain they are inflicting. We believe that the principal should meet with each of the four boys as well as their parents to discuss what has been transpiring. Every school should have strict rules and guidelines against bullying, and the principal should make certain that these four students understand these rules and the consequences that follow should the rules be broken. We do not believe it is in the best interests of these four students to let the situation continue.

On another issue, if in fact, your son is doing some things that are provoking other children, then it would be important for the principal to discuss this with you and your son. Some children, without realizing it, may say or do things that upset their peers. We do not know if this is the case with your son but if it is, then your son can benefit from learning new ways of relating. However, even as the principal seems to be suggesting your son is engaging in behaviors that demonstrate poor social skills, this should not exonerate the behavior of the bullying students.

Although your first meeting with the principal was not satisfactory, we suggest you schedule another meeting. At this second meeting you can ask for more specific feedback about your son's behavior, but you can also strongly state your opinion that the situation should be addressed with these other students. Until it is, we are concerned that your son will continue to be anxious and upset about attending school.

Question
In one of your workshops you actually advocated that students be involved in creating classroom rules and consequences. I think one of the reasons we have so many discipline problems in society and in school is because we have given too much control to kids. I think teachers should tell their classes what the rules, expectations, and consequences are and kids have to learn to follow them. What purpose does it serve to have students decide what rules to have? Isn't that the role of a teacher or any adult?

Answer
We believe that it is the responsibility of teachers to set and guide discipline. However, this does not mean that students should not be involved on some level in the disciplinary process, especially if we keep in mind that discipline can best be understood as a teaching process. Our work and research has convinced us that disciplinary practices in schools should be guided by the goals of creating safe and secure environments while developing self-discipline and self-control in students. To accomplish these goals, we believe that teachers should discuss the topic of rules and consequences with students. Certainly some rules are nonnegotiable. These include issues related to safety, security, and treatment of others.

However, we believe that once nonnegotiable rules are discussed, students can be involved in answering the following questions: "What rules do you think we need in this classroom for the classroom to run smoothly and for students to learn best?" "What is the best way to be reminded of rules so it doesn't feel like we are nagging each other?" "What should the consequences be if we forget a rule?" In answering these questions, teachers still maintain their authority but by involving students they help them to understand that there are reasons for rules and consequences. Such an exercise helps to promote self-discipline and self-control. It does not give too much control to students but rather teaches them more responsibility and control.

Question
In your workshops you have talked about creating a positive school environment that fosters self-worth and motivation. As both a parent and middle school teacher, I really struggle with grades and how for some kids grades appear to

lessen their self-esteem. I feel some kids put in so much effort but are not great students and never earn high grades. They never see their name on the honor roll. We have assemblies celebrating the achievements of honor students, and I look around and can see the faces of the kids who will probably never be celebrated in this way. Also I feel that some students work just to get high grades and that is all that counts to them. I guess I am wondering how does one acknowledge the accomplishments of honor roll students without diminishing unintentionally the self-esteem or resilience of the C student? Also, what can we do to enhance the academic self-esteem and motivation of those students who work hard yet receive just average grades?

Answer

It is our strong belief that every student possesses at least one skill or island of competence that can be highlighted or displayed in schools. If schools only recognize academic competence, then many students will fail to be appreciated for accomplishments other than those shown in test scores or grades. As you point out, academic excellence will not be part of every child's experience. For some it may be certain extra-curricular activities such as student government or athletics. We don't advocate that the awards assemblies for academic excellence be eliminated, but we do believe that additional awards (not just trivially created so that everyone gets something) be added to such assemblies.

The issue of report cards that do not discourage students with average or below average grades is an important one. We have spoken with many educators who question the heavy reliance on grades but lament that they are necessary when students apply to college or for jobs. Ideally, report cards should reflect more than grades. They should include a narrative of a student's progress and of areas of strength and weakness. We realize that this would involve extra time on a teacher's part and we know how busy teachers already are. However, we should continue to search for ways to capture on a report card each student's strengths not only in academics but in a variety of areas; we should attempt to describe academic struggles within a framework that articulates the kinds of assistance that are required to help each student perform more successfully. This is not an easy task, but in a society that emphasizes a respect for diversity, we must develop ways of assessing students that capture the unique strengths of each.

Question

As a high school teacher, I loved Dr. Julius Segal's notion that teachers are important, charismatic adults in students' lives, that teachers play a major role in fostering resilience. But I wonder how I can be a charismatic adult and make a difference in the lives of my students when I have more than 150 students in my different sections. Any suggestions?

Answer

We appreciate that becoming a charismatic adult in the life of a student is typically more challenging for a secondary school teacher than an elementary school teacher. High school teachers compared with elementary school teachers interact with more students each day and also have less time with each one. However, we have been impressed with the ways in which high school teachers have still been able to develop a personal relationship with their students, a relationship from which their students in Segal's words "gather strength."

It is important to remember that it is often the simple things that have a lasting impact. For instance, teachers learning the names of their students, greeting them with a smile, being available and accessible, having a sense of humor, treating each student's opinions with respect, and discussing mistakes as experiences from which to learn, have all been descriptions offered by students as the characteristics of caring educators. We believe these behaviors can be exhibited even when a teacher has 150 students.

We knew of one high school teacher who told his class on the first day of school, "Sometimes I don't have a chance to get to know you as much as I would like so during the year I plan to call each of you twice at home in the evening just to find out how you are doing." This teacher said it only took him about seven or eight minutes each evening to make a couple of calls and the benefits were noticeable in the behavior and academic performance of his students. The students were so impressed with this act of caring that he was often nominated by them as the outstanding teacher in his school district. He was a wonderful example of being a charismatic adult for more than 150 students each year, having a lifelong impact on them.

13

Todd's Story

The Process of Resilience

W hen we first decided to write this book, a volume of questions and answers, we wrestled with how to provide a concluding chapter in this format that would convey to readers the true power and potency of resilience in shaping each and every life. We decided it wasn't enough to remind readers that resilience was important only because it conveyed a sense of optimism, ownership, or personal control. We have, in all of our works, emphasized the paramount importance of raising resilient children to ensure future success for every individual and for the collective culture. We hope through the information we have provided in this text, to educate and reinforce the important role every adult can play in a child's life, believing in them and providing them with opportunities to reinforce their islands of competence and feelings of self-worth.

Recently, during filming our documentary, "Tough Times/Resilient Kids," the material to close this volume presented itself. As part of this documentary, veteran broadcast journalist Mike Schneider, former host of NBC's "Weekend Today" and news anchor at ABC's "Good Morning America," had the opportunity to interview Todd Rose and his family. Short parts of those interviews appear in the documentary. The transcripts from those interviews have been edited and appear in this chapter.

The second author of this book met Todd thirteen years ago when Todd was fourteen years of age. As a seventh grader, despite good intellect and strong academic skills, Todd had a disastrous school history. His problems developing self-control led him to lack sustained attention in school and to frequently act thoughtlessly and impulsively. His functioning then and now met the criteria for Attention Deficit Hyperactivity Disorder. Over the following years, Todd's life has exemplified the power and process of resilience. Though his road to adulthood has contained many bumps and twists, the qualities of resilience we have described as reflecting the mindset of parents capable of fostering resilience and the mindset of children who demonstrate resilience, are exemplified in this family's story. We leave you with their words, words that we hope will not only inspire but guide each and every one of you with your children.

Mike: When you look back on your childhood, Todd, what word or words would you use to describe yourself?

Todd: I have actually thought a lot about that. I would say turbulent. Turbulent comes to me because it is hyperactive and a little bit destructive at the same time.

Mike: When did you internally become aware of this turbulence? Is there something that was felt that you couldn't put your finger on?

Todd: Not necessarily. It is an interesting thing because for most of my life I didn't realize that I was acting or behaving any differently than anybody else. I just didn't understand why people didn't like me and didn't want to be around me. You just think you are behaving in the same way and so it takes a while. I don't think I really became aware of it until I was nineteen or twenty when I started realizing maybe I need to think through the way I act, behave, and think.

> I didn't realize that I was acting or behaving any differently than anybody else.

Mike: When you were younger were you aware that people may not have liked you or that you had some issues with authority figures perhaps?

Todd: Certainly. It was interesting because I wanted so much to be like every young kid, to have friends and things like that. You feel a little bit of animosity from other people. But you really don't know why and you just sort of think it is their issue. I don't know why they don't like me; I'm just like everybody else. I wasn't very good at picking up on those cues as far as what it was about my behavior that was sort of offish and defiant.

Mike: Think back to when you were nine or ten years old. When you got up in the morning can you remember what you were out to accomplish?

Todd: If it was the start of the school year I really did have a strong desire to go. Each year I told myself that this was the semester I was really going to do well. I'm going to sort of hunker down and get the job done. I always wanted to make contracts with myself. Okay, I'm going to make friends today. But over the course of a day or over the course of that semester it kind of all falls apart and you just sort of throw your hands up in the air and start over.

> I would just think I wanted people to like me so much, and I just wanted to have a normal childhood but for the most part I just didn't.

Mike: How did that make you feel?

Todd: It was very difficult. It was so devastating inside. I would just think I wanted people to like me so much, and I just wanted to have a normal childhood but for the most part I just didn't. I don't know, it's hard to explain.

Mike: You use the word *normal.* Did you feel that you were not normal?

Todd: Yes, I did. But as a young child I didn't realize I wasn't normal per se. At some point I realized that something was different. That was a difficult thing to face. Hey, there is something different about me. I have to take this certain medication to make me like everybody else. That's an adjustment in and of itself.

Mike: You used the word a little while ago, *destructive.* Did you break things? Did you steal things? Did you fight kids?

Todd: Oh, yes, yes, yes. It is bizarre to me. I look back and I can't explain why I did some of the things I did. When I was younger, I would steal things. I was always getting in fights with people, usually not winning. I wasn't the biggest kid. I would steal things, and then I would lie a lot to cover it up even when the truth was easier to tell. I look back and I think, what was I thinking? I have no real answer for that.

Mike: I'm sure Mom and Dad tried to set you straight. How did you react to that? How did you interact with your parents?

Todd: I see now what they were trying to do. They were more focused on long-term issues, but sometimes as a kid you don't think much beyond that day and so it is difficult to see it from their perspective. I was focused on my desires: I want to have friends and I want to do this and I want to do that. These were all very short-term goals. They were trying to focus on building character and building confidence so that when the time came, when I realized I needed to do something different, I would possess those foundations.

Mike: If you don't mind, give me an example of a low point. There must have been a time when you and your parents just went at it. What caused that? What happened? Give me a real sense of what it was like to be inside your skin at that age with your parents in your home.

Todd: I'll tell you it probably culminated in a lot of frustration on their part trying to show me the value of education and realizing it wasn't sticking with me. Every semester, promises, promises, and then D and F averages across the board and getting in a lot of trouble as far as getting kicked out of school and things like that. It culminates in a lot of frustration on everyone's part. I remember when my principal in high school told me I couldn't graduate with my class. That was a very frustrating thing for everybody because at that point that was what I was working for: getting through high school and hopefully moving on. That wasn't an option anymore and things were looking somewhat bleak and I had my own ideas, right? I still thought it was more external than me. Everyone else was at fault.

Mike: Their fault, why is the world against me?

Todd: Right, yes, and so you say it to yourself. I've gone through making some athletic teams in high school and getting kicked off every time. They were seeing the destructive behavior that it was causing, and I just thought we had different perspectives. I didn't set long-term goals. Long-term goals for me meant next week. The basketball game next week—that was a long-term goal. They had a lifelong perspective for me, and I didn't, and so when this all bubbled over it was very stressful for everyone.

Mike: Was there a moment that just . . . in terms of an actual incident . . . where you and your parents just went at it?

Todd: No, you know we never really went *at it*. That was the thing. It wasn't about anger. More about disappointment and almost like, fine you know we have tried so hard, and it is interesting because, there never was anger. It was more just disappointment. I never had a time when I just felt okay.

Mike: When you were told you couldn't graduate, what happened to your life at that point?

Todd: In my mind I didn't realize I didn't possess a long-term strength and I needed to graduate. I had a girlfriend, who is my wife now. I didn't have a high school diploma. I was working as a stock boy for minimum wage, and we found out we were about to have a family. That was as rock bottom as you can get because I hadn't been very successful at anything and so there wasn't much reason to think that would change anytime soon. There was just a lot of frustration. My parents were trying so hard, and it just didn't seem to be taking with me.

> My parents were trying so hard, and it just didn't seem to be taking with me.

Mike: When did things start to change?

Todd: Actually I can give you an exact moment for that one. That is pretty easy. I was nineteen when my wife and I had our first child, Austin. I remember we were sitting in the hospital, and I do remember as if it was yesterday. My wife was asleep from the delivery, and they brought in our son and asked if I wanted to hold him. I said okay. I didn't know what to think—it was all kind of overwhelming—and I just sat there and I realized, just that very moment, that this is not about me anymore and things need to change because there is a young lady and now a young child who are totally dependent upon the outcome of my life and that was so overwhelming to me. Now, it still took me a good nine months to a year to get off the dime; I mean it is easy to change your thoughts, behavior is a little different. But that was the true moment for me.

Mike: Sounds like you became aware at that moment that you knew your life, your behavior, affected somebody else in a profound way.

Todd: Growing up I never really thought much about it. I didn't care that much about my behavior. I didn't really value my life. I don't mean that in a sense that you think about taking your own life at all, it is just that it didn't seem to really have much consequence for me. I could deal with the fact that if people were disappointed; well, I was used to that. Mostly they were always disappointed. But it is an unbelievable feeling when you have somebody else that says look, I believe in you, right? I believe that you will make it alright for us. It is an overwhelming feeling, and it was the first time I have ever felt that sense of responsibility on that scale.

> It is an unbelievable feeling when you have somebody else that says look, I believe in you.

Mike: So where did you take it from there?

Todd: Well, I sat there and I realized things need to change. I can't make $6.00 an hour forever. That wasn't really going to do well for our family, and I just thought I needed to go to school. It is interesting because people have asked why did you choose school after such a horrible experience? I thought that was amazing; I really don't have an answer to that. I realized that after all the frustrations and struggles that your parents and you go through, it

comes down to that example they set for you. I look at my mom
and dad and the educational example they set for me, and there
wasn't a doubt in my mind that's what I needed to do. So it is
kind of amazing. After the horrible educational experience I had,
that I would say at nineteen, okay, I'm going to go to school.

Mike: How did you end up going back to school? You had been invited
to leave.

Todd: Yes, yes, that's exactly what I thought. I decided against returning
to high school, and I took the GED and did well on that.

Mike: Proud of yourself?

Todd: Yeah, it's not that difficult of a test. Then I said okay, what now,
what do I do here? I applied to a number of colleges in the state
and was promptly rejected. Nobody wants a high school dropout
with a GED and low ACT scores. There was a university in
Ogden, Weber State, that said okay, you can come, but you have
to attend off-campus classes at night. So I said, okay, that's great.
My wife actually went down there and enrolled me the first time.
I would say I'm going to go to school, and she would say, yeah,
you told me that last semester. She went down and enrolled me
and said I signed you up for a few classes and if you don't like
them, you better go down there. So I did because I thought I
better take classes I want. But she really got the ball going.

Mike: When you found yourself back in a classroom, let alone college,
how did it go for you?

Todd: You know what? It's interesting because there was a lot of self-
doubt. I had no expectations for myself. I don't think anybody
really had many expectations for me except they were happy that
at least I was making this effort and so the compliments were sort
of the let's-just-wait-and-see kind of attitude from all of us,
including myself. But the one thing I remember that was
important was that nobody there knew who I was. That was
important because in high school teachers knew who I was, right?
I mean I could move from grade to grade and they knew about
me. I had plenty of experiences where they knew about me and I
think that in some ways it affected my performance and sort of
the interactions we had. But nobody in college knew who I was.

Mike: Fresh start?

Todd: Yeah! In my mind I decided I wanted to make a change. I think that is ultimately what I needed. Nobody knew me. I could be whoever I wanted to be and that was a big deal for me.

Mike: What happened when you had to do all the things you probably disdained in high school, reading, assignments, tests? Did you prepare yourself?

Todd: Yeah.

Mike: It happened just like that?

Todd: No, definitely not. I think one of the products of not really putting a fairly good effort into school most of your life is that you end up with really poor study habits. I used to literally hate to read. Most of my life it was difficult, and I didn't like it, which is a big difference today. But, it is funny because I took a class in economics that was pretty difficult, and this teacher would say you know what, none of you are going to do well on this test. He was very arrogant but that was good for me because I was competitive. At first it had nothing to do with I really want to learn, it was more I am going to show him. So that class was alright, and I took a psychology class and had a professor with whom I interacted well. We formed a good relationship to the point where I remember not turning in an assignment on time, which I was going to do when I got around to it, and she came up to me and asked is something the matter? What happened? And I was like, um . . . I actually made up an excuse like oh, it's my printer, you know? So she said get it in. My office is here, bring it in tomorrow. I thought, oh, my goodness, she is really going to stick with me on this one, so I did it. So to say that all of a sudden I was this great student is a far stretch. It was an incremental process that took a lot of time.

Mike: You didn't feel you had the baggage of your high school legacy or reputation?

Todd: Right, that is a good word for it. As a matter of fact, there were times early on where I would get into classes where there were a few people from my high school and I actually withdrew from those because I knew there was a sense inside of me that as soon as I got into that situation I felt a desire and a need to act a certain way. I couldn't explain it. Sort of brought me back to where I had been. So I tried to stay away from classes that I knew people in and that was good for me.

Mike: Tell me a little bit about the work you did with Dr. Sam Goldstein. In the process of moving from who you were to who you are now, there was some work you had to do.

Todd: Yes, surely. My work with Dr. Goldstein was on two levels. First was a sense of a good diagnosis to get a finger on it and say this is what is affecting my life. I actually still have the fourteen-page diagnostic report. To this day I read it and have highlighted it and made comments. For me that was actually the number one thing that got me this far in school. I said, look I want to know what this was that affected my life.

Mike: How old were you at this time? When you were diagnosed.

Todd: I believe I was in seventh grade. So for the longest time it was sort of well, you're just a bad kid. This was sort of the perception that came across. You are a bad kid, you don't try, you don't want to succeed. Actually, to be able to say, this is the issue and there are things we can do about that, helped. People would want to talk to me all the time about what I was doing, and I just got the sense that no one really understood what it really meant to have an attention disorder. I felt Dr. Goldstein in our conversations did. I remember that and I remember his first words to me. We walked into his office. I remember it very vividly. He said, "Let's figure out what's wrong with the rest of the world." Rather than let's figure out what's wrong with you (laughing), and I remember that. It set me off to where I wasn't defensive. Because I was defensive at first; I didn't want to go to a psychologist and be discussing this sort of thing. I remember thinking, maybe I'll give this a chance because this person is not out to figure out what's wrong with me. Because again I didn't think anything was wrong with me. So I think I was able to open up a little bit better. It was the first step.

But probably more important for me was, as I progressed in college and did better for the first time, the thought of actually going to graduate school entered my mind. It was kind of a silly thought really. It was sort of fleeting. I knew I really enjoyed psychology and the brain and I sent a letter to Dr. Goldstein, just real broad. I didn't even look at the questions I asked—and I probably didn't need to ask those silly questions—but I just said I was interested in this and I didn't know what to expect. I didn't really expect a response. I got a prompt letter that said this is what I know, this is what you should do, and I kept that letter. One of the biggest things that affected my going on to where I am now was the ability to do research, and that is something he said I ought to look at. That opened my eyes. And when I was invited to do that I don't think I would have actually taken that opportunity because it was a lot of work had I not known that was an important step.

Mike: It seems to be almost a total opposite for somebody who has an attention "disorder" to be able to focus on anything in general, much less research. That seems like once again the mirror image, the flip side actually.

Todd: That was actually a process, too. When I was younger when I took medication, people noticed I was able to focus. In fact, I didn't want to take it. I didn't want to have to take a pill. I wanted to be the same as everybody else. So I didn't take it. That was probably one of the worst choices I ever made, because your parents can tell you here is your medicine this morning but when I get to school it's up to me, right (laughing) . . . and so I actually stayed off it. When I got into college I realized there was a point, the first year, that I said I can't fool myself. This legitimately helps me to be able to focus and be able to learn, and so I went to my doctor and started medication again, which was a big first step because it does level the playing field. I know there is a lot of differing opinions on that, but it certainly was the first most important thing for me because it allowed me to stay on task and complete my homework and even begin thinking about long-term things. It was interesting.

Mike: In your college years, when did it occur to you that not only could you survive a college environment but you could thrive in it and consider the notion of going on and continuing on in your education? When did that hit you?

Todd: That didn't hit me for a long time. This is how it happened. I never wanted to take real difficult classes. Every semester I would try a harder class because at some point I was going to figure out there was a reason why I was doing well and it didn't have a lot to do with me.

Mike: You thought the classes were too easy?

Todd: Right, and I think a lot of people thought that. I got a lot of comments. Even my relatives would say, Todd got straight As, and then, let's see what happens when he gets into upper division classes. It was good because for a long time my motivation, as I commented, was very external. That was good, alright . . . I'll show them. You think that but ultimately inside I thought there is going to be a point to where my intelligence is going to hit a brick wall and there is going to be a class that just knocks me off my seat and brings me down to reality. So I just kept taking harder and harder classes, and I remember saying, okay, this anatomy class is going to be the one, or this statistics class is going to be the one. I was so poor in math for so long I thought statistics would be the one, and, actually, I excelled in that and was invited to be a supplemental teacher the next semester. So at that point I thought, okay, you know what, I think I can do this. But in the back of my head was the concern that there was a standardized test I was going to have to take to get into graduate school. I have never done very well on standardized tests so I thought, I'll keep telling myself I'm interested in going to graduate school but ultimately thinking that test would be the doom for me.

Mike: What happened when you went to take the test?

Todd: Actually, I had developed strong study habits and I went through a class to prepare for it at the University of Utah. I made myself physically ill preparing for that test. It was one of those immediate gratification tests. It is computerized. Instant scores (laughing). I get these scores and I was proud, I'll tell you that.

Mike: Tell us how well you did.

Todd: I was in the upper percentiles. I definitely didn't hurt myself, I'll put it that way.

Mike: So you figured, okay, I'm going to graduate school.

Todd: Actually I never thought that. My mentors were telling me I'd be just fine. I'm thinking I don't know. So I applied to thirteen schools not knowing what to expect. I applied to three lower-end schools that I felt pretty confident I could get into. A lot in the middle where I thought maybe, maybe not. I picked three dream schools where I would just love to be if I could, because it doesn't hurt to try.

Mike: Which ones did you pick?

Todd: I selected California Berkeley, Columbia, and Harvard.

Mike: How did you do?

Todd: I got into Berkeley, I got into Harvard, and I was a finalist at Columbia.

Mike: So here you go, a kid that dropped out of high school. Accepted. The letter comes from Harvard. Tell me about that day.

Todd: Well, it is funny because Harvard wanted the freaking moon. I mean . . . (laughing) . . . everybody else wanted a one-page essay. They wanted seven pages. I thought, is this really worth it? It was $100 to apply and I have a family and this money is coming from somewhere to apply for this, and I tell you I thought maybe I shouldn't apply for this. This is kind of silly. I could use the $100. I thought no, let's just do it. You won't regret anything. I had read a lot of work by a particular psychologist, Curt Fisher at Harvard, and I wanted to work with him. You don't want to get your hopes up, and so I went and sought out letters of recommendation. Dr. Goldstein provided an excellent one for me. Those were the things that made a huge difference. People wanted to go to bat for me. I applied to Harvard and I started getting some acceptance letters first from other schools and so it was a good sign. I had been accepted to the lower echelon schools, and I thought well, at least I'm going. I was very excited. Well, maybe I'm going to be a doctor, be a psychologist.

   The letter from Harvard didn't actually come first. I got a call from Curt Fisher, but I wasn't there. He called and talked to my wife. I get home from school and they are all grinning ear-to-ear, standing on the porch waiting for me. They said there was going to be a letter coming. Well, a letter came from Harvard and my wife screams, "Open it, open it," and I wondered why she was so excited. Actually, the letter indicated I forgot to fill this out and this out and I'm wondering why are you smiling so much about this. She was all excited; then she said, Curt Fisher called. He said you got in. I didn't know if that meant master's program, doctorate, you know, I didn't know what to expect and I didn't know what to think. I was speechless.

Actually the thing that went through my mind was they made a mistake. I thought I was going to call and they would say something like, Todd Rose, oh, it was Tom Jones, we're sorry. He left his home phone number—Curt Fisher that is—and said call me back. So I called and I'm sitting there—this is a person whose work I've read and am very interested in—I didn't have a single thing to say . . . I just sit there going *um*. He said, "Well, why don't you E-mail me?" and I go, "Okay, bye" and hang up the phone and go, "Oh gee, that's not very good." I wanted to call everybody and couldn't get hold of anybody, you know, my family. So I'm sitting there and it was just very exciting because that really was the place I wanted to be. There are times, even now, when things are difficult and there are some tough classes, I realize how lucky I am to be given that chance.

Mike: It is luck and it is also hard work and the realization of what we're talking about here, the resilience that you have managed to demonstrate. Why do you think you had that sense of resilience? Did you develop it? You mention the word *process*.

Todd: *Process* is a great word for it. Resilience for me, and I am very interested in that now, because I see a lot of children. When this whole thing went through, going to Harvard, I got a lot of responses from people who were struggling. I realized there is not a lot of difference between me and these kids because when I see them and talk to their parents I realize that was me. That's exactly me. So I thought, what's the difference? Is it luck, is it chance, what? I think *resilience* is the term that best defines it and even that is hard to define. This is what I think it is. My parents were smart enough to look at the long-term perspective and realize that we're having battles with this kid on a daily basis and it is frustrating and it can be rocky but ultimately there has to be a foundation that he can fall back on, and that was it. The funny thing is that while I may have disappointed them a lot, my family never gave up on me. I had that experience throughout my youth, I remember.

It is funny because I remember a very specific incident I had with my grandmother. I believe that everybody has to have one person that can just be crazy about them no matter what. I remember getting kicked out of school for throwing a stink bomb (laughing). People knew who I was; at least class was entertaining when I was there. My parents were frustrated. They had to be. I remember we didn't have a lot of money back then, and what was in style were spandex shorts. I don't know why and I'm glad I don't have any pictures from back then. My grandmother, who also didn't have a lot of money, showed up at our house that night with a pair of shorts and said here is a present for you. She said it's not because I'm proud of what you did but because I love you, and the thing is, that seemed so contrary to everything I had learned so far that she should reward that kind of behavior, but I so remember that. That this person loves me.

> I realized there is not a lot of difference between these kids and me because when I see them and talk to their parents I realize that was me.

Mike: As a parent, do you try to remember that with your kids? When they put you through the test that kids always put parents through, do you try to draw on that, knowing full well that you probably won't be able to until you are a grandparent?

Todd: It is such an interesting thing because it is such a balance. These kids and myself go through so much, and some of it was my fault and some of it wasn't. Your parents fight for you all the time, and I think that they get to a point where you just want to go, look, I'm just going to be so nice to you and let you get away with whatever you want to do because you are having such a tough time. But you have to be strong as a parent. Luckily, my parents knew that there was a balance. You've got to know that you're loved and have a foundation that will help you to overcome this in the long term.

That to me is what resilience is and was: sort of just knowing that I was loved, knowing that I was cared for, but also knowing that I wasn't going to get away with whatever I wanted. They were going to be tough on me and that was what I thought sitting in the hospital and saying something has to change. I think about the kids in similar situations but without the family support. Luckily, in my family education is a big, big priority. My dad overcame some terrific odds to get a degree, and so for me that was a no-brainer. I saw what happened to our lives as children because he went to school, went to school at night when he worked full time. So to me it wasn't a difficult thing. Those examples are very important. Over the course of your whole lifetime they build up your character and resilience. I don't know why I was lucky enough or whatever to be able to turn my life around, but I am glad I did.

Mike: How do you try and apply it now as you become a psychologist? As you continue as a parent?

Todd: I am much more aware of how daily events affect a child's overall perspective on life and attitude toward things. I attempt to see growth as a process. Mistakes are experiences to learn from. As a child it was just so hard when all you do is fail. The fact is, I didn't try in school because honestly, in the back of my mind, I knew if I try at this and fail I have nothing left. Everybody would say, will you just try it. And I would say, you're right, if I would just try and the fact is I'm not trying because I can still hold on to that. That way I haven't failed at this, and I remember that. I want to teach my children that there are opportunities to learn. Everybody makes mistakes and fails, but you have to be able to say okay, what can I learn from this experience. That is an important lesson parents can teach you.

Mike: It is interesting the way you define *failure*. You can define failure to mean almost anything, but you choose to define failure as not

trying, then anything else you do will be something short of
failure.

Todd: Yeah, I think that as a child I expressed a lot of failure. You end
up thinking that you need to be perfect, that okay, I'm going to
commit to being better, and I did. Every single year I was going
to change. A lot of kids that were in my situation are still
struggling, but most of them know they want to be different. It is
a very difficult process. It is having this structural support of
people around you that follow you through your life that is so
important. It is funny, there was no reason for Dr. Goldstein to
correspond with me. We have corresponded for years, just on his
own time. I think, hopefully, he saw that I was sincerely
interested. To have support not only from your family but also
from someone in the field that you are interested in. It is amazing
what that does for your self-esteem.

Mike: I don't think a lot of people understand in the entire process you
thought you were failing because you were trying hard every day.
I mean, there was a lot of work involved in this, which maybe the
outside world doesn't quite understand sometimes.

Todd: Yeah, the behavior looks like not trying, lazy, doesn't care. That
can't be further from the truth. It was an internal battle every day
with myself. I would do things, and as I got older I would realize
that was really dumb, you know. But then your self-esteem is so
fragile that you are not going to admit that, and you end up
wanting to fight the world over it. But I remember a situation, it
was so funny but it is a good story for me that I keep . . . because
a lot of my problems in school were my fault. I mean, not my
fault but I did have a responsibility. It wasn't just like the school
coming down on me for no reason. I remember being in an
English class. The one thing I turned to even when I was doing
poorly was writing. I loved to write poetry. It was just easy for me.
It came to me and I really, really enjoyed it.

So I was in seventh-grade English class and the teacher said we
are going to write poetry. I thought, hey, this is something I know
I can do. Not only was this going to be graded, but the winner is
going to get a king-sized Snickers bar. In seventh grade this was a

big deal for me. So I went home and I spent so much time writing this poem on ski jumping. I thought it was a great poem (laughing). I wrote it out and my parents were there and I took it back to school and turned it in. Actually, I was sort of bragging, *cocky* would probably be a good word, sort of scared inside but you didn't want to show that. I'm going to win this, you know, I wrote a great poem. So the time comes to get them back a week later and I get my paper back and not only did I not win, which was fine, I got an F. I thought, gee, I thought it was really at least worth something. So I asked my teacher and he told me, You couldn't have written that poem. There is no way you could have written that poem. I went home just devastated because I really tried. I don't mean to put all the blame on someone else because there was interaction over the course of the semester that would say this person isn't really trying. But my parents called and said they were there when I wrote it. He never would give in. So I failed.

I remember walking out of that junior high school and thinking I give up, I quit. I really, really do. Like I said, I don't mean to blame one incident, but I just remember that thought in my head like, what do I have to do?

> I remember walking out of that junior high school and thinking I give up, I quit.

Mike: Even when you try they don't believe you did it.

Todd: In my head I had already changed, right? I want to do better and I expected the rest of the world to sort of see that. Read my mind and give me all the chances in the world.

Mike: Do you ever think about going back to that teacher and just writing a little letter on Harvard stationery?

Todd: (Laughing) You know it's funny because one of the other interesting processes that took place, as I said wanting to do better at first was very external for me, was to show other people, right? I am going to prove you wrong, and I started to do better. But over the course of my undergraduate studies it became a very internal thing, and at this point I don't care anymore. I love learning so much that I see the inherent value of it aside from making money or things like that. So I want to say that was an unfortunate experience but ultimately I don't want to say I would do things differently because it led to who I am today and how I think. So I just keep it as part of my story and hopefully there will be a day when I can use that anecdote to help other parents and kids who are suffering.

Mike: Lyda and Larry, listening to Todd today you must be very proud of him. Parents always have dreams for their kids and then somewhere along the line sometimes we all wonder whether our dreams have exceeded our children's grasp. There must have been times along the way where you began to think there is no way this kid is going to get anywhere that is going to make his life even close to what I envisioned it being. Tell me about some of those times.

Lyda: This is not going to sound true, but I always had faith in him and maybe that's just a mother's instinct, but I knew what he was capable of deep down inside. My whole thing was holding out until he could realize his potential.

Mike: He'd outgrow all that?

Lyda: Yeah. A lot of disappointments along the way. I try to not make long-term goals for my children in my own mind because you need to let them develop. I knew he had it in him. Which is probably different than my husband.

Mike: A sort of balancing act. Larry, did you have the same confidence or did you have more profound doubts?

Larry: I don't think anybody ever gives up on their children, but there were many times I wondered if Todd would ever make it in life. Yeah, I had my doubts. I didn't know if he would make it.

Mike: When you go through doubts as a parent, whom do you blame? Do you blame your kid? Do you blame yourself? Do you blame life? What?

Larry: Personally, I don't think I ever tried to assign blame. First of all, Todd was our first child. We didn't know what we were getting into. We thought all kids were this way. It was not until we had more children that we realized that Todd was different. We also realized he was smart. Lyda had a lot more faith than I did in his future, but, I've said this before, I thought he would be a smart criminal rather than a smart student.

Mike: When did it begin? Was it when he got to school? Was it the report cards coming back saying Todd works below his potential or disrupts the class? How did you first become aware of "his problem"?

Lyda: He had behavior problems in kindergarten. They did testing back then and found he was above average, way above average. So as he advanced through, maybe by third grade, teachers started complaining and by the time he was in sixth grade it was a full-blown problem, with his peers, with our neighbors, and our family members.

> Everyone wanted to blame you as a parent or tell you what you were doing wrong. That's the difficult part of having a child that does not fit into society's norm.

Mike: What kind of problems? Was it fighting? Was it arguing?

Lyda: Todd was very impulsive. He would act out and be out of control. Everyone wanted to blame you as a parent or tell you what you were doing wrong. That's the difficult part of having a child that does not fit into society's norm.

Mike: You tended to personalize it?

Lyda: Definitely.

Mike: You feel that you've let your child down? You were not a good parent.

Lyda: Yeah, especially when everybody is telling you what you should be doing.

Mike: What did they tell you?

Lyda: That we needed to be more strict. We just weren't strict enough and so he was so out of control. But then if we were strict, they would say maybe you're too strict on the child. You have to come to terms with yourself and your confidence in yourself, and that's what we finally did. We shut out the voices of people from the outside who didn't know what we were dealing with.

Mike: How long did it take you to get to the point where you were confident enough in yourself or you had reached the end of your tolerance to listening to other people tell you what you should have been doing?

Lyda: I think when he was in junior high. The later years of junior high.

Larry: We had a lot of people—friends, neighbors, relatives—trying to give advice. They were sincere, but until you have lived with a child that has problems, you can't even begin to understand what is going on. We kept trying.

Lyda: You have to go on your gut instinct, that you know your child. I mean, I've known him from the day I brought him home. I know what his potentials are. You just work on trying to build self-confidence and a sense of love. That's what we set out to do.

Mike: So did you try to get him involved in out-of-school activities, things like that?

Lyda: Anything he excelled in, we supported 100 percent.

Mike: Tell me a little bit about that. What activities and what was the end result?

Lyda: He loved basketball and he played on a church basketball team, which is not that big of a deal but we were at every game to support him. Bought him basketball shoes and really supported anything he excelled in so that he could feel good about himself in some area.

Mike: Did he stick with it?

Lyda: Yes. He would make the school teams but because of his grades he couldn't play.

Mike: Every time?

Lyda: Yeah. The school system back then was more of a frustration to us because they were not willing to work with us or understand the problem.

Mike: Going in for parent-teacher conferences must have been an experience. Tell me about that.

Larry: Oh, boy. I think you started sending me all the time, didn't you?

Lyda: But you learn to tune that out too because you would come home and just want to lay all this negative stuff on your child, and pretty soon it got to where if they said he really did good in art, that is what I would come home and tell him.

Mike: Look for the victories?

Lyda: I would look for anything. But for a long time we were listening to everybody, feeling like failures. I would come home and you just want to attack Todd verbally. "Look what your teacher said, this and this . . . what's wrong." We tried to flip that a little as he got older.

Larry: There were a wide variety of teachers though. Some were very good and understood that there was a problem. Some had a hard time dealing with Todd because Todd was very disruptive. It was just his personality and the way he behaved. So, we always tried to have some sympathy for the teachers, tried to explain, and hoped they would be patient and work with him.

Lyda: Some would and some wouldn't.

Larry: Yeah. Some were tough.

Mike: When did you decide that you needed outside professional help with this? How did that process come along?

Lyda: It was the summer before seventh grade. I thought, he can't go to junior high. He is just not going to make it. That is when we went.

Mike: And what happened? Tell me about the process.

Lyda: We went to our family practice doctor. One thing I still appreciate is that he made the diagnosis, but he would not put a child on any medication unless they saw a psychologist, just to make sure. That was probably the greatest turning point in our life was that he sent us to Dr. Goldstein, and I appreciated that, because that really gave us a strong basis to work from.

Larry: I was a little less enthusiastic about it because I was thinking, oh great, another doctor bill with no results. Even at the time I don't think I appreciated the input or the value of what that particular doctor appointment meant to us as a family and to Todd until years later. There was a lot there.

Mike: Tell me about your first session. I assume the three of you met with Dr. Goldstein together and exchanged some ideas. When you drove home after that first appointment, what did you say to each other? Were you hopeful?

Lyda: I was relieved because there was someone who really understood. A lot of doctors are great at diagnosing, but they don't have the comprehensive background to deal with it. I was relieved because to Dr. Goldstein it was, hey, that's how they act. It was a relief to me. I think I maybe expected a little more from the medication and so that's where you have to be more realistic.

Larry: Of course, we did not know how consistently he was taking the medication. Sometimes he would take it and sometimes he wouldn't.

Lyda: And they're teenagers.

Mike: Did you kind of expect a cure? We got the label, now here is the cure?

Lyda: Yeah. We have this doctor who is so smart and we are going to put him on medication and he is going to turn into a normal child. That's not fair to the child. But that is how you feel as a parent. You are just desperate. You really are desperate.

Mike: So when did you, as you went through that, I guess, the initial couple of months with the medication and some of the sessions, when did you start to notice changes and how did they manifest themselves?

Larry: I can say that the first couple of months there was a drastic change in Todd's behavior. It really had a positive impact, but it didn't last very long. He quickly drifted back to his old ways.

Lyda: Possibly because we waited until he was older and he had developed a lot of learned behavior. Now I'm an advocate for getting early intervention.

Mike: So there were improvements for him. But obviously, even through high school, you had some negative experiences.

Lyda: When he was going into high school he decided he really didn't need his medication anymore. You can't argue with a sixteen-year-old. You can't force them.

Mike: You can argue, but you can't get them to do it.

Lyda: You can't force them to take the medication and that was his
         thing—"I can do this without medication."

Mike: Why do you think he did that? Why do you think kids in general
         do that, but specifically why do you think Todd said no more?

Lyda: Growing up you want to be part of a crowd and you want to be
         like everyone else, and to take a pill sets you apart because you are
         not normal so to speak. You know, you don't fit in with the
         normal. It has to be frustrating.

Mike: Did you ever reach a point when you just felt sorry for him?

Lyda: Oh, I spent many times crying. You'd cry yourself to sleep. It is
         very painful as parents to watch your child because you want
         them to reach their full potential and all along the way people are
         holding him back. Todd was holding himself back. It is very
         painful. It's a painful process.

Mike: I presume, in a way, there is a lot of guilt that goes with it too. Do
         you blame yourselves at all?

Lyda: Maybe, at the time.

Larry: I know now that I'm older, I would have done things differently.
         Back then my solution to this problem was very strict, structured
         discipline. There were some positive results from that, but I'm not
         sure that it was the best solution to try to cure Todd's problem. I
         think back and I probably would not have been near as strict with
         Todd, structured but not as strict. I don't know what the book
         says to do, but on the other hand, Lyda was always trying to work
         the other side of it, the motherly love thing. Maybe it was a good
         balance. I don't know.

Lyda: When I talk with parents I tell them to do the best you can and
         don't look back. That's the best advice. Just look forward and do
         the best you can at any given moment.

Mike: When he was invited to not come back to school, I presume that
         either you had to go to the school or you got a letter from the
         school. What happened?

Larry: We made the decision that Todd was done with school. The
         school would have probably kept him there through the year and
         tried to work with him. We decided that it was not in his best
         interest or in the school's best interest to have him there because

he was not going to graduate and he was more into the playing
around and partying. We felt that it was time to put an end to the
whole school situation and let Todd go to work and get out on his
own. I still think that was a good decision because he was not
accomplishing anything in school.

Lyda: There has to be consequences. School is not a place to go and
cause trouble. It is a place for learning. By that point, I was tired.
I didn't want to fight anymore. I had fought everybody for so long
that it was almost a relief to just say, let's pull you out, get you on
your own, and see what you can do.

Mike: Let's fast forward a bit to his decision to seek higher education.
What did you guys think of that?

Lyda: That was great.

Larry: It was wonderful to see him do it. Even though, I have to admit, I
had big doubts that Todd could handle that.

Mike: How did he tell you or how did you become aware of the fact that
suddenly this young man who disdained high school, apparently,
was thinking about taking college courses?

Larry: I think it kind of came on gradually. It was not a big
announcement. He talked about it off and on, I'd like to get some
education. We'd always say, yeah, yeah, you go ahead. It came on
gradually. We had several years between being pulled out of high
school and him actually starting school. Several years and many
jobs. It just came on slowly.

Lyda: You just offer advice because we had both gone to the university
and graduated, so we would say, hey, this is great and this is how
you do it. Then you just stand back and cross your fingers.

Mike: At that point you have eliminated expectations. You just say,
"We'll see"?

Lyda: Yeah, just let him learn how he can do on his own.

Mike: When he started to flourish, you must have been, I guess
shocked, but I mean *delighted* is probably a better word.

Larry: Both.

Lyda: I knew he was smart though. I've always known that he was very
brilliant. So it felt good to see that he could also feel that in
himself.

Larry: I knew he was smart too, but I had doubts that he would be able to focus and really pull it all together. There is a big difference between high school–level education and college-level education. I thought it was almost impossible for Todd to pull that off. I had doubts for a long time. In fact for the first three quarters, I felt that his grades were probably due more to the curriculum.

Mike: Taking easy courses?

Lyda: Manipulating the teacher.

Larry: I took engineering courses and I thought they were tough. I thought the psychology courses must be easier up there because Todd is getting great grades. It was not until he took statistics. He took that class and I told many people at work, this will be the test for Todd. If he can make it through statistics he will be in good shape. I had a lot of doubts, but he ended up student teaching the class the next semester. That was definitely the point in time when I knew that Todd had made it.

Mike: It made you a believer?

Larry: I was a believer. I was convinced.

Mike: Now the next step is graduate school. Now this has to just be incredible.

Lyda: It's great.

Mike: He was going to apply to some safe schools and then some schools that were probable, and then what they called reach schools. So when you heard he was going to apply to Harvard, what went through your mind?

Larry: Well, first of all, usually Todd, at least in his younger years, would brag first and try to accomplish later. He was very reserved about applying to Harvard, Berkeley, and Columbia. He would say, "I'm going to apply, but I really don't have much hope for that." I have to commend him on that. I think he knew he had it in him. He knew he had the grades and references, but I was surprised.

Mike: Was it because he got there in an unconventional way, that this legendary school might hold it against him?

Lyda: I thought it would work in his favor because he had proven himself on the lower level. I just thought they might be willing to give him a shot.

Mike: What did you think when the letter and the telephone call came?

Lyda: He called me on my cell phone. I was driving, and he said, "I can't believe it, I can't believe it."

Mike: I guess that kind of brings it full circle now as parents, running the gauntlet . . .

Lyda: Of emotions!

Mike: Are you surprised to hear Todd in retrospect felt your strength and support?

Lyda: Yeah. Because you don't feel like you're getting through. It's constant battles over everything in their whole life. So that's really surprising.

Larry: You always feel like you are teetering on the edge of complete failure in that situation, so it is very surprising to have Todd give you that kind of feedback. It is very rewarding.

Mike: This may be an important thing to bring up too. Sounds like you need to really work as a team.

Larry: I can't imagine trying to handle this situation alone, yet I know many parents do.

Mike: It must put enormous strains on all relationships.

Lyda: That happened with us, too. I would get frustrated, but I didn't want the yelling and screaming because it felt worse. But you need to have the discipline and consequences for their behavior. It's a juggling act. You just find what is best for you.

Mike: And it is not just the child and it is not just the parents. It's the whole family.

Lyda: It's the combination, yes.

Mike: How do you think your family came through this? Are you better for this ultimately do you think?

Larry: Definitely.

Mike: Do you think you are closer because of it?

Lyda: We are closer, and I think the other kids can look at Todd and his accomplishments and put that into their lives, although they do not have the same situation. If Todd can do it then I can surely do it. Also, more tolerance. I think it helps you to look at the rest of your children and other people's children in a different light.

Larry: Seeing Todd's successes actually help them. They saw where he was heading and where he was going and now they see the result of a complete turnaround. That can't help but be a positive influence on their lives.

> You just have to believe in yourself, and you have to believe in your child.

Mike: What would you say to other parents going down this road right now? The ones whose kids have not reached that turning point in their lives where things have started to come together for them.

Lyda: Hang in there. You just have to believe in yourself, and you have to believe in your child. Just take the road as it comes. It is easier if you don't try to fight it along the way. You have to get somewhere that they can come to feel good about themselves. That's important and that's hard because it is exhausting for a parent. It's very exhausting.

Larry: And never let them know that you have given up or don't give up. Because once you have done that I think they have lost all hope. You have to always keep a glimmer of them believing in you as a parent. That you trust them and you think they can do what they are capable of.

Recommended Reading

Brooks, R., and S. Goldstein. 2001. *Raising Resilient Children*. New York: McGraw-Hill.

Goldstein, S., K. Hagar, and R. Brooks. 2002. *Seven Steps to Help Children Worry Less*. Plantation, FL: Specialty Press.

Heininger, J. E., and S. K. Weiss. 2001. *From Chaos to Calm: Effective Parenting of Challenging Children with ADHD and Other Behavioral Problems*. New York: Pedigree Books.

Ingersoll, B. D., and S. Goldstein. 2001. *Lonely, Sad, and Angry: How to Help Your Unhappy Child*. Plantation, FL: Specialty Press.

Shure, M. 1996. *Raising a Thinking Child*. New York: Pocket Books.

———. 2000. *Raising a Thinking Preteen*. New York: Henry Holt.

Zentall, S., and S. Goldstein. 1999. *Seven Steps to Homework Success: A Family Guide for Solving Common Homework Problems*. Plantation, FL: Specialty Press.

Index